The Trapper Murders

A True Central Oregon Mystery

by

Melany Tupper

Central Oregon Books, LLC, Christmas Valley, Oregon

PRINTED IN THE UNITED STATES OF AMERICA

Visit our website at: www.christmasvalley.net

First Edition published 2013

ISBN: 978-0-9831691-5-4

To the Families

CONTENTS:

You cannot kill another person without
killing a part of your own soul,
unless your own soul is already dead.

Author's Introduction:

In the spring of 1924, citizens of Bend, Oregon were stunned by the news that a horrendous triple murder had occurred just west of town. Three men who were trapping around the Cascade Lakes had met a violent end, and their bodies had been shoved through a hole in the ice of Big Lava Lake. That was terrifying news, indeed. For the killings were so brutal that many believed they must have been the work of a madman. The gory scene was discovered in April by family members who had gone searching for the men, and as events were reconstructed, it became clear that the crime had been the work of two killers working in partnership. A prime suspect was identified almost at once, because of a dispute with one of the victims, but the second man, who was very likely the brains behind the operation, was never identified.

Television and Hollywood have given almost everyone a basic understanding of how a multiple murderer operates, working to educated us since the mid-1970's when the term "serial killer" first came into the vernacular of law enforcement. Although serial killers are a rare sort of creature, the pathology, the need to kill for psychological gratification, did exist in society long before it was officially recognized or understood. However, in order to deliver a product that can resolve all aspects of the story line in a short and snappy manner within an hour or two, television and movies invariably oversimplify the way that the psychopath operates, his modus operandi, and several TV victims are usually killed within a short span of days or weeks. In real life, victims of such killers are usually spread over several decades.

He, because very few serial killers are female, usually kills for the first time around the period when he reaches adulthood. The first attempt tends to be disorganized to the point that the initial victim might actually survive. The first is often a male family member, and the next will also be taken from near where the killer lives. Subsequent victims are usually spaced several years apart, but as the killer hits his stride at the peak of his 'career,' around age 40, he will kill with greater frequency and less control. He might get sloppy, and might kill several people at once. Unlike the television psychopath, who commits identical crimes, the modus operandi of true serial killers evolves from one crime to the next. Each murder will be different, yet elements of the previous crime will be carried forward, and each murder will contain new aspects that may be manifest in the murders to come.

The killer becomes a master of the game he plays with law enforcement, and winning that game is important to him. Toward the end of his 'career' the pace of his killing will slow, becoming more regular, and his last victims will again be taken from near where he lives. Because a serial killer is often also sociopathic, with a true criminal mind, he may go to prison for any number of deeds, putting an end to his killing. These reptilian creatures tend toward the habits of stealing, lying, raping, swindling, cruelty and violence.

He might be 'taken out' by a member of society who innately recognizes him for what he is. Or, he might get caught in the act of killing. Law enforcement was more easily fooled in the days before ballistics, DNA testing, and fingerprinting. In those days, he could kill undetected, hiding in plain sight.

He might be forced to stop killing by age and infirmity, and when that happens, he often takes his own life, because what thrilled him most, the act of killing, is no longer available. A profound, lifelong sense of deep self-loathing and a numbing boredom feed his drive to commit suicide.

Ray Van Buren Jackson was just such a man. He grew up in the Sweet Home area of Linn County, Oregon, and his career as a killer spanned several counties of central Oregon, including Deschutes, Lake, Harney, and Klamath. In *The Sandy Knoll Murder, Legacy of the Sheepshooters*, I described some of Jackson's first and last victims, all killed near where he lived. One of those victims was a very prominent man named John Creed Conn, whose murder occurred in Lake County. Details of the Conn murder appeared on the front page of the *Oregonian* for nine months in 1904, making it one of the most sensational murders in the history of the state.

The easiest, while admittedly oversimplified, comparison that can be drawn between Jackson and any 'known' murderers is to think of the killers in the popular 1996 film, *Fargo*. What drove those killers, what really made them tick, was material gain, and they would kill anyone who got in their way. For Ray Jackson, particularly in his earlier crimes, the killing seemed almost incidental to his primary focus, that was obtaining wealth and power. It is easy to imagine the two men who formed a partnership in *Fargo* having killed before, and it is a well-documented fact that psychopaths sometimes pair up to accomplish a thing that one could not accomplish alone.

This book explains how Jackson spent the intervening years of his life, from about 1907 through 1924, and describes additional crimes that may be attributed to him. It is with great sadness and loathing that I write the following, but do so in hopes that it may bring a sense of resolution to the families of the victims. All of the events described are true, and any suppositions I have made regarding these murders have been framed as such. If there is one thing that I learned while writing *The Sandy Knoll Murder*, it was that death would follow Ray Jackson, just as surely as night followed day.

Mug shots from Jackson's second stay at the Oregon State Penitentiary, after he and an accomplice, John Ryan, were convicted of robbery in Baker County in 1899.

Ray Van Buren Jackson spent the last 20 years of his life in Harney County, and was buried at the Burns Cemetery. He died from a gunshot that was determined to have been self-inflicted.

Chapter One

The Smoking Herd

When we step back from the psychological and emotional aspects of *The Sandy Knoll Murder*, as we have the luxury of doing one century later, and look logically at the nuts and bolts of the crime, it allows us to then move forward through time and inspect other murders pragmatically.

A psychopath does not experience life in the same way that most people do. They don't experience all of the lighter shades of fear like worry, concern, and caring that add minor drama to everyday life and keep it interesting and challenging. As a result, people in the sociopathic to psychopathic range suffer from chronic boredom.

If Jackson was a typical psychopath, his violent behavior would have peaked around the time he reached the age of 50, around 1920. Toward the end of his life, Jackson probably descended into alcohol abuse, depression, and depravity in his personal life and failed to take care of himself. He no longer had the physical strength and vigor required for violence, and was not able to relieve the emotional deadness that he had always carried with him.

There would be no more intensely sadistic exploitation of victims, and no more of the calm and relief that the sadism gave him from his profound self contempt and chronic boredom. He could no longer inflict terror, pain, and helplessness on others to obtain a feeling of mastery over his own childhood abuse experiences.

It can be shown by the injuries to the front of the head and the face of some of Ray Jackson's victims that the attack was made in close contact and from the front, and that frontal view of the destruction of a life was something that thrilled Jackson no end.

In the book *Bad Men Do What Good Men Dream*, Robert I. Simon defined a paraphilia as "recurrent intense sexual urges and sexually arousing fantasies that involve either nonhuman objects, or the suffering and humiliation of oneself or children or other non-consenting parties." Ray Jackson's paraphilia included abnormal desires that involved extreme or dangerous activities, and that paraphilia is an important facet of his character when it comes to the task of pinpointing him as a psychopathic killer. He was sadistic, and displayed antisocial aggression toward women and children, and he derived pleasure from inflicting suffering on a live victim.

A number of serial killers have been found to have displayed, as children, a triad of behaviors comprised of bedwetting, fire setting, and cruelty to animals and other children, known as the Macdonald Triad. Such children are more likely to become vice presidents of corporations than to become serial killers, but a large number of serial killers display that triad as children, and carry forward some of those habits into adulthood in the form of arson, rages, overkill, sexual aggression, cruelty, sadistic poisoning, and mutilation. The terrible triad is considered a sure sign of a child in deep trouble psychologically.

Considered separately, fire expresses a hyperactive excitement and deep seated anger and an expression of sexual and aggressive overstimulation or abuse. Torturing, killing, and mutilating animals shows sadism and cruelty. Bedwetting can imply emotional disturbance and poor impulse control. The triad can sometimes be traced to neurological damage.

Childhood abuse seems likely in Jackson's case. He was known to have been extraordinarily cruel to the children left in his charge as a teacher, and most serial killers have either a cruel and insensitive father, or a father who essentially abandons them before they reach the age of twelve. Many serial killers experience severe abuse as children, and Jackson's predilection for attacking the heads of his victims may point to another explanation of how he came to be such a monster. Psychologists vary in their opinions on how serial killers are created, with some pointing more to physical characteristics of the brain and heredity, while others lean toward environmental factors. Many claim that both nature and nurture must be deviant to create a psychopath who kills, and neurobiological disorders are amazingly common among criminal defendants. In one study, 15 death row inmates were chosen for examination, and in each the research found evidence of severe head injury and neurological impairment. Did Jackson himself suffered a head injury at the hands of a harsh disciplinarian father?

"Many such killers, over the course of their abusive upbringings, suffered head injuries and trauma directly for example, Henry Lee Lucas, Albert Desalvo, and Bobby Joe Long," wrote Stephen J. Giannangelo in *The Psychopathology of Serial Murder*. Interesting, too, is a 1994 brain scan study that showed violent convicts having impaired function in an area of the brain linked to impulse control. That area, perhaps not coincidentally, is the prefrontal cortex, where blows are most likely to land.

One psychologist described serial killers as "power mad in the extreme," as men who crave control of another to build their own fragile egos while demonstrating the weakness of others. In the case of Creed Conn, Jackson worked systematically to dismantle the man's life, to take and destroy all that he was. And, in retaining control and possession of Conn's body for seven whole weeks after the killing, Jackson displayed a degree of necrophilia, which has been described as "the malignant form of the anal character."

Ray Van Buren Jackson was 34 years old when he murdered Creed Conn at Silver Lake, Oregon in 1904. Most psychopaths, if they are killers, will begin killing before that age. But even though the Conn murder was probably not his first, it had to have been one of the most sensational. The front page stories that ran in the *Oregonian* for nine months after Conn disappeared contained important details about the crime scene, described as "a small sandy knoll" where Jackson had deposited the body. In the Conn murder, Jackson exercised a great degree of control over all aspects of the crime, and practically everything about the disappearance and murder of Conn, and the later reappearance of Conn's body, was organized. Much can be inferred about Jackson from the clues that were left, and it was those clues that convinced the author that the crime might be solved using research methods.

The crime scene at the Sandy Knoll showed evidence of what is known as "signature aspect." That being, things that were done by the killer for his own psychological gratification, his internal motivations. The murder scene or "dump site" of a psychopath will show evidence of activity that appears strange, or unnecessary for the perpetration of the crime. Those are things that serve no apparent purpose, and may include repetitive, ritualistic behavior seen in his other crimes. Examples might be posing the body of the victim, mutilation of the victim, symbolic gestures, items being taken from or deliberately left at the scene, and other unusual behavior beyond what is needed. Signature behavior will evolve somewhat over the killer's lifetime, but the general theme of it will persist. Internal motivations were what drove Jackson to kill, rather than some actual motive as in the great majority of murders. And, because the signature behavior was a part of him, the strongest and worst part of him, it was an inescapable element of Jackson's psychology that was revealed in subsequent and prior crimes.

> *"The murderer's modus operandi may change... but his distinctive trademark does not. These are the killer's calling card. This man leaves his mark on his work, like a painter leaves his signature on a canvas."*

> *Sir Arthur Conan Doyle*
> *The Case of the Silk Stocking*

The first noteworthy signature aspect of the Conn murder was that Conn's head had been horribly damaged sometime after he was killed. Creed Conn had striking good looks, with strong features, light blue eyes, and dark hair, and was very highly regarded in the community. When his body was found at the Sandy Knoll, his face was damaged to such an extent that his gold watch and personal effects had to be used to identify the body. The words "maimed" and "mangled" were used to describe his face. His features had been "obliterated."

What does that attack of the head and face say about the psychology of the killer? Was he envious of Creed Conn? Did he wish that he himself was better looking? Or, did he have an inferiority complex about his own intelligence? Could it imply a compensatory facade, a killer who constantly attempted to elevate himself in terms of his own intelligence? Or, was he merely repeating some of what had been done to him as a child? Because the attack on the face was not considered as a contributing factor or a cause of death, it had no practical purpose. It was done for psychological gratification, and with great vigor. That could indicate poor impulse control that would allow the behavior to be repeated at a later date.

In a so-called "normal" murder, a motivated killing, the killer will usually do what is most simple and practical. Creed Conn's cause of death was a gun shot to the heart. If it had been a simple act of revenge or a crime of passion, the easiest thing would have been to fire that shot, then quickly leave the area or dispose of the body. But, this killer felt the need to carefully position Conn's body, like a billboard on that knoll, so that it could be seen by anyone traveling the main highway into town. Conn was placed on his back, with his feet close together and his hands up over his head "as if in repose," like he was asleep or dozing. His hat had been crammed down tightly on the back of his head. The killer took a chance of being caught while positioning the body in a manner that would have been embarrassing to the victim.

Creed Conn was known as a "wide awake Republican." The positioning was a signature behavior that did not serve the practical purpose of making Conn any more dead, and also revealed that the killer wanted to control the experience of discovery of the body, when and how it was found, and was using it as a communication medium. Was this a killer who enjoyed humiliating others? A similar behavior was found in the Whitechapel murders committed by Jack the Ripper, who placed his victims in humiliating poses. Jackson put an unopened bottle of laudanum in Conn's vest pocket, that could have been another way of mocking the merchant, because laudanum was a common sleep remedy of the day.

The high level of control that Jackson exercised in the Conn murder, and in the handling of the body, make it seem likely that Jackson was a 'control freak.' The people who knew him probably had the impression that he was 'on a power trip.' He felt compelled to hold, to own, Conn's body for seven weeks after the killing, keeping it close at hand and under his control. That, too, points to a pathology, because Creed Conn happened to be the brother of a district attorney. No man in his right mind would want to be found anywhere in the vicinity of the body of the district attorney's murdered brother. Especially when large rewards were being offered. What can be inferred about the mind of

Jackson from this? Surely, holding the body in that way made him feel more powerful. He owned Creed Conn, and that could indicate that he sought to emulate him. Those seven weeks made him feel so much more intelligent than everyone who was searching for the missing man, because he was the only person who knew where Conn was. He waited for snow to fall, and when it did snow for the first time in seven weeks, he hauled Conn's body out of town and placed it on that knoll. When the sun came up in the morning, around the time the body was found, and several hours before the investigators arrived from the far away county seat, the snow and his footprints had dissolved, erasing every trace of Jackson and every indication of where the body had been hidden.

District Attorney Lafayette "Lafe" Conn, doctors T.V. Hall and A.A. Witham, and Sheriff Horace Dunlap were confounded by the set of clues left at the Sandy Knoll, and that was exactly what Jackson intended. It was a game for him. The supreme game in which the stakes were very high. Lafe Conn must have believed that the killer would be found, because anyone who would have dared to kill his brother, dared to kill Creed Conn, must have had a huge motive to have taken such a huge risk. He was looking for a red flag, something major that Creed Conn had done that had enraged another man. What Lafe Conn did not know was that Jackson killed because of what he felt inside of himself, his internal motivations. Although no clear motive was revealed by the evidence at the Sandy Knoll, it did prove one thing beyond a reasonable doubt, that Jackson loved to toy with investigators.

Jackson had done some tampering with the body when he deposited it on that knoll. He shot a bullet through the body, that entered at a point three inches above the first and went into the ground. That might make the sheriff wonder if Conn had been killed on that spot, and would have left powder burns that could point to suicide. By the time the body was found, nearly every newspaper in the state had published the theory that Conn had been murdered by a gang of sheepshooters, a scenario that might involve multiple gun shots. The Sandy Knoll was and is located on property owned by the ZX ranch, a large cattle operation, and

Jackson may have wished to dabble in sheepshooter theory, leading the investigators even further astray.

Creed Conn seems to have been everything that Jackson wanted to be. He possessed many of the external symbols of wealth and success that Jackson lusted after and admired, like fine horses, nice clothes, and his own business. Conn was liked and respected by all of the local stockmen, and had a very fine freight team and good looks that were the source of his celebrity and charisma. Jackson seemed to believe that if he had Conn's wealth, he could be all that Conn was, and more. In the years that followed the murder, there were even a few indications that Jackson sought to emulate Creed Conn. Jackson started a mercantile store at Paisley in 1911, and soon after Conn's death, had the audacity to purchase Creed Conn's flashy buggy team from his estate. He became politically active too, and in 1908 was elected as superintendent of schools for Lake County.

> *Freight teams and wagons supplied the life blood of the early eastern Oregon communities. They took products to market and brought in clothing and supplies. Bells on the lead team announced their arrival. Men who managed the horses and drove them received the same hero worship from small boys that pilots do today.*
>
> *Carrol B. Howe*

Jackson seems to have hoped to become everything that Conn was. It was a powerful love-hate relationship, in which Jackson loved most in Conn the qualities and attributes which he believed to be lacking in himself, while hating Conn for those very same qualities. The murder of John Creed Conn had to have been very meaningful to Jackson. If not the pinnacle, it was certainly a high water mark in his career. And, understanding Creed Conn's life gives us great insight into the psychology of Jackson, for Jackson felt intimately tied to Conn by his lusting after everything that Conn was and what he represented.

Prior to the day of the murder, Conn suffered considerable, anonymous harassment at the hands of Jackson, who burned his freight wagons, poisoned his freight team killing one of Conn's 'leaders,' and seems to have poisoned Conn himself. All of those things point to a deep-seated resentment, and an irresistible urge to bring Conn down. Many psychopaths kill with poison, and it might one day be found that Jackson's had a prior victim killed in that manner. Psychopaths also often have a lifelong love affair with fire and the effects of arson, and will burn several things before they reach adulthood. It makes them feel powerful to watch people scramble around at the scene of a fire.

> *"This is one of the best known freighting outfits in Eastern Oregon, and many snapshot photos have been taken of it."*
>
> *Ashwood Prospector*

The targeting of the freight team was significant because it was the outward symbol of Conn's success, and in many respects that team *was his identity.* The valuable animals were recognized throughout east Oregon as one of the very finest teams in existence. They were bred from the Percheron stock that his father, Henry, had brought on the Oregon Trail from Indiana in 1854, and were specialized animals, a combination of mules, some of them enormous, and horses, with two nimble and brainy white horses in the lead. Conn owned fourteen freight animals, but seems to have varied the configuration of the team to match the length of the trip and the terrain. Around 1900, a tradition existed among teamsters that if one man's team could pass another on a steep grade it would win the bells of the inferior team, and Conn's team had many, many bells. A short newspaper item taken from the date of the sale of the animals after his death tells us that the Conn team would draw a crowd as it passed through a town, and the few people who owned cameras would run out into the street to take pictures of it. Conn understood visibility and promotion, and knew that his team was a traveling advertisement for his business.

A short 'blurb' that appeared in the *Shaniko Leader* in November of 1900 was picked up by the *Oregonian*, and described how Conn's team had delivered 13,500 pounds of wool to Shaniko, and returned to Silver Lake with 16,000 pounds of freight. In early August of 1902, the *Lake County Examiner* described Conn's ten mule team traveling from the rail head at Shaniko with twenty thousand pounds of freight for the Conn store at Silver Lake.

The *Bend Bulletin* described the great team as it passed through town in June of 1903 with three wagons and five teams comprised of eight mules and two horses. Each wagon carrying two barrels of water, one on each side. Another team followed with feed for the freight team, and the writer commented that "freighting is expensive business this season." Again, in August of 1903, the Conn team made the paper when it passed through Bend on the way to Silver lake with five spans of mules and one span of horses, carrying 20,000 pounds of barbed wire on three wagons. "Cheerfully they walked along, seeming not to feel their heavy burden," commented the *Bulletin*. Later that month the Conn team was in Bend again with 20,000 pounds of wool on a round trip to Shaniko that required 28 days.

Creed Conn seems to have been poisoned about a month before his death, because he had been taking laudanum "for some bodily ailment." Laudanum is a liquid opium solution that was widely prescribed and sold over the counter in the days before common pain killers, like aspirin, were mass produced. It was used to treat insomnia and was, and remains today, an effective remedy for dysentery. Conn was suffering from "hemorrhages," which probably referred to a bleeding from the bowels that could have been a symptom of arsenic poisoning.

In *The Sandy Knoll Murder* the poisoning death of little Ethel Martin during the time that Creed Conn was missing was described as having occurred while the girl was at school with Jackson, who was the teacher at Silver Lake. Everything points to the girl having been poisoned by Jackson just before she returned home, and could have been the result of the girl having discovered where the body was hidden or other particulars about Jackson's guilt. The poisoning of Ethel Martin and the freight team at about the same time opens the possibility that Jackson used poison on Conn, a murder attempt that failed and only made the man sick. After all, if Jackson would use poison on animals, and on an eleven year old girl, what was to stop him from using poison on a man?

After Creed Conn became an independent businessman with the J. C. Conn General Merchandise Store at Silver Lake, he seems to have fallen into the all too common human trap of overextending himself. After graduating from Willamette University, he had gone to work in the Paisley mercantile store of his brothers, George and Virgil, in 1886, located near the center of Lake County. He opened a store at Silver Lake in 1892, and built a new store building between 1897 and 1899, but remained in partnership with Virgil until about 1899.

He began borrowing money in 1900, $1,580 from Louise and George Gilfry, on which he was only able to repay the annual interest. He borrowed $1,500 from Al Geyer in 1903. He owed over $40 to the blacksmith, William D. Robinette, who worked at the big Silver Lake livery stable owned by Warren Duncan. About $358 in back wages was owed to his clerk, Frank Payne. And, he held a promissory note to Martha Lane in the amount of $3,270. At the time of his death, Conn had not even paid his dues to the Baptist church, or what he owed on his newspaper subscription. All of those debts and loans and more were due to be paid in full at about the same time. So, it seems that around March of 1903, Conn and his new friend, school teacher Ray Van Buren Jackson, concocted a plan to make some fast cash.

Jackson arrived in Silver Lake in the summer of 1902, and was also in a tight spot financially. The school superintendent who hired him seems not to have known that Jackson had been in the Oregon State Penitentiary from June of 1896 until the summer of 1898 for forgery committed in April of 1895, and then went back to prison from July of 1899 until May of 1900 for a burglary in Baker County.

In January of 1900, a note for $500 had been due to his brother, William L. Jackson. After prison, Ray had gone to live in Harney County, and seems to have owned a small herd of cattle there since about 1895. By 1902, he owned 75 head with the "Circle 7" brand that he kept at Big Stick Creek near The Narrows and the headquarters of the Double O ranch. In September of 1902, Jackson borrowed $450 from the First National Bank of Burns and used his livestock as collateral.

In October of 1902, Jackson's brother sued him for recovery of the money that he had loaned him, and on October 29 his cattle were seized. On November 10, 1902, Sheriff Horace Dunlap of Lake County served Jackson with a summons to appear in court in Harney County to satisfy the debt to his brother. Jackson failed to appear. On December 15 his cattle were auctioned off to satisfy his debt to the bank. By April of 1903, when he entered into the deal with Conn, Jackson had just been laid off from his teaching job for the spring and summer, still owed $784 (including interest and attorney's fees) to his brother, and had earned only $40 per month for six month's teaching at Silver Lake.

Jackson and Conn filed on side by side claims under the Timber and Stone Act, near Mush Spring in north Lake County. According to Creed Conn himself, the men who located Conn and Jackson on their claims were John Bloss and George F. "Frank" Scott, who seem to have been intimately tied to sawmill man William T. E. Wilson. Several of Frank Scott's neighbors from the Black Butte area were located on timber lands near Mush Spring in 1903, about the time that Scott arrived in Oregon.

The timber deal that the two men entered into seems to have been orchestrated by Jackson, because he had connections to the Wilson family, and because it would not be the only time that Jackson posed as a timber expert. Wilson's brother, John O. Wilson, had been in the same grade with Jackson in the tiny school at Waterloo in Linn County from 1879 until about 1887. W. T. E. Wilson had a ranch on Squaw Creek, and a water power sawmill on Pole Creek, both near Sisters, and Frank Scott and John Bloss both lived in the Sisters area. Moreover, Conn had numerous friends who filed on timber claims, but none of his friends were located by Bloss and Scott, or had claims near Mush Spring.

Buying and selling government timber land was all the rage in central Oregon around 1900, and could be compared to the housing craze that swept through central Oregon a hundred years later. Many saw it as a way to make a fast buck.

The government, under the Timber and Stone Act, would sell to an individual 160 acres of valuable timber land for the paltry sum of $410, just so long as that person promised to keep the land for their own individual use. But many people soon realized that they could 'flip' their timber land, selling it to a big corporation at a profit of one or two thousand dollars. Citizens began to form cooperatives, under which they illegally agreed in advance to sell their claims to a timber company, and banded together to file on adjoining claims to create uninterrupted blocks of land. The timber companies were happy to pay a premium for those lands, because adjacent claims were much easier to log.

Jackson and Conn filed on side by side claims in section 11 of township 27 south, range 12 east on April 7, 1903. It is not known if Conn initially offered to put up the $410 in costs and fees that Jackson would need to buy the land from the government. But, by December 29, when Creed Conn made final proof and paid for his own timber land claim, Jackson stated that he had relinquished his claim. The two men had agreed to act as witnesses for each other through the claims process, and Jackson did appear for Conn on December 29, stating that he believed that Conn was taking the timber land for his own individual use. There was nothing to suggest that, by December of 1903, Jackson was anything other than completely flat broke.

Then, as he had for most of his life, Creed Conn seemed to have every advantage. The money he would make from the sale of his timber claim would certainly discharge his most pressing debts. Jackson, on the other hand, the man who had gone through life with a gigantic chip on his shoulder, the man who was chronically envious of practically everyone, especially Creed Conn, was up the creek without a paddle. The seizure of his livestock, hugely important to him as a symbol of wealth, must have been a bitter blow. It is easy to see how, inside the mind of a deeply disturbed man, who had endured privation and prison, the outcome of the timber deal would have fueled his envy of Creed Conn.

It was under those circumstances that Jackson determined that he would get back what he considered to be "his money" and his cattle. As described in detail in *The Sandy Knoll Murder*, around the first of February, over $3,000 disappeared from Conn's bank account, the money that Conn was holding on deposit for Martha Lane. Shortly afterward, Conn began to suspect that his bank account had been tampered with, and may even have known that the cash was withdrawn using a forged promissory note. At that time, Conn became ill, probably from arsenic poisoning. On February 12, Jackson torched the ZX barn containing Conn's three freight wagons. On the 29th, he poisoned his team. On March 4, 1904, he lured Conn to a secondary location and shot him in the heart.

A story of a riderless horse surfaced in 1904, four days after Creed Conn disappeared. A young man by the name of Fred Collins stole a horse from the Innes ranch at Summer Lake and later released the animal. The *Lake County Examiner* printed an anonymous innuendo about Collins, implicating him in Conn's disappearance, and that little news item could have been another facet of Jackson's game. The young man was arrested and sent to prison by Lafe Conn, but only charged with the theft of the horse and some petty larceny, committed on February 29.

Perhaps the most important clue to the identity of Conn's killer lies, not in what was found at the Sandy Knoll, but in what was not found there. Creed Conn always carried a small pocket journal with him that was mainly a financial record. It was used to note transactions made when he was away from the store, and could be compared to a check register or a passbook. When he returned to his store, Conn would transfer his notes to his main set of books, writing in the appropriate debits and credits. Jackson took that journal, because it was not found on Conn's body, or in his hotel room, or at his place of business when the brothers turned the store upside down looking for it. If Conn had possessed some proof or evidence of a forged promissory note, or even the actual cashed and canceled note itself, it probably was kept in that journal, considered a safe place because he had it on his person at all times.

When Conn's brother, District Attorney Lafe Conn, dove into trying to solve his brother's murder, he was a highly intelligent and well educated, yet rather inexperienced, investigator. The course of his inquiries seems to have followed the standard used for a typical motivated crime. He searched in vain for a true motive, looking for someone who had a concrete grudge against Creed, an enemy or a rival. He probably closely examined all of the people that his brother owed money to, and even considered a couple of them as suspects. But Lafe Conn was lead astray by his own conviction that a man had to have a motive to kill, and a very strong motive to kill the brother of a district attorney.

The idea that a man would kill for no reason other than psychological gratification, that a man could be overwhelmed by the compulsion to kill just for the sake of it, was only understood by a handful of doctors working in psychiatric hospitals at the time. The possibility of it may never have even entered Lafe Conn's mind.

Jackson, like the other men who Lafe Conn mildly suspected, had an alibi, and had no real, known motive. Not in the traditional sense. He told the district attorney that he had been at the schoolhouse at the time of the murder, as witnessed by his students. It is important to note here that, by the time he murdered Conn, Jackson already had the money. Money and material wealth were the things that drove him to kill throughout his life. Financial gain was what 'made him tick.' In the case of the Conn murder, and his prior crimes, getting his hands on the money was his top priority. Jackson got the money before he murdered Conn, and felt empowered and more daring. His ego was boosted by all of that ready cash. And, as a man who would not hesitate to engage in risky behavior, he hardly thought twice about the acts of harassment against Conn. Jackson probably believed that, if he could ruin Conn in business, and he knew full well that Conn's financial condition was very strained, the problem of Conn's suspicions, and the merchant himself, would simply go away. By the first of March, things came to a head, and Conn may even have indicated to Jackson that he suspected him.

Lafe Conn may have suspected the livery owner, Warren Duncan, partly because of the trauma to his dead brother's head and face, apparently caused by a hammer. But, around 1900, when horses were used universally, most people owned farrier's hammers, as did blacksmiths, to nail on horseshoes. Creed Conn's freight team was probably Duncan's largest and most important account, but Conn had not paid the blacksmith in more than four months, a debt that Duncan must have truly resented.

The district attorney probably also closely examined the cowboys of the ZX ranch, because it was on their property where the body had been found, and where the Sandy Knoll was located. The ZX was also the place where Creed Conn's wagons had been burned about three weeks before his disappearance, and may also have been the place where he pastured his team when they were poisoned. But, since no one from the ZX was ever arrested or held as a suspect, and no warrant was issued for the arrest of any ZX employee, it can safely be said that Lafe Conn found no evidence against anyone there.

Some longstanding Lake County innuendo and folklore puts suspicion on Virgil Conn as being responsible for the murder of his younger brother. And, it is possible that even Lafe Conn suspected Virgil for a time. A study of the probate records of Creed Conn reveals that Creed owed a large sum of cash for the purchase of grain, $1,800, since 1898. That debt was allegedly due to George Winkelman, and was charged to the estate and paid on September 3, 1904. Because that amount of money could buy a huge amount of grain at the time, and because of the date named, it seems likely that Virgil was trying to recover the cost of having fed Creed Conn's famous freight team during the years of their partnership. Creed had always at least paid the interest on his debts during his lifetime, but on that alleged debt to Winkelman, no interest payment was ever made. If Virgil Conn did hold a grudge against Creed over grain consumption, it was satisfied by regular means of cash from the estate, so we cannot safely assume that Virgil resorted to something more desperate.

Another victim who can probably be attributed to Ray Jackson was Julius Wallende. As described in *The Sandy Knoll Murder*, Wallende was just 16 years old when he disappeared from Silver Lake. According to the book, *Profilers*, by Campbell and DeNevi, serial killers are stimulated by the memory of their murders, and find themselves deeply preoccupied with those memories to the point that the memories contribute to fantasies for subsequent killings. Consider that factor as we review the circumstances of Wallende's death. Some of the information from that crime bears repeating here, because it will illustrate how the modus operandi of Jackson evolved from the Conn murder, to Wallende, and also shows some elements that would be carried forward into the future.

Some of the common elements between the Conn and Wallende cases are interesting because they show how the second Silver Lake murder allowed Jackson to relive, and revel in, the satisfaction of the Conn murder all over again. On December 27, 1907 Julius Wallende, like Conn, disappeared shortly after leaving a hotel in Silver Lake. When Wallende left the hotel, it was believed that he, like Conn, was going to meet someone.

According to an *Oregonian* reporter, writing from Silver Lake around March 16, Silver Creek had been frozen over during the winter, but had begun to thaw around March 6. Around March 9, an anonymous letter was sent out from Portland to Silver Lake. It is not known to whom the letter was addressed, although it may have been sent to the ranger station there. It arrived on March 12, and bore news that prompted the local citizens to begin searching for the body on the day that it was found. Private detectives were put on the case at Portland to trace the origins of that letter, but the writer was never discovered. The author believes that Jackson was the source of that letter, because it is surprisingly common for psychopaths to communicate with investigators about their crimes, and they love to involve themselves in investigations.

Another anonymous communication is worth mentioning because it may have come from the killer, and carried a theme that was used in the Conn murder as well. After Wallende's body was found, on March 20, Sheriff Dent of Lake County issued a warrant for the arrest of Allie Hamilton, about 28 years of age, who had been present at the inquest, and who was Wallende's employer. Dent notified the *Oregonian,* about the suspect. On March 22 or 23, a second suspicious communication was sent, this time to the *Oregonian* and probably by telegram, for it was printed on March 24. The source of the telegram was not an *Oregonian* staff writer, because the dateline labeled it as a "special" from Silver Lake.

> *"Olie Hamilton, accused of murdering Julius Wallende, was heard of near Odell at the foot of the mountain, on this side, and is no doubt trying to cross the mountains to Lane County by the old military road. He has abandoned his horse and has gone on afoot. The reward for his arrest and conviction offered by Silver Lake citizens now amounts to $450."*

It should be noted that the spelling of the man's name was odd, and that the official investigators had used either "Ole" or "Allie," but never "Olie," to refer to Mr. Alec Hamilton.

The ranger station at Silver Lake, where Jackson had worked as an assistant to the ranger during the warm months of 1907, was equipped with a telegraph set, and so was the ranger station at Odell. Also note that the theme of a young suspect who fled the scene and turned his horse loose was used in the Conn murder as well. It is quite common for psychopaths to attempt to pin their crimes on others, as a part of the game, and that report sticks out like a sore thumb, because the official investigation and pursuit of Hamilton had taken a different course entirely. The source of that telegram was not the Lake County Sheriff. At the time that it was sent, the sheriff was on his way to Klamath Falls in pursuit of Hamilton, on information that the suspect had registered under an assumed name at a hotel there.

Wallende's body had apparently been stored over the winter and, like Conn's, was "in an excellent state of preservation." It had been placed in Silver Creek the night before, and was found on Friday, March 13. As in the Conn murder, the body had been placed in plain sight of anyone traveling the highway. It was positioned near the Silver Creek Bridge, very near the spot where Creed Conn had been shot. Another similarity was the way that the killer controlled when and how the body was discovered. The choice of Friday the 13th as the date of discovery may have been an attempt by Jackson to make a coy allusion to the culture of the sheepshooters, who the media had blamed for Conn's murder, or just another way of toying with investigators.

The evidence that the body was placed in the stream the night before came from an oral history account that was recorded by Teressa Foster in her book, *Settlers in Summer Lake Valley*. Ethel Ewing Billings was the wife of Ranger Nelson "Jay" Billings. In 1908 the couple lived at the Silver Lake ranger station, situated near Silver Creek and just in front of the present day Forest Service building. Ethel Billings described how her dog, Pedro, had made a great commotion at the edge of the stream on the night before the body was found.

Several details from newspaper accounts of the discovery make it seem that Wallende's body had been tied at the spot by a rope. Silver Creek would have been running very high at that time of year, and a rope would have been one sure way to keep it in the exact spot that Jackson had chosen. The *Oregonian,* on March 15, stated that the thaw had come and the snow had melted. "The body was found by Bert Gowdy, who overheard some boys talking about an old coat they had seen in the water of the creek and which they had been unable to pull to land," reported the *Oregonian* of March 19. "He and the men with him secured a long pole and managed to get the body up to the bank where it was tied with ropes, and Judge J. S. Martin, as acting coroner, was notified." On March 27 the *Bulletin* at Bend, in a story they picked up from the *Silver Lake Oregonian,* reported "the body was discovered floating in Silver creek." How could a body float in a thawed, raging stream, without moving, unless it had been deliberately anchored in place?

From the fall of 1906, through the end of March of 1907, Jackson taught school at Paisley, about 60 miles south of Silver Lake, and developed the reputation of being a very mean school teacher, as documented by writer, Earl F. Moore and others. From April through August of 1907, Jackson worked as an assistant to Ranger Gilbert Brown at the Silver Lake Ranger District. In the fall of 1907, he went back to teaching at Paisley, and school was out of session during the holiday season when Wallende was killed. In early March of 1908, Jackson put himself forward as a candidate for superintendent of schools for Lake County. On the night of Thursday, March 12, he took Wallende's body from its hiding place and put it in the stream. In the April primaries, Jackson received the nomination from the Democratic Party of Lake County, and in the first week of June, 1908, he was elected school superintendent.

The Bend *Bulletin* of March 20 reported that Wallende's "head had been mutilated and the skull fractured." And the *Oregonian* of the 15th said that Wallende's head had been "frightfully battered" and that his skull had been fractured "in numerous places." Ten wounds were counted on his head, apparently made by some heavy, blunt instrument. One of those blows had fractured the top of the skull. Wallende's arms were badly bruised with defensive wounds, and his nose had been fractured, showing that the killer faced him during the attack, and probably did so for the thrill of it. Like Conn, the damage to Wallende's features was so severe, that by six days later, the authorities still had not fully established the boy's identity. Wallende had been missing for 75 days.

The *Oregonian* of March 19 speculated that the wounds were made with the butt end of a revolver, but it could be argued that a heavier weapon would have been required to do so much damage in close quarters with a short swing of the instrument. When the top of the human skull is fractured, only the most severe blows will break the bone all the way through so that the fracture is visible on the outside of the head. Lighter blows may splinter the bone on the inner surface of the skull only. A blow to the thick part of the skull on the top of the head that broke the bone all the way through would require something heavier than a pistol, and also something with a longer reach, such as a hammer or a hatchet.

The pistol that Jackson was known to carry at the time was a pearl handled Colt revolver that would have weighed about two and one third pounds, with most of that weight in the center, cylinder portion of the gun. And, because of his new seasonal job in forestry, Jackson would also have probably owned one of the marking hatchets that were standard issue for men working for the U.S. Forest Service. The hatchet was used for marking timber and a variety of tasks. It was made of hard steel and weighed about two pounds, with most of that weight in the head. The butt end of the tool was shaped like the head of a hammer and was about the size of a half dollar coin. It had the raised letters "U.S." molded into it. Timber was marked by cutting a blaze in a tree, and then stamping the blaze with the letters "U. S.," or by stamping the cut end of downed trees. Such an instrument could have been used to knock Wallende down, fracturing the top of his skull.

Remembering that financial gain was what made Jackson 'tick' requires us to inspect Wallende's financial condition. The young man had received his pay from Alec Hamilton, about $90, when he finished work around 4 p.m. on the day that he disappeared. He left the hotel around 9:30 p.m. That money, and his gold watch and chain, valued at $35, were not found on the body. Wallende had filed on a homestead claim near Christmas Lake on October 3, 1907, in township 27 south, range eighteen east, section twelve, six miles east of what is now the main intersection in Christmas Valley. The young man was able to lie convincingly about his age on his application, stating that he was 25 years old, so he was probably large for a boy of 16. By law, a citizen had to be over 21 years old to file on federal land.

Alonzo Long, father of Reub Long, acted as a witness for Wallende's mother and half-brother, Lena M. and Otto A. Samson, in 1913 when they completed the legal requirements to prove up on the claim. Long stated that he did not believe Wallende had ever established residence on the land. Another witness who had known Wallende in 1907, Henry Hach, stated, "He was murdered at Silver Lake, Oregon about December 27, 1907. He had the lumber purchased for his house when he was murdered." Between the good paying job that Wallende had, and his recent lumber purchase and intention to buy a homestead from the government, it would have been evident that the young man had some ready cash.

Jackson had a predilection for punishing young men, as revealed by former student Earl F. Moore, who described in detail the cruel and humiliating way that Jackson treated the children left in his charge, and how Jackson's treatment of the older boys was nothing short of sadistic.

> *"This is where the rawhide whip came in. Lash after lash cut red welts over the shoulders and back until the area looked as though a red rope had been coiled up on it. Then you were forced to try the torturous procedure again or until the strength refused entirely. The bigger the teenager, the more Jackson seemed to enjoy the cruelty."*

Moore described another incident in the classroom where Jackson's attack on a teenage boy resulted in a fist fight and brawl that left the young man with a broken hand.

So, how did Jackson escape detection in the Conn murder, and then go on to commit a second atrocity at Silver Lake? District Attorney Lafe Conn had at least a passing interest in Ray

Jackson, because Jackson had been questioned about his movements and details of the morning of March 4, 1904. Jackson had always admitted to having had breakfast with Conn immediately before he disappeared.

But, there were no eye witnesses to that murder, and even as Lafe Conn's insight into Jackson's true character grew over the years, nothing short of a signed confession by the ex-convict could have put him behind bars. Until 1910, Lafe Conn had nothing to go on, other than a small error in the timing of events, as reported by Jackson. Lafe Conn knew that there was an adequate gap in time between when Jackson and his brother left the hotel where they had breakfast, and the time that Jackson appeared at the schoolhouse. The exact time of his arrival at school was a nagging question, because he was taking Jackson's word for it. Conn disappeared between 7:45 and 8:15 a.m. but, according to the school laws of the time, the school day did not begin until 9 a.m.

Brothers Virgil, Lafe, and George Conn all had a good understanding of Creed's exact financial condition and debts after his death, and were fully aware of the debt to Martha Lane, and repaid it, on October 1. Suspicion had to have fallen on the Lane family, at least during the seven weeks that both Creed Conn and the cash were missing. The brothers moved quickly to settle Creed's estate, in those days when debt was considered a scandal and a disgrace equal to outright theft. When Creed Conn had been missing for less than four weeks, without a body or a witness to a murder, without any proof of death, and without jurisdiction, Lafe and Virgil Conn essentially had Creed declared dead and began to sell off his worldly goods. It was probably done to avoid a scandal, and to quiet the rumors that the indebted member of a politically proud family had absconded with Lane's money.

Lafe Conn seems to have continued to keep a wary eye trained on Jackson, even though Jackson never acted guilty and was even helpful to the investigation. Jackson never attempted to leave the country, as would be expected from a man who had suddenly come into a large sum of money. But, in mid-October of 1910, while Lafe Conn was still practicing law at Lakeview, Jackson, in the capacity of school superintendent, was indicted for having embezzled from the Lake County school system. The brothers rapidly exhumed Creed Conn's body from the Silver Lake Cemetery on November 19, then took it to Klamath Falls, where it was autopsied for the first time on about November 21. On November 25, the body was interred on land that had been a part of their father's farm, at what is now Roseburg Memorial Gardens. The brothers' knowledge of the three thousand dollars that disappeared in 1904, and the way that the autopsy followed Jackson's indictment for embezzlement, all indicate that Lafe Conn suspected Jackson of the murder of his closest brother.

What seems to have earlier escaped the attention of Lafe Conn was that Jackson bought about three thousand dollars worth of cattle after the murder of Creed Conn and the disappearance of Martha Lane's money. On June 21, 1904, the unemployed school teacher, who should have been almost penniless at the time, was stopped while attempting to cross the Cascade Forest Reserve going east with 250 head of cattle, without a permit to do so, by the diligent ranger, Addie L. Morris. Possession of that 'smoking herd' indicates that Jackson came into a large sum of money in early 1904. Jackson was stopped near Lowell in Lane County, and was no doubt intending to take the old military road east, the same road described in the anonymous telegraph about the flight of the alleged suspect, Hamilton, in 1908.

It is easy to see that Jackson's love of money came to him before his desire to kill for it, but after the satisfaction he derived from the Conn murder, the thrill of killing was tremendously magnified in him, and it must have occurred to Jackson that killing before stealing made the stealing infinitely easier. As time passed, his confidence grew, because he had gotten away with it.

Jackson would kill for material gain, used arson and poison, and attacked the heads of his victims. His crime scenes were organized, and he liked to communicate with newspapers and the authorities, especially when he could implicate another person. He liked to involve himself in the investigation of his own crimes, and to possess the bodies of his victims for a time. He had killed a celebrity who was the brother of a district attorney, and accomplished another satisfying murder at the same place. He now believed that he was capable of anything.

Ray Van Buren Jackson used the middle initial of "V" early in life, as in this 1896 photo from his forgery conviction in Oregon. Shortly after arriving in Lake County in 1902, he switched to using the middle initial of "B."

SOURCES:

The Sandy Knoll Murder, Legacy of the Sheepshooters, by Melany Tupper, 2010 Central Oregon Books, LLC. Book details the murder of John Creed Conn, as well as the murders of Ethel Martin, Julius Wallende, and Ira and Harold Bradley.

Bad Men Do What Good Men Dream, A Forensic Psychiatrist Illuminates the Darker Side of Human Behavior, by Robert I. Simon, M.D. 1996, American Psychiatric Press, Inc., Washington, D.C., p 291-292, 297, 299-300, 307-309.

The Psychopathology of Serial Murder, A Theory of Violence, by Stephen J. Giannangelo, 1996, Praeger, Westport, CT, p 3, 10, 22-23, 26, 36-38.

Crime Classification Manual, by Burgess, Burgess, Douglas, and Ressler, 2006, John Wiley & Sons, San Francisco, CA, p 19-40.

"J.C. Conn's Body Found," *Crook County Journal,* April 28, 1904.

Editorial, *Crook County Journal,* June 23, 1904. Picked up from the *Central Oregonian* at Silver Lake.

"Reign of Terror," *Oregonian,* May 10, 1904.

"First in Heart," *Oregonian,* July 14, 1904.

"Murder or Suicide," *Oregonian,* June 12, 1904

"Weather Report for March," and "Weather Report for April," *Lake County Examiner,* July 21, 1904.

"Was Not Suicide," *Oregonian,* June 9, 1904.

C. P. Marshal to G. P. Tarpey and Johanna Tarpey, February 11, 1903. G. P. Tarpey and Johanna Tarpey to Chewaucan Land and Cattle Company, March 25, 1903. Deed and Title Records, vol. 13, p 318 , Lake County Courthouse, County Clerk's Office, Lakeview, Oregon.

"New Firm at Paisley," *Lake County Examiner,* June 9, 1910.

"Supt. Jackson Talks of Schools," *Lake County Examiner,* May 6, 1909.

Personal conversation between the author and Mr. John Robertson of Roseburg on March 13, 2011. Robertson is a great nephew of Creed Conn, and is also President of the Douglas County Historical Society. According to Robertson, Henry Conn Sr. and his son James both raised Percheron horses.

Historic Douglas County, Oregon 1982, by Douglas County Historical Society, 1982, Roseburg, Oregon, History of the Henry Conn Family, p 108.

The Growth of Lake County, Oregon, by G. E. B. Stephenson, 1994, Book Partners, Inc., Wilsonville, OR. Photo of a freight team on page 34 of this book is the only photo that the author has found of a team that matches the description of Conn's team.

Reflections, Short Stories of Old Lake County, Lake County E. S. D., 1982, Lakeview, Oregon. During his interview for this book, Ted Conn said that Conn's team included two horses.

"Local Interest," *Ashwood Prospector,* May 24, 1904.

"Oregon Notes," Oregonian November 24, 1900.

"Local Happenings Told in Paragraphs," *Examiner,* August 14, 1902

"Local Events of the Week," *Bulletin,* June 12, 1903

"Local Events of the Week," *Bulletin,* August 7, 1903

"Local Events of the Week,"*Bulletin,* August 21, 1903

"Death of Ethel Martin," *Lake County Examiner,* April 7, 1904.

In the Matter of the Estate of J.C. Conn, Deceased, Probate file of John Creed Conn, Order Appointing Appraisers, April 9, 1904. Probate Case Files, 18751927, Clerk's Basement South Storage Room, Lake County Courthouse, Lakeview, Oregon.

Inmate record (and photo) of R. V. Jackson, inmate #3680, sentenced from Clackamas County, June 9, 1896, Oregon State Archives, Salem, Oregon.

The State of Oregon vs. R. V. Jackson, Oregon Circuit Court at Clackamas County, indictment, November 16, 1895, Circuit Court Case Files, Oregon State Archives, Salem, Oregon.

Inmate Record of R. Jackson, #4134, 1899. Oregon State Archives, Salem, Oregon. Record contains only a photograph of Jackson, but he and his accomplice, John Ryan, are also listed in the penitentiary's Convict Record on page 102.

W. L. Jackson vs R. V. Jackson , in the Circuit Court for the State of Oregon, for County of Harney, Default and order for sale of attached property, case #666, October 20, 1902. Harney County Circuit Court, Burns, OR.

"W. L. Jackson vs. R. V. Jackson," *Harney Valley Items*, May 2, 1903. Default and judgment and order for sale of attached property.

Profilers, by John H. Campbell and Don DeNevi, 2004, Prometheus, Amherst, New York, p 77.

R. B. Jackson to First National Bank of Burns, September 10, 1902, Mortgage Records, Harney County Clerk's Office, Burns, OR

"The School Teachers of Oregon," editorial, *Roseburg Plaindealer*, May 16, 1904. Oregon teachers were among the lowest paid in the country in 1904.

"Getting Along," *Oregonian*, March 8, 1910. This short item was picked up from the *Examiner*, and is a fine example of Jackson's habit of newsprint braggadocio. In it, he claims to have gotten his start in the cattle business in 1902 with only $40, but fails to mention the bank loan, the loan from his brother and, of course, the money stolen from Conn.

U.S. Census Bureau, Twelfth Census of the United States, 1900, Hardin pct, Wayne County, Nebraska.

U.S. Census Bureau, Thirteenth Census of the United States, 1910, Black Butte pct, Crook County, Oregon.

General Land Office Records, U. S. Department of the Interior, Bureau of Land Management, search results for all of township 27 south, range 12 east, Willamette Meridian, available online at: http://www.glorecords.blm. gov/results/default.aspx?search Criteria=type=patent|st=OR|cty=|twp_nr=27|twp_dir=S|rng_n r=12|rng_dir=E|m=33|sp=true|sw=true|sadv=false

Timber and Stone patent application file of John C. Conn, serial #ORLAA 058633, Bureau of Land Management, records of the

General Land Office, National Archives and Records Administration, Washington, D.C. Patented October 22, 1904.

The State of Oregon vs Fred Collins, Information for Larceny of a Horse, May 16, 1904, Circuit Court Journal for 1904, p 410411. Lake County Courthouse, Circuit Court Basement West Storage Room, Lakeview, Oregon. Collins was found guilty and sentenced to three years in prison on May 20, 1904. Lafe Conn was the prosecuting attorney.

The State of Oregon vs Fred Collins, information for larceny in a dwelling house, May 19, 1904, Circuit Court Journal for 1904, p 420-421. Lake County Courthouse, Circuit Court Basement West Storage Room, Lakeview, Oregon. Collins stole a coat and vest from the home of George Winkelman.

"News Notes From Paisley," *Lake County Examiner*, March 10, 1904.

"Collins is Arrested," *Lake County Examiner*, March 17, 1904.

Inmate record for Fred Collins, #4900, May 30, 1904, Oregon State Archives, Salem, Oregon.

"Mysteriously Disappeared," *Plaindealer*, March 17, 1904. Article was originally published in the *Central Oregonian* at Silver Lake soon after Conn's disappearance.

Twelfth Census of the United States, 1900, South Dakota, Edmunds County, Pembrook township. Shows Julius Wallende at age 9 living with his brother Ernest and parents Lena and George W. Sampson (Samson).

"Mute Evidence of Crime," *Oregonian*, March 15, 1908.

Homestead patent application file of Julius Wallende, serial #424854, Bureau of Land Management, records of the General Land Office, National Archives and Records Administration, Washington, D.C. Patent was issued to Wallende's mother, Lena Samson, in 1913 with the help of Governor Chamberlain.

Settlers in Summer Lake Valley, by Teresa Foster, 1989, Maverick, Bend, Oregon, Appendix p 2.

A History of the Fremont National Forest, by Melva Bach, 1990, Forest Service, USDA, Pacific Northwest Region, Fremont National Forest, p 19, 21, 24, 29, 33, 35.

"Silver Lake Aroused," *Oregonian*, March 18, 1908.

"Found with Ugly Gashes," *Oregonian* March 19, 1908. Dateline is Silver Lake, March 16.

Early Days in the Forest Service, volume 1, account of Albert E. Cole, Senior Ranger Deerlodge (retired 1935). Web site of the Forest History Society: http://foresthistory.org /ASPNET/ Publications/region/1/early_days/1/sec4.htm

Newly Published Histories by Retirees, Recollections, by Ira E. Jones, submitted by Evan Jones, from the web site of the National Association of Forest Service Retirees, NAFSR: http://www.fsx.org/history.htm

Morris's Human Anatomy, by Sir Henry Morris, 1921, P. Blakiston's Sons & Co., Philadelphia, p 13-35.

"Silver Lake Murder," *Bend Bulletin*, March 20, 1908.

"Suspect Allie Hamilton," *Oregonian*, March 21, 1908.

"Seek Slayer of Wallende," *Oregonian*, March 22, 1908.

"Suspected of the Murder of Julius Wallende," *Oregonian*, March 25, 1908. Photo

"Fugitive in Mountains," *Oregonian*, March 24, 1908.

"More Particulars Given," *Bend Bulletin*, March 27, 1908. Cites the *Central Oregonian* as its source.

US genweb archives, Special Projects, National Search Engine, Tombstone Project, Silver Lake Cemetery, County of Lake, Silver Lake Oregon. Available online at http://files.usgwarchives.net /or/=lake/cemeteries /silverlakecem.txt Julius Wallende is incorrectly listed in the index, that gives his name as "Julius Wallmade." Date of death is also incorrectly given as March 8, 1908. Wallende was believed to have died on the night he disappeared, December 27, 1907.

Western Echoes, by Earl F. Moore, 1981, Tremaine Publishing, Klamath Falls, Oregon, p 72-73.

"In the Circuit Court," *Lake County Examiner*, October 20, 1910.

"Grim Reminder of 1904 Range War," *Lake County Examiner*, November 24, 1910. Story was picked up from the *Silver Lake Leader*.

The Codes and General Laws of Oregon, compiled by William Lair Hill, vol 2, second edition, 1892. Bancroft Whitney, San Francisco, p 12-47.

Untitled article, *Umpqua Valley News*, November 24, 1910.

Untitled article, *Roseburg Evening News*, November 23, 1910.

Untitled article, *Roseburg Review*, November 22, 1910.

"In the matter of the resignation of R. B. Jackson," *Lake County Examiner*, September 28, 1911.

Diary Book 4, March 1904 September 1904, Addie L. Morris, Cascade Reserve Ranger 1899-1905, p 15 June 21, 1904. Letter of S. C. Bartrum, Forest Supervisor, to Addie L. Morris, June 24, 1904.

Charles Hyde Kimzey's mug shots from his first stint in prison at the Idaho State Penitentiary in 1915. Kimzey managed to escape from the Homedale Work Farm on a stolen horse just four months after he was incarcerated. He remained a fugitive for 18 years by moving around and using several aliases.

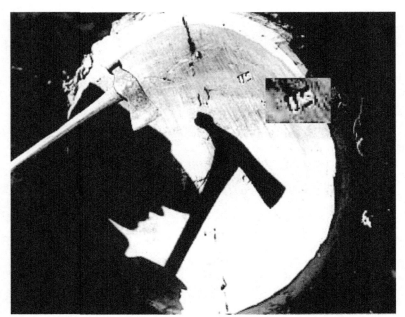

Photo silhouette of a Forest Service worker using a marking hatchet to 'stamp' the letters "U. S. (see insert) in the end of a log for a government timber sale.

Chapter Two

Getting Away With It

Soon after being released from prison, on January 25, 1898 Ray Jackson borrowed $500 from his brother, William L. Jackson, and headed east. He had been sentenced to two years in the Oregon State Penitentiary on a forgery charge on June 9, 1896, but apparently was released about six months early. In one version of Jackson's obituary, written in 1938, we learn that he first came to central Oregon in 1898, and went to work for the Double O ranch as a bookkeeper.

The old records for the Oregon State Penitentiary show that one "R. Jackson" was incarcerated on July 3 of 1899 from Baker County on a charge of robbery, along with a man named John Ryan on the same date. Prisoner numbers for the two men were recorded as 4133 and 4134. On July 3, 1899, the *Daily Journal* at Salem made note of the arrival of the prisoners. "Sheriff W. H. Huntington, of Baker county, today brought down J. Ryan and R. Jackson each to serve a term of one year for robbery." Several traces of Ray Jackson can be found around the Baker area during that period. On March 3 of 1900, he had a team of horses and harnesses that he mortgaged to a nearby prominent stockman, James Fleetwood, who owned a large ranch on Burnt River. Since the mortgage was recorded about two months before Jackson was released from prison, it seems likely that Jackson had worked for Fleetwood before he was arrested, and that Fleetwood was in possession of the team and demanded payment for their upkeep.

Around the turn of the last century, when agriculture was the main industry in Oregon, prisoners were often paroled into the custody of prominent ranchers to work off their debts. On June 13 of 1900, Jackson was counted in the census of the Unity precinct, and lived with a man named William Chamberlin in Baker County. Both men made their living as farm laborers, possibly in the employ of Mr. Fleetwood. Also worth noting is that the parents and family of Miss Bernice Case arrived at nearby Sumpter between 1897 and 1900, so Jackson may have first met the young school teacher there, and may even have tried to find work in his former profession as a teacher at Sumpter.

The five hundred dollar loan, in the form of a promissory note, was due to his brother in January of 1900, but he never repaid it. His next move seems to have been attaching himself to the family of his childhood friend, Willis G. Bardwell. In an oral history recorded in 1980, Mrs. Jessie Bardwell Williams, a daughter of Willis, said she moved to the Double O ranch with her family when she was four years old, or around 1899. In July of 1901, Willis Bardwell and Anna E. Hurlburt acquired some water rights along Big Stick Creek near Iron Mountain, in sections 5, 8, 9, 10 and 11 of township 26 south, range 26 east where they had a dam, reservoir, and a long irrigation ditch. Bardwell patented a homestead in that same township in 1906. When William Jackson sued Ray to try to recover his money in 1902, he told his attorney that he believed Ray had partial ownership of those water rights. Although the author found no proof of Ray Jackson having actual legal water rights at Big Stick Creek, proof of the Bardwell and Hurlburt rights was found, and that indicates that Ray Jackson was ranching in the Iron Mountain area by 1902.

On September 2, 1902, Jackson registered his "Circle 7" brand with the Harney County Clerk, and gave his address as "The Narrows," pointing to the same area and the neighborhood between Harney and Mud Lakes. Over the summer, Jackson had arranged a teaching position for himself in Silver Lake, in Lake County. On the same day that he registered his brand, Jackson mortgaged 75 head of cattle to the First National Bank of Burns for $450. On October 29, his cattle were seized as William sought to recover his money. On November 10, a summons was delivered to him at Silver Lake by Lake County Sheriff Horace Dunlap. In December the cattle were finally auctioned off at he Hurlburt ranch. The buyer was William Hanley, owner of the Double O.

Ray Jackson was a sly character, there can be no doubt about that, and he had the gift of glibness that enabled him to charm his way into numerous favorable situations. When he arrived in Lake County around June of 1902, he met fellow teacher, Gilbert "Bert" Brown, whose real name was actually Daniel, like his father, but he preferred to be known by his middle name. Both Jackson and Brown were hired to teach school in Lake County in

1903, and Brown would later prove instrumental in securing a job for Jackson with the Forest Service.

Also very early on, and certainly by the summer of 1902, Jackson had warmed up to the influential Conn brothers, George, Creed, and Virgil. All were very well respected in business and politics, and Jackson's friendship can be shown by his repeated associations with those men. As late as May of 1914, Jackson acted as a witness for George Conn in a civil case in which he sued J. D. Farra to recover over $1,000 on a bad check written for the purchase of hay.

In October of 1911, when Paisley became an incorporated town, Jackson and Virgil Conn were both voted in as aldermen, or city councilmen, along with M. C. Currier, P. J. Brattain, V. O. Morgan, and B. F. Cannon. In September of 1912, Jackson and Virgil Conn attended the Irish Picnic together, traveling from Paisley with Mike Sullivan for the big annual event held at Camas Prairie, near Lakeview.

For whatever reason, possibly an acquired 'sixth sense' about people, Creed Conn seems to have seen through Jackson's manipulative ways; his flattery, superficial charm, and pity ploys. After all, Creed had spent more time working directly with the public in the mercantile business than had either of his two older brothers, who had other pursuits, like Virgil's management role in the mercantile company, and seat in the state legislature during the 1890s. And, George's farm, orchard, and flour mill. Even after Jackson was indicted for embezzling from the school system in October of 1911, it is plain to see that his friendship with George and Virgil Conn endured. Virgil's political influence and experience as school clerk and school director at Paisley for 17 years prior to 1910 probably helped in arranging Jackson's move to the position of principal of the Paisley school after he abruptly resigned as principal at Silver Lake in mid-January of 1906.

Jackson's teaching career provided him with a ready supply of attractive young ladies. His first wife, Alda "Jessie" Parrish, who seems to have divorced him when he went to prison in 1896, had been a school teacher. And, his resignation from the Silver Lake school seems to be connected to the relationship he had with a Silver Lake teacher, Miss Bernice R. Case. She probably arrived in Lake County in August of 1904, the month that she applied for a county teaching certificate at Lakeview. By that October she was teaching at the Salt Creek School, about six miles north of Lakeview. But, some time in early 1905, Miss Case moved to Silver Lake and began teaching there under Ray Jackson, who was now principal.

About that same time, there appeared an interesting, yet anonymous, short opinion piece in the *Examiner,* suggesting that teachers of Lake County should be paid a stipend to attend the teachers' congress at Portland, that happened to coincide with the upcoming Lewis and Clark Exposition.

Because the letter was so poorly written, and because it so closely reflected Ray Jackson's selfish desires when it came to the teachers' institute fund, the author believes that the letter came from the pen of Jackson himself. It is provided here in all of its incoherent glory, exactly as it appeared in the *Lake County Examiner* of January 26, 1905.

> *At a meeting of educators from various parts of the state, the propriety of diverting county institute funds to the purpose of making the educational Congress to be held at the Lewis and Clark exposition a success and at the same time, give valuable experience to the teachers of the State, this seems well, but can it be done? The law seems to require teachers county institutes to be held and requires teachers to attend them under penalties for failure. They cannot be held without funds. Again can the funds for this use be turned to another however, closely related not provided for by law.*

It is not known what Jackson meant by "a meeting of educators from various parts of the state," unless he was referring to a chat that he had with his friend, Gilbert Brown, who was teaching at Paisley at the time. There had been no meeting of teachers in Lake County over the holidays, or for several months prior.

In early July of 1905, the *Bulletin* carried the scandalous news that "Professor R. B. Jackson and a Miss Casey (sic), a teacher in the Silver Lake school, passed through Bend this morning on their way to Portland to visit the exposition. They are driving across country, going by way of the McKenzie route."

A few months later, Christmas vacation occurred for Lake County schools, and it was during that week, between December 22 and January 2, that Ray Jackson made contact with his estranged father, who had virtually washed his hands of his sociopathic younger son. Around January 5, Martin Van Buren Jackson was in Lakeview on his way to Silver Lake "to visit his son, who is sick" reported the *Examiner*.

Five months after Jackson and Miss Case had made their little excursion to Portland, Jackson suffered some sort of nervous collapse. "Prof. Jackson, principal of the Silver Lake school, has resigned his position. He has had several nervous spells recently, caused by overwork, and is now confined to his bed with a severe attack," reported the *Examiner* on January 18. It was not until March 21 that Jackson was able to return to teaching. "Prof. R. P. (sic) Jackson, who resigned the principalship of the Silver Lake public school some weeks ago on account of poor health, has sufficiently regained his health as to accept the Paisley school and began teaching there last Monday a week ago," noted the *Examiner* of March 29.

The author found another example of Ray Jackson suffering a nervous fit, of sorts, in an oral history account by a man who had been a friend and occasional visitor of Jackson's during the 1920s when he lived on the east side of Wagontire Mountain. It occurred just after the shooting death of young Harold Bradley, and Jackson reacted dramatically when he became frightened that Link Hutton might come after him.

In a 1991 interview, Shelby Petersen described that January 1926 visit to Jackson's house. Petersen's arrival after dark sent Jackson fleeing from the house in a paroxysm of fear. Later, after Petersen turned the lights out and went to bed, Jackson crept up on the porch of his own house and called out to whoever was inside. Jackson had been so agitated that he forgot to grab the pistol that he kept under his pillow as he exited the house. According to Petersen, the highly agitated Jackson kept him up most of that night talking, talking fast, about the frightening events of the Bradley murder, and told Petersen that he was very afraid of

Link Hutton, the man who owned the ranch where Harold Bradley was killed.

Whatever became of Miss Bernice R. Case is not known. Did Jackson's father hand deliver a payment to the unfortunate lady? It would be perfectly understandable for him to have done so, for a scandal could have spoiled the reputation of his other son, William L. Jackson, who was a highly respected educator and superintendent of schools in Linn County, and Martin Jackson certainly would have known better than to entrust Ray with any sum of money.

The school laws of Oregon contained a provision about the morality of teachers, and in those days, teachers were required to present "certificates of good moral character" before they were granted teaching credentials. The board of directors for the school district had the power to dismiss teachers for good cause. The last trace of Miss Case was found in the *Advertised Letters* list published in the *Examiner* on August 2, 1906, a list of un-claimed letters that were being held at the Lakeview Post Office. Wherever the lady was, she had left Lake County by the summer of 1906 without collecting her mail.

Another man who relocated to Paisley from Silver Lake in March of 1906 was Frank W. Payne, who had been the clerk in Creed Conn's mercantile store before, during, and after the mur-der. Virgil Conn had kept Payne on the payroll to run the Silver Lake store for two years after his brother's death, and seems to have closed it around March 1 when he moved Payne down to Paisley to work in his large mercantile store there.

Jackson and Payne had definitely known each other for a few years, and probably since about 1902 when Jackson arrived in Silver Lake. In 1906, they entered into a cattle ranching partner-ship, and that winter were feeding their band of cattle at the head of the Chewaucan Marsh. In May of 1907, Jackson registered his diamond brand for cattle and horses at the Lake County clerk's office, and in October of that year, Payne and Jackson sold some of their cattle to Jack Horton at Bonanza.

Ray Jackson seems to have begun working for the Forest Service in the spring of 1907, and his friend, Gilbert Brown, who was the first ranger to ever be stationed at Silver Lake, entered his new duty station on April 1, 1907. In February, the *Examiner* reported that "Prof. R. B. Jackson and E. O. Lamb came down from Paisley last week to investigate the stock range question inside the reserve," a news item that indicated Jackson may have already been working on the forest in some capacity.

In an account that Brown wrote for *TimberLines*, a newsletter created by and for alumni of the Forest Service's Region Six, Brown counted R. B. Jackson among the "old time rangers" that he had worked with. In another account of his days at Silver Lake, Brown wrote, "As my assistant R. B. Jackson and I were leaving Silver Lake one morning, the saloon keeper stopped us and said that a certain man had threatened to kill me; that he was drinking and dangerous." Jackson and Brown did encounter the angry drunk later that evening, but the matter was resolved during supper around the campfire.

Jackson seems to have slid easily into the role of 'pseudo ranger,' and even had the county paper convinced that he was the real thing when he left the Forest Service in more or less of a cloud in September of 1907.

> *"R. B. Jackson resigned his position as ranger the first of the month. Mr. Jackson will take charge of the Paisley school as principal on the 16th of this month."*

It is very common for psychopaths of all stripes to finagle their way into positions of authority, and they particularly like situations where they can have control over a small group of people, like a group of teachers, a classroom of students, or a board of directors. They are power hungry individuals, and many have finally been caught when they went a bit too far by impersonating some authority figure, such as a doctor, psychologist, or policeman.

Just as he had become a self-described "professor" of higher learning when he began teaching a handful of grade school kids at Silver Lake, when Jackson put on that wide brimmed Forest Service hat in 1907, he became a self-styled timber expert, although his actual forestry experience was limited to chopping kindling for the wood stove of the school house. Many male school teachers were hired by the Forest Service in those days because they were available during the warm months of the year, and because they were well educated and literate enough to pass the civil service exam. Jackson saw the chance to make some good money on the side, and he parlayed his newfound authority into a timber locating business for himself.

In September of 1907, Jackson located William W. Hampton, his neighbor, on a timber claim near the Klamath County line, telling the rancher that it contained three million board feet of lumber, and collected $150 as his fee for having pointed out the corner markers on the quarter section. It is interesting to note that $150 was roughly three times the going rate for locator services at the time, and was more than most men earned in three months. Jackson might have gotten away with his little money-making scheme for a long time if the claim of Mr. Hampton had not been contested by another man, a Mr. Henry, who filed on the same land.

That fact that Hampton's claim was contested points to some inexperience on Jackson's part. The case and conflict created a small stir in the close-knit community of Paisley, and would certainly have caught the attention of Ranger Gilbert Brown. Strictly speaking, employees of the Forest Service were not allowed to capitalize on their positions in order to line their own pockets, a practice that, in modern times, would be referred to as a conflict of interest. After 1905 and the takeover of the forestry department by the USDA, the new Forest Service went through a series of housecleaning cycles that removed many corrupt rangers and inspectors who were taking money on the side, among other things. Jackson's exploits in the timber game would have been severely frowned upon, to say the least. Jackson never worked for the Forest Service again after 1907.

As we reflect back on the life of Ray Jackson, a pattern of sociopathic behavior emerges. He repeatedly manipulated situations and people to advance himself, but always took a chance, broke a rule or law, and blew his opportunity. His lack of conscience and shortsightedness allowed him to step over the line where a normal man never would. He also had the habit of forming partnerships, involving one or more people in his schemes. He did that with John Ryan in the 1899 robbery in Baker County, and Creed Conn in their 1903 timber claims, and partnered in forest work with Gilbert Brown in 1907. He convinced Frank W. Payne to become his cattle ranching partner around 1906. He involved his friends, George Emery, George Harper, and Frank Dobkins, in his timber locating scheme by having them act as witnesses at the land office. It might even be said that he had a sort of partnership with Miss Case in the Silver Lake school. Ray Jackson was fond of partnerships

A career in education provided Ray Jackson with a ready supply of attractive young ladies, who included his first wife, Jessie A. Parrish, Bernice Case, and the unfortunate Emma Dobkins.

SOURCES:

State of Oregon vs. R. V. Jackson, Circuit Court of the State of Oregon for the county of Clackamas, April 20, 1896. Jackson was charged with "forging an order and evidence of debt and falsely uttering the same as true and genuine with intent to injure and defraud."

W. L. Jackson vs. R. V. Jackson, Circuit Court of the State of Oregon for the county of Harney, ." April 25, 1903. Default and judgment and order for sale of attached property, case no. 666. Complaint originally filed on October 20, 1902.

"Pioneer Rancher Takes Own Life," *Harney County American,* February 4, 1938.

Convict Record, Oregon State Penitentiary, page 102. Shows convict #4134, R. Jackson, from Baker County, crime of robbery, sentence of one year, received July 3, 1899, discharged May 11, 1900, age 29, single, no creed, read and write, laborer. Convict # 4133, John Ryan, is listed just above Jackson, with the same crime, received on the same date, with the same sentence, also from Baker County.

Untitled article, *Daily Journal,* July 3, 1899.

Twelfth Census of the United States, Oregon, Baker County, Unity Precinct.

Twelfth Census of the United States, Baker County, North Sumpter Precinct.

"Mortgages," *The Sumpter Miner,* March 14, 1900. Chattel mortgage on March 3, R. B. Jackson to Jas Fleetwood, two horses and set double Harness for $105.

Harney County History Project, AV-Oral History #274, sides A/B, Jessie Williams, Winter 1980, Burns, OR, by Richard Cowan, p 12, 89.

"Suicide is Verdict of Coroner's Jury in Jackson Death," *Burns Times-Herald,* February 2, 1938. Describes W. G. Bardwell as "a boyhood friend of Jackson. Bardwell was also a member of the coroner's jury.

Water Right of Anna E. Hurlburt and W. G. Bardwell to all of the water of Big Stick Creek, July 1, 1901. Water Rights Record, vol.

A3, 18741959, microfilm. Harney County Clerk's Office, Clerk's Basement Storage, Harney County Courthouse, Burns, Oregon. Claim included the W. G. Bardwell dam and reservoir, and ditches in township 26 south, range 26 east, sections 5, 8, 9, 10, and 11.

Homestead patent of Willis G. Bardwell, serial #078245, township 26 south, range 26 east, sections 3 and 10, 160 acres, patented December 17, 1906. U.S. Department of the Interior, Bureau of Land Management, General Land Office Records, http:// www.glorecords.blm.gov/search/default .aspx

Record of Marks and Brands of R. B. Jackson, residing in Harney Co., OR, September 10, 1902. Cattle branded with a circle 7 on left ribs and swallow fork in left ear and overslope in right ear. Clerk's Basement Records Room: Record of Marks and Brands [with index], vol. A, 18891905 (1 volume), p 127. Harney County Courthouse, Burns, OR.

R. B. Jackson to First National Bank of Burns, chattel mortgage of 75 cows and steers with circle 7 brand on left ribs, for the sum of $450, for a term of six months, September 10, 1902. Clerk's Basement Records Room: Index to Mortgages Direct, vol. 1, 18851895 (1 volume), Harney County Courthouse, Burns, OR Jackson gave his mailing address as "Narrows."

Summons to R. V. Jackson, in the Circuit Court of the State of Oregon, for the county of Harney, W. L. Jackson vs. R. V. Jackson, received by Harney County Sheriff Tom Allen on October 27, 1902. The summons was served on Jackson by H. R. Dunlap, Sheriff of Lake County, on November 10, 1902.

Timber and Stone patent application file of John C. Conn, serial #ORLAA 058633 , Bureau of Land Management, records of the General Land Office, National Archives and Records Administration, Washington, D.C. Patented October 22, 1904. In his cross examination, a document signed by Jackson as a witness to Conn's timber and stone claim on December 30, 1903, Jackson stated that he had known Conn "about 18 months," or since approximately June of 1902.

Settlers in Summer Lake Valley, by Teressa Foster, 1989, Maverick Publications, Bend, OR. p 1920, 59-60, 88, 94, 124, 157-161. According to a student's account, Jackson began teaching at Silver Lake in very early 1903 .

"Co. School Report," *Lake County Examiner,* July 23, 1903.

"Lake County Teachers," *Lake County Examiner*, October 23, 1903 shows R. V. Jackson assigned to Silver Lake, and Gilbert D. Brown assigned to Warner Lake School.

Tenth Census of the United States, Californian, Solano County, Vacaville Township.

Twelfth Census of the United States, Oregon, Klamath County, Klamath Lake Precinct.

"Co. School Report, Register of Teachers," *Lake County Examiner*, July 23, 1903.

"Geo. Conn Secures Judgment Against J. D. Farra for Note," *Lake County Examiner*, May 28, 1914.

"Brief Mention," *Lake County Examiner*, May 28, 1914. Jackson is named as witness in the Conn vs. Farra civil case.

The Centennial History of Oregon, 1811-1912, vol 4, S. J. Clarke Publishing Co., Chicago, IL, 1912. Biography of Virgil Conn, p 1064-1065.

"Governor Reports on Recent Trip," *Lake County Examiner*, July 20, 1911.

"Governor's Visit to Paisley," *Lake County Examiner*, July 20, 1911. Article was picked up from the *Chewaucan Press*.

"43 Votes Cast at Paisley Election," *Lake County Examiner*, October 21, 1911

"School Apportionment," *Lake County Examiner*, May 5, 1910.

"Lakeview and Vicinity," *Lake County Examiner*, March 29, 1906.

"Teachers' Examination," *Lake County Examiner*, August 11, 1904.
"Lakeview and Vicinity," *Lake County Examiner*, October 6, 1904.

Untitled and anonymous letter to the editor, *Lake County Examiner*, January 26, 1905.

"Paisley Pointers," *Lake County Examiner*, January 12, 1905.

Untitled article, *Bend Bulletin,* July 7, 1905. Jackson and his companion pass through Bend on their way to the expo.

The Codes and General Laws of Oregon, compiled by William Lair Hill, vol 2, second edition, 1892. Bancroft-Whitney, San Francisco, p 12-33.

"Additional Local," *Lake County Examiner,* January 11, 1906.

"Lakeview and Vicinity," *Lake County Examiner,* January 18, 1906.

Harney County History Project, AV-Oral History #381, sides A/B, Shelby Petersen, August 4, 1991, Burns, OR, by Edward Gray, p 114.

Portrait and Biographical Record of the Willamette Valley, Oregon, Chicago, Chapman Publishing Co., 1903. Biography of William L. Jackson, p 816-817.

"Advertised Letter List," *Lake County Examiner,* August 2, 1906.

"Lakeview and Vicinity," *Lake County Examiner,* September 27, 1906. Mentions that F. W. Payne is working in Virgil Conn's store at Paisley. According to the probate records of Creed Conn's estate, Payne last drew wages in the month of February 1906.

Untitled short article, *Lake County Examiner,* January 31, 1907. Jackson and Payne buy hay to feed their band of cattle.

Untitled short article, *Lake County Examiner,* October 17, 1907. Sale of cattle by "Payne & Jackson" to Horton.

TimberLines, thirty year club, region six, U.S. Forest Service, vol XIV, June 1960, p 4953.

History of the Fremont National Forest, by Melva Bach, 1990, Forest Service, USDA, Pacific Northwest Region, Fremont National Forest, p 21, 35.

"Lakeview and Vicinity," *Lake County Examiner,* February 28, 1907

Record of Marks and Brands, Brand certificate for cattle and horses of R. B. Jackson, residing in Paisley, Lake County, Oregon, May 4, 1907. Lake County Clerk's Office, Lake County

Courthouse, Lakeview, OR. Jackson used the diamond brand on the left stifle of horses and on the left ribs of cattle.

"Silver Lake Leaders," *Lake County Examiner,* September 12, 1907. Short news items extracted from the *Silver Lake Leader,* announced that "R. B. Jackson resigned his position as ranger."

Timber and Stone patent application file of William W. Hampton, serial patent #100769, township 36 south, range 16 east, section 32, 160 acres, patented January 6, 1910. Bureau of Land Management, records of the General Land Office, National Archives and Records Administration, Washington, D.C.

Ray Jackson was known to carry a pearl handle Colt pistol very similar to this one, and was fond of displaying it when he believed that he was being challenged.

Chapter Three

Black Cat

The key to understanding the fate of Eli Barnum, who died by gunshot in Lakeview, Oregon on December 7, 1910, is to first understand his strong family values. He loved his wife, Myrtle, and wanted to remain married, and he was devoted to their three young children. Then, a black cat crossed his path, for Eli Barnum's death was intimately tied to Ray Jackson's short career as superintendent of schools for Lake County.

Jackson, a Democrat, was elected in June of 1908, and beat the Republican incumbent, J. Q. Willits, by a single vote. Perhaps Jackson would have received more votes if he had not misspelled the word, superintendent, not once, but twice, in the political advertisement that he placed in the county paper. A noteworthy thing for an educator to do.

> *For County School Superintendant*
> *To the Democratic Voters of Lake County, Oregon.*
>
> *I hereby announce myself a candidate for the office of County School Superintendant, subject to the decision of the Democratic Party, at the Primary Election to be held April 17th, 1908.*
>
> *R. B. JACKSON*

As previously mentioned, Jackson, in his position as superintendent, or "superintendant," embezzled money from the school system, was indicted for it, and was asked to resign. The question of just how he acquired that money, and how much money was embezzled, remained unanswered until now. A superintendent, unlike a sheriff, county treasurer, and some other elected officials, is not a bonded individual. His official duties, as described by state law, offer him few opportunities to handle actual cash, and that fact considerably narrows the possibilities as to the exact nature of Jackson's crime.

Although the superintendent was responsible for apportioning the county school fund among the various districts, that was not an instance where he was allowed to handle money. The school fund was held and monitored by the county treasurer, and the superintendent only worked with figures. Throughout the state of Oregon, and probably in other states as well, the education laws required an annual event known as a "teachers' institute" that would have given Jackson access to a sum of cash to be used to defray the expenses of the event.

The teachers' institute could be thought of as a sort of three day conference for teachers, who would travel from all over the county to attend. There, they would share war stories, listen to speeches by esteemed educators, and take classes on teaching methods. But, a careful study of the newspapers of the time allows us to rule out those events as the target of Jackson's thievery. Jackson never was handed a large sum of expense money for holding teachers' institutes for the simple reason that no teachers' institutes were held in Lake County during Jackson's tenure.

Those annual events for teachers were supposed to be funded by the fees that teachers paid for examinations and certificates that allowed them to teach in Lake County. Teachers who were new to the county were required to take the tests, and veteran teachers were required to test for new certificates at regular intervals, every one to three years, depending upon the grade of the certification.

According to state law, the exam fees were supposed to go into a special fund, held by the county treasurer, and saved for the annual institute events. The reason that Lake County held no teachers' institutes during the time that Jackson was in office was that Jackson himself proctored the exams and collected the money. And he kept it.

By doing so he committed the crime of "peculation," the embezzlement of public funds that was, and still is, a felony. It will be remembered from Jackson's 1905 letter to the editor, reproduced on page 34, that Jackson endorsed the policy of diverting those funds for his own use, and he did, indeed, make a practice of pilfering the teachers' exam money. The only explanation for that odd behavior has to be that Jackson was a hedonistic sociopath who could not resist money, and would take it whenever he got the chance. And he did so despite having several large business investments and assets, and a steady job.

Just after Jackson became superintendent in September of 1908, the Ana River Land, Water, and Power Company was organized in Lake County with a capital stock of fifteen thousand dollars. Author Teressa Foster credited Jesse Nelson, who lived on Ana River, with the development idea, and the first officers were Frank W. Payne, Jesse Nelson, M. W. O'Brien, and civil engineer Curtis Duvall. Their plans included building an earthen dam 250 feet long, and irrigating three or four thousand acres with the flow from the four bountiful artesian springs that produced about 150 cubic feet per minute. The October 1, 1909 annual meeting of the irrigation company was attended by officers M. W. O'Brien, Jesse Nelson, F. W. Curron, Curtis Duvall, and S. W. Barry. A short news item in the *Examiner* described their work as "encouraging" for the new settlers.

In early June of 1909, Jackson became president of a group of investors who bought out the old Paisley Mercantile Company of Lawrence S. Ainsworth and Chester L. Withers, and called the corporation the Chewaucan Mercantile Company. The new company was worth forty thousand dollars, with Stephen P. Moss as vice president, and Bill Y. Miller as secretary and treasurer. Jackson's friends, Frank Dobkins and Frank Payne, were stockholders.

For over three years, from the time that Jackson took office until the fall of 1910, the teachers' institute fund stood at exactly $21.50. No one seemed to notice, even though Jackson was recruiting and testing numerous teachers twice a year, in February and August, as required by state law. The summer that Jackson began as superintendent, he wrote temporary teaching permits, allowing a few teachers to legally teach school until the time of the next examinations. He charged those five teachers $2.50 each, and pocketed that money as well.

The exact nature of Jackson's crime was discovered by a careful examination of the financial statements of Lake County, published twice each year in the *Examiner*. That was where the unchanging balance of the institute fund was found.

Before Jackson's predecessor, Superintendent J. Q. Willits, left office he added $39 to the fund, that showed as the line item "received from examination fees," and left a balance of $21.50. Jackson's forced repayment into the fund showed up as a differently worded line item in the fall of 1910, "received from R. B. Jackson $231."

It is worth noting that Jackson was a rather unmotivated superintendent. His first apportionment of school money left the districts high and dry in the fall of 1908 because he finished the work two months late. He was also required to make an inspection of every school twice each year, a duty that he was known to have performed only once, in June of 1909. He did not care a jot about his duty to organize the institutes for the teachers, having found a better use for that money himself. But, he was very punctilious when it came to organizing the teachers' exams, because there he saw the opportunity for personal gain, and actively recruited teachers before the exams with editorials and notices in the county paper.

Lake County Examiner
May 6, 1909

"There are a number of openings in the county for competent teachers at good wages, and not less than six months employment each year. The wages cannot be less than $60, and there are several schools that command from $120 to $150 per month. There are opportunities here in way of securing land, deeded or government, that can be availed of by teachers that in time will make them comfortable and desirable homes."

Jackson displayed all of the shortsighted impulsiveness of a textbook sociopath when he collected those examination and teaching certificate fees. At each testing session he probably collected no more that $50, an amount that was about equal to his monthly salary. Why was he willing to risk disgrace, prison, loss of prestige, and career suicide for such a small amount of money? What *was* he thinking?

~48~

His peers, the teachers of the county, were the people most negatively impacted by the thefts. Jackson might have derived some satisfaction from undermining them, which fed his love of power, and his grandiosity. Then, there was the little thrill he got out of it, because it carried the ongoing risk of getting caught. Sociopaths crave stimulation of that kind constantly. They are addicted to risk. Jackson went through life with a chip on his shoulder. A feeling that the world had shortchanged him some-how. And, he had poor impulse control that made it easy, almost natural, for him to grab what he wanted, force himself upon women, abuse alcohol, and lash out in a fit of rage. Any one of those internal motivations, or all of them, could have prompted Jackson to repeatedly take that money. Whatever the reason was, it was a reason beyond reason. It was not something that a rea-sonable person with a conscience would ever do.

Yet, no one, not County Clerk Frank Payne, County Judge Bernard Daly, or County Treasurer Frederick O. Ahlstrom, nor any of the commissioners noticed the stagnation of the institute fund, even though the balance of $21.50 was published twice per year in the *Examiner* in the county financial report. No one, that is, until the arrival of James F. "Fred" Burgess.

Burgess was hired around the first of September, 1909 to serve as the new principal of the Lakeview school, a position that he held for many years, and where he also taught high school courses. At the same time, his daughter, Bessie, was hired to teach the 7th grade there. In July of 1910, he attended the State Teachers' Association meeting at Salem. In the spring of 1911, the dynamic new principal organized a public performance by the children, and used part of the proceeds to buy three unabridged dictionaries for the school. The Burgesses were a public-spirited family, and active in the Chataqua Circle, YMCA, Lakeview Commercial Club, Ladies Aid Society, and the Methodist Church sunday school.

There can be no doubt about it, Burgess was a real pro, and he knew his way around the education system very well. He may even have known a thing or two about the education laws of Oregon, the same laws that described how exam fees were to be paid over to the county treasurer, to be put in a special fund for use in the teachers' institutes. And, since those institutes were a 'codified' annual ritual all around the country, it was likely that Burgess had attended a few himself. As the new principal, Burgess would have naturally desired such an event, and probably made some inquiries.

Emma Dobkins, a teacher who sometimes acted as Jackson's assistant and was a sister of Jackson's friend, Frank Dobkins, died tragically on March 2, 1910. The exact cause of her death is not known. Her death certificate gave her cause of death as "angina pectoris," a type of pain that is a symptom of inadequate blood and oxygen supply to the heart. That document also provided the information that she was not teaching at the time of her death, and gave her occupation only as "domestic duties." She was attended by Dr. A. A. Witham for only 30 minutes prior to the time she expired, from 8:00 p.m. to 8:30 p.m. She died at Paisley, probably at the home of her parents, and the information on the certificate was provided by her brother, Frank.

Thirty minutes of care does not seem to match the theory put forth earlier by the author, that Emma Dobkins may have died in childbirth. If she had died after a long and difficult labor, one would hope that the duration of care by Dr. Witham would have been longer. That circumstance makes the possibility of poisoning seem all the more likely.

Some sources in folklore say that Emma Dobkins committed suicide. Angina is a symptom of something else, like a heart attack. It could be caused by extreme fatigue, or by the action of some toxin that cut off the supply of oxygen to the heart. Regardless of how Emma Dobkins died, people who knew the family almost universally agreed that Jackson had a hand in her death. Given the indications that Jackson used poison to his advantage on several occasions, it is worth considering that he may have acted to avoid a scandal similar to the one with Miss Case that derailed his career in 1905.

Emma Dobkins died just before the Democratic primaries in Lake County, and was buried next to her grandmother, Margaret, at the Paisley I.O.O.F. Cemetery, where a large marble pillar, with the words, "gone, but not forgotten," marks her grave. Her parents, William and Eliza "Jane," and brother, Frank, are all buried in the same plot, number 41. In an adjoining plot, number

40, that is near Emma's headstone, there is buried an unknown infant that could have been her child.

As time went on, Jackson continued his senseless pilfering of the teachers' exam money, and in April of 1910, he delivered about 1,000 head of cattle for the sum of thirty-three thousand dollars to Alexander A. Davis of Klamath Marsh. The source of the information about that sale, furnished to the *Examiner,* was undoubtedly Jackson himself.

> *The exact price paid per head for these cattle is not known, but is considerably in advance of anything sold before in the country.*

In August of 1910, Jackson held another exam session at Lakeview, in the school where Burgess was now in charge, and Fred and Bessie Burgess both attended, took the exams, paid their fees, and passed. A total of nineteen teachers from all over the county took the exams. Sixteen passed, three failed, and all paid fees to Jackson.

Burgess' role in the drama may have been simply asking the county treasurer about the funds available, and the possibility of holding a teachers' institute. Burgess definitely did say something because, around the end of August and shortly after the Burgesses passed their exams, Jackson was ordered to pay over all of the exam fees that he had collected over the past three years. Perhaps the most shocking aspect of the whole affair was Jackson's refusal to repay the money when he was caught.

> *"R. B. Jackson, county school superintendent, was indicted for refusing to pay over public money at the time provided by statute. He paid the money into the county treasury after the time provided by law had expired, but such act apparently does not clear him in the eyes of the law."*

Burgess' enthusiasm for the annual events can be seen in the April 1912 institute, after Jackson was out of the picture. Burgess played an active role in that event and delivered a lecture on teaching mathematics. Yet another indication that Burgess was the one who blew the whistle was that, when Jackson's court date came up on about May 4, 1911, Fred and Bessie Burgess were called as witnesses, probably to describe how they had seen Jackson collecting fees at the exams.

Just after he was confronted, Jackson went on a drinking and shooting spree, riddling the town of Paisley with bullets on the weekend of September 3, 1910. "Sometimes a cornered sociopath will adopt a posture of righteous indignation and anger in order to scare off her accuser," wrote Martha Stout in *The Sociopath Next Door*. "Frustration may engender anger or rage in a sociopath."

Now Jackson's fat was really in the fire, and he knew it. Not only was he going to have to come up with the $200 he had pilfered, he was certainly going to lose his job, had to pay attorney's fees to W. Lair Thompson, and was facing the possibility of a long term in prison because this was the second time that he had been caught stealing money from a school system.

The file of "The State of Oregon Vs. Ray B. Jackson," circuit court case 40, has been lost, so it may never be known exactly what role the Burgesses played in the indictment. Jackson must have been told that 'the jig was up' around the end of August, and we have to wonder exactly how the charge against him became "refusing to pay over public money at the time provided by statute" instead of the much more serious charge of peculation, which his crime clearly was.

There could have been a plea bargain agreement, or more exactly, a "charge bargain," in which Jackson paid over the money on the day before his indictment, in exchange for the lesser charge. There was no possibility that Jackson could have sustained the claim that he did not know that the law required him to turn over the exam fees to the county treasurer. An awareness of the law is the responsibility of the individual, as John Selden put it, "ignorance of the law excuses no man." Then, there was the inescapable fact that the law describing the deposit of exam fees was printed in the same section of the school laws, section five of superintendent duties, as was the requirement to hold teachers' exams beginning on the second Wednesday of August and February, a duty that Jackson performed with exacting diligence. A new edition of *The Oregon School Laws* was published in 1909, and sent out to every school district in the state by J. H. Ackerman, Oregon Superintendent of Public Instruction. Jackson would certainly have had a copy of it in his office.

> *"Well, old Ray was pretty smart too, but he didn't seem to get too far."*
>
> Shelby Petersen

Although Jackson made that profitable cattle sale in April, since that time he had invested heavily in the new Chewaucan Mercantile Company at Paisley, and was president of that firm. The store was scheduled to open in the spring of 1910, but the opening was delayed until about June 1, possibly for financial reasons. Frank Payne was a stockholder in the new firm.

Jackson had apparently also invested heavily in the Ana River Irrigation Company because, at their next annual meeting, October 1, 1910, he emerged as the new company president. An infusion of three thousand dollars in cash that year allowed the men to order a large pumping plant for irrigation. Officers under Jackson were M. W. O'Brien, Curtis Duvall, and stockholders were J. F. "Frank" Barnes and Jesse Nelson. Frank Payne may have continued to hold stock in the company.

The Ana River company was hard at work trying to recruit investors and settlers to buy land from them in the new town site platted by Nelson and named "Spring River," and they opened a realty office in Paisley to handle sales. Then, on October 20, 1910, the *Lake County Examiner* carried the shocking news of the indictment of the company's president. Regardless of the taint that the news put on the reputation of the company, Jackson remained in his position as president for a time.

It is important to remember that Jackson got caught for embezzlement during the time that he was closely associated with County Clerk Frank Payne; in cattle ranching, in a mercantile company, in county politics, and in an irrigation company. So, it was quite possible that Jackson turned to his friend, Payne, for help. Payne, according to Payne himself, had a good friendship with Judge Daly, and all three men were Democrats. Daly, as county judge, did not try Jackson's case because it went before the circuit court.

Jackson's case was on the court docket for May of 1911, but it seems to have been settled out of court or dismissed because, if there had been a trial, some mention of the details would have found their way into the county paper, and that was precisely the thing that the county officials wanted to avoid. The only hint of the outcome of "The State of Oregon Vs. Ray B. Jackson" was noted by the *Examiner* as, "A number of civil actions were considered Monday and Tuesday, several of them being settled and dismissed."

Jackson could not have asked for a better attorney than W. Lair Thompson, one of the finest legal minds to ever come out of the state of Oregon. Thompson's office, for about a year, was conveniently located above Daly's Bank of Lakeview. When the Oregon Valley Land Company put him on retainer, he moved his office into their building. In November of 1910, Thompson was elected joint representative of the Oregon House for district 21. In April of 1911, Lafe Conn succeeded Thompson as attorney for the Oregon State Land Board.

To put it very simply, the county court probably convinced W. Lair Thompson that its interests, and the interests of the county schools, would be best served by keeping the details of the matter out of the papers, and out of the court room, by getting back the stolen money and by permanently removing Ray Jackson from the school system. After all, a conviction would have brought great disgrace and shame upon the whole county court. All were elected officials. County Treasurer Ahlstrom, Judge Daly, the County Commissioners, and County Clerk Payne, had all failed to notice Jackson's thefts taking place right under their noses. Moreover, the news of Jackson's indictment came about one month before the Lake County general election of 1910.

The matter was kept rather quiet, and Jackson repaid the money some time between October 3 and 18 of 1910. The time of the repayment was obvious, because on September 30, the balance of the institute fund remained unchanged. But, by the time of his indictment on October 18, the stolen money reappeared in the account. That year, Judge Daly, Clerk Payne, Myrtle Barnum's stepfather, Commissioner Rehart, and Treasurer

Ahlstrom, all were reelected. Since Jackson was an elected official, the county court had no power to fire him, and his circuit court ordered resignation took effect on September 1, 1911. The county court faced the added problem of finding someone to replace Jackson, as no one from either the Democratic or Republican parties had put themselves forward as a candidate in 1910. The election had come and gone, and not even a write-in candidate emerged for the post.

It is worth noting that Lafe Conn was a good friend of W. Lair Thompson. Their friendship was made obvious in the article recounting their partnership in the defense of the accused murderer, Louis Veyssade in November of 1910. Jackson must have engaged Thompson as his defense attorney in the first week of October, and probably discussed his prior conviction on a similar charge and desire to keep out of prison.

> *"He was a school teacher for a while. But he was a deadbeat, he was kind of a crook."*
>
> *Russell Emery*

It also seems likely that, shortly after Thompson took Jackson's case, he told what he knew of Jackson's past to his friend, Lafe Conn, and renewed old suspicions about Jackson. About a month later was when Lafe and George Conn exhumed Creed Conn's body and had it autopsied in Klamath Falls on its way to reburial in Roseburg.

When deputy district attorney, John D. Venator, visited Paisley on October 7, and served Jackson with a summons to answer to charges, the charges named were probably both peculation and failure to pay over public money, because Jackson was surely guilty of both crimes. District Attorney Delman V. Kuykendall certainly had adequate evidence to convict Jackson on the more serious charge of peculation. Numerous teachers could testify that they had paid Jackson for their exams and certificates, and the county treasurer would be able to testify that he had never received that money. The crooked superintendent would not be able to make the false claim that he had paid the money over, because no receipts existed.

Since there was an excellent chance that Jackson would be convicted, Kuykendall had to have been motivated by other considerations to make a charge bargain in exchange for certain concessions. Another question facing the district attorney was whether or not the public interest would be served by convicting Jackson of peculation. There would be an expensive trial, and Jackson could be sentenced to prison without repaying the money he had embezzled. Would the interests of the teachers of the county be better served by getting that money back?

So, it came to pass that Thompson and Jackson offered to plea guilty to the lesser charge of failure to pay over public money, offered to put the $231 back into the teachers' institute fund, and tendered Jackson's resignation to take effect on September 1, 1911. Jackson may even have been barred from future employment by the county, because he never taught school in Lake County again.

We have to consider the possibility that Frank Payne helped Jackson's cause in some way. His close association with Jackson at that time is beyond doubt, and Jackson, with his talent for manipulation, could easily have convinced Payne that he had done Payne several big favors in their shared business ventures.

"'You owe me' has been the standard line of sociopaths for thousands of years, quite literally, and is still so," wrote Martha Stout in her *thirteen rules for dealing with sociopaths in everyday life.* "It is what Rasputin told the empress of Russia."

Perhaps the most obvious indication of all that someone helped Jackson's cause was his seemingly magical avoidance of prison. Another minor miracle was that Lair Thompson took Jackson's case at all. At the time he took Jackson on as a client, Thompson was running for state representative, and when the case went to court in May of 1911, Thompson had 12 other items on the docket. Moreover, Thompson was very much occupied in September and October with preparing the defense for Louis Veyssade, accused of shooting John P. "Jack" Barry in August of 1910 inside of a Lakeview saloon. It was a large and complex case with many witnesses, and teamed with Lafe Conn, Thompson won that particular courtroom battle. It is quite possible that Judge Daly and Clerk Payne themselves convinced Thompson to take Jackson's case. Aside from Payne's obvious friendship with

Jackson, both Daly and Payne would have been most anxious to see a bargain agreement that would keep the matter out of the courtroom and out of the public eye so close to election time.

Jackson usually involved others in his schemes. He worked his manipulation by finding the innermost wants of people after getting to know them. He would pretend to be of a like mind by telling people he was "just like" them. That he understood them, and agreed with their views. Once he learned that person's views, he would give that person just what they wanted, or at least a taste of it. That way, the new 'friend' would feel beholding to Jackson. That he owed him something. Then Jackson had him in the palm of his hand.

Take the 1903 timber deal with Creed Conn as an example. Conn was cash poor, and had several debts that were coming to a head. Jackson saw Conn as an influential ally that he could use to advance his own interests. So, when Jackson got to know Conn a bit, he concocted a timber deal so that Conn could file on a claim, then set him up with sawmill man Frank Scott and locator John Bloss. Then, Jackson asked Conn to put up $410 so that he could file on an adjoining claim. He might have put the idea forward as just a loan, because Jackson was notorious for not repaying his debts. Or, he might have offered to act as a 'dummy' entryman for Creed Conn so that he could obtain two adjoining parcels for himself. But, Conn was a shrewd businessman and probably well versed in government regulations around the Timber and Stone Act. Jackson ultimately had to relinquish his claim because he was not able to convince Conn to put up the money.

In October of 1910, not only Ray Jackson, but also his friend, Frank Payne, found themselves in wrenching and embarrassing situations. During March of that year, Payne began employing various women to perform clerical assistance in the county clerk's office. That was mainly due to the large number of deeds flowing in from the sale of real estate by the Oregon Valley Land Company.

One of the women hired by Payne was Myrtle Barnum, wife of Eli Barnum and stepdaughter of county commissioner Charles A. Rehart. Eli was a co-owner and operator of what his advertisements described as "the largest feed stable in southern Oregon or Northern California," the Mammoth Stables in Lakeview. In

March of 1910, Barnum received a kick in the knee from a horse and was laid up and unable to work for a time due to the injury. It is not known exactly when that spring Myrtle Barnum went to work for Payne, but the time of Eli's injury seems likely.

Payne's relationship with Myrtle must have been platonic at first. The 1910 census, taken in late April, showed that Payne's wife, Florence, (nee Martin) was also an employee of the county clerk's office. Despite the growing tide of O. V. L. Company filings, Payne, surprisingly, let go two of his helpers at the end of June, telling the *Examiner* that the office had caught up on the work and no longer needed them. That act could have coincided with the time that Payne's wife, Florence, began to suspect that something was going on. For the months of July and August, Payne had three assistants again. Two of them were Myrtle Barnum's sister, Nell Simpson, and Mae Barnes, daughter of irrigator J. F. "Frank" Barnes. The third was undoubtedly the justifiably jealous Florence Payne. Despite the apparent expulsion of Myrtle Barnum from the clerk's office, her love affair with Payne continued, and had tragic consequences. By the time of Jackson's October indictment, Payne's marriage was on the rocks and Florence had gone to Portland to stay with relatives. She sued Frank Payne for divorce on grounds of adultery.

Consider the position that Eli Barnum was placed in as those events unfolded, the heartbreak he felt over his wife's affair with Payne, and the sorrow for his children. William E. "Earl" Barnum, at eight years of age, was the oldest. Orva Ann was six, and Esther T. "Thayne" was only three. Eli's great sadness over the affair was expressed in an *Examiner* article after his death.

> *His troubles were of a domestic nature.... The deed was committed in their home on Water Street, and seems to have been the result of a determination on the part of both not to live together longer. He doubtless thereupon concluded that life was not worth the cost, and quickly ended all.*

Unlike Florence Payne, Myrtle Barnum had no legal grounds for divorce, and would not have been able to get free from her marriage unless Eli brought suit against her, something that he was apparently unwilling to do. For two months after the affair became common knowledge, until December, the Paynes and Barnums found themselves in a horribly embarrassing scandal.

Consider, also, the differences in occupation between Payne and Eli Barnum. Payne had gone to college and worked as a clerk or at a desk for all of his life. Barnum must have been a man of considerable strength, because most of his work involved large heavy items like sacks of grain, bales of hay, and horses. Barnum's obvious love of his wife makes it seem likely that Payne felt intimidated by Barnum, who may even have threatened him. On December 8, the *Examiner* reported:

> *The community was shocked yesterday after-*
> *noon by the report that Eli Barnum had sui-*
> *cided by shooting himself with a 32 calibre (sic)*
> *pistol. The bullet entered the body just above the*
> *heart, and he died about half an hour after*
> *committing the deed. He was unconscious from*
> *the time of firing the fatal shot until he passed*
> *away. No inquest was deemed necessary by the*
> *authorities and his remains will be laid to rest*
> *tomorrow in the Odd Fellows cemetery.*

On December 15 the *Examiner* published the following:

> *Last Sad Rites Over Eli Barnum*
> *Many Sorrowing Friends Present at Funeral*
> *Last Saturday*

> *The funeral of the late Eli Barnum took place*
> *last Saturday afternoon. Rev. Melville T. Wire*
> *conducting the services. There were a large*
> *number of sorrowing friends of the family in*
> *attendance, and the sympathy of all went out to*
> *the bereaved relatives. Mr. Wire delivered a*
> *very strong address and many present, both*
> *strong men and women, shed tears.*

Not for many years has this community been wrought up to such a pitch and for a time it was feared that violence would result over the circumstances attending the sad and untimely death of Mr. Barnum. It is without doubt the most regrettable affair that has ever occurred in Lake county, and the heartfelt sympathy of all goes out to the relatives of the deceased in the sad hour of their bereavement.

Note the contradictions implied by these accounts. Eli Barnum felt great sadness over the prospect of losing his wife, and remained with her long after he learned of her affair--yet supposedly agreed to a separation--and then, the devoted family man inexplicably decided to commit suicide. While it is true that people in the throes of marital troubles often do crazy things, surely a man of Barnum's devotion would have wanted to attend to the welfare of his children. Doesn't it seem more likely that Myrtle Barnum was the one who wanted out of the marriage, and that the manner of Eli's Barnum's death was something quite different than suicide?

> *"We must look for consistency. Where there is a want of it we must suspect deception."*
>
> Sir Arthur Conan Doyle
> The Problem of Thor Bridge

Although the head is a much more common target than the chest for men committing suicide by gunshot (statistically three times more common), it is not known how often a man attempting suicide aims at his own heart and 'misses.' But, the likelihood of that should also be questioned, because the bullet wound of Eli Barnum was "just above the heart." Yet, despite those facts, and the well known Payne-Barnum affair, the authorities who responded to the scene, probably coroner William Wallace, County Physician T. V. Hall, and Sheriff Warner Snider, found no motive and jumped to the conclusion of suicide. No investigation was carried out, no inquest was held, and scandal in the county seat was once again avoided. The only public information about the death of Eli Barnum was rather sketchy, and contained in newspaper articles.

The passage of many years, the benefit of history, allows the researcher to take a holistic view from the vantage point of "now." As we reflect back on the 1904 murder of Creed Conn, we can easily draw some parallels. Conn was killed by a single gunshot to the center of the chest, fired from a pistol. There were powder burns on his clothing, and his own pistol, presumably acquired by burglary, was found next to the body. Conn's death was, at first, ruled a suicide. Jackson and Payne were both key witnesses in that case because of their association with Conn and because they were two of the last people to have seen him alive.

We can also spin the wheel of time forward from 1910, to the year 1925 and Harold Bradley's murder. Bradley died on Link Hutton's Wagontire ranch, and the author put forth the theory in *The Sandy Knoll Murder,* that Jackson had been having an affair with Hutton's wife, and tried to assassinate Hutton early one morning, before dawn. As Bradley and Hutton passed back and forth in front of the garage, silhouetted by lantern light, Bradley was struck by two gunshots.

Jackson's material motive in the Bradley case was supposedly to acquire Hutton's valuable ranch property, that adjoined his own. Jackson 'happened along' immediately after the shooting, and was later alone with Bradley at the moment of his death. According to the tale put forth by Jackson in a statement he made to the coroner's jury, he and Bradley had met with the Huttons the night before to discuss dissolution of the Hutton's marriage. According to Jackson, Hutton, quite uncharacteristically, volunteered to give over all of his ranch holdings to his wife, Leona. That scenario offers several more obvious parallels to Eli Barnum's tragic and untimely death and marital problems.

Did Jackson take what he learned from the Conn and Barnum killings and carry it with him into his later life on Wagontire Mountain? After Hutton was tried for, and found innocent of, Bradley's murder, he continued to live on his Wagontire ranch for many years--not exactly the behavior of a man who would easily give up his property to an unfaithful woman.

History offers many examples of predatory murderers who killed for both their own mysterious, internal motivations, and for profit, and Ray Jackson could have been just such a killer. Richard Kuklinsky of New Jersey, who was convicted of multiple murders in 1986, told an interviewer that he had murdered over 100 people as a young man, before he began his career as a contract killer.

Could Jackson have lain in wait inside of the Barnums' house, and stepped out from his hiding place when Eli arrived home? If Barnum had a second or two to react, that could explain why the bullet struck him high in the chest. The lack of an inquest or investigation in the case has left us with an unfortunate lack of detail. How could the officials have been so certain that a suicide had occurred? Usually, if there was an eye witness to a suicide, that person was named in the newspaper account. In Barnum's case, no such person was ever named. The statement that Barnum lived for one half hour after he was shot could have come from anyone in the neighborhood who responded to the sound of gunfire. Myrtle Barnum would have known the time to expect Eli at home, and also where he kept his gun.

Did Jackson appeal to his friend, Frank Payne, to help him, to 'pass go,' collect two hundred dollars, and get out of jail free, in exchange for a resolution to Payne's romantic dilemma? The timing of the events of Jackson's indictment, Payne's affair, and Eli Barnum's convenient death was absolutely uncanny. Knowing all that we do about Jackson's sociopathy, his craving for financial gain, and the way that death followed him, we have to ask the question: If Jackson were ever hired to kill a man, would it not look an awful lot like what happened to Eli Barnum?

Less than a year after Eli's death, Frank Payne and Myrtle Barnum were married in a quiet ceremony at her parent's house. What became of the Barnum children is not known. A most searching examination of family and census records and newspapers of the period failed to disclose their whereabouts after the death of their father.

~~~~~~

Lake County Examiner
November 16, 1911

Popular Clerk Weds

County Clerk Frank W. Payne was married last evening to Mrs. Myrtle Barnum, who has for some time been employed in his office as stenographer and typist. The happy couple will reside in the Dan Godsil house which has been newly painted and papered for their reception. The ceremony was held at the residence of the bride's parents, Mr. and Mrs. C. A. Rehart, before a few immediate friends. While Judge B. Daly performed the tying process in his usual graceful manner.

~~~~~~

SOURCES:

"For County School Superintendant," *Lake County Examiner*, April 2, 1908.

"Official Returns of the Election," *Lake County Examiner*, June 11, 1908.

The Oregon School Laws, With Rules and Regulations of the State Board of Education, Blank Forms, Etc., prepared by J. H. Ackerman, Superintendent of Public Instruction, State of Oregon printing office, Salem, OR 1909. Pages 153-157 describe teachers' examinations and certificate fees.

"Examination of County Records," *Lake County Examiner*, July 16, 1908.

"Semiannual Statement," *Lake County Examiner*, October 8, 1908.

"Semiannual Statement," *Lake County Examiner*, April 8, 1909.

"Semiannual Statement of Our County Officers," *Lake County Examiner*, October 14, 1909.

"Semiannual Statement," *Lake County Examiner*, May 5, 1910.

"County Expenditures," *Lake County Examiner*, November 3, 1910.

"County Holds Busy Session," *Lake County Examiner*, January 11, 1911.

"Financial Statement," *Lake County Examiner*, April 27, 1911.

"Semiannual Statement," *Lake County Examiner*, November 9, 1911. These financial statements make plain the condition of the institute fund, and show that after October 1, 1910 $231 was added. The source was Jackson's repayment.

"Big Irrigation Enterprise," *Lake County Examiner* October 1, 1908.

"Ana River Irrigation," *Lake County Examiner*, October 7, 1909.

"New Firm at Paisley," *Lake County Examiner*, June 9, 1910.

The Centennial History of Oregon, 1811-1912, by Joseph Gaston, S. J. Clarke Publishing Co., 1912, Chicago, IL. Biography of Chester L. Withers, p 473.

"Superintendent of Schools Makes Some Recommendations," *Lake County Examiner,* October 15, 1908.

"Teachers Examination," *Lake County Examiner,* August 11, 1910.

"Teachers Examination," *Lake County Examiner,* February 2, 1911.

"Schools Are in Good Shape," *Lake County Examiner,* June 10, 1909.

"School Opens Monday," *Lake County Examiner,* September 9, 1909

"Personal Mention," *Lake County Examiner,* June 9, 1910.

"Died," *Lake County Examiner,* March 10, 1910. Obituary of Emma Dobkins.

Certificate of Death, Emma A. Dobkins, March 2, 1910, State of Oregon, County of Lake, #736.

William "Bill" W. Brown 18551941: Legend of Oregon's High Desert, by Edward Gray, 1993, Your Town Press, Salem, OR, p 171-173.

"Getting Along," *Lake County Examiner,* March 8, 1910.

"County Teachers Pass Examination," *Lake County Examiner,* August 18, 1910.

Circuit Court Case Files, ca. 18751922, clerk's vault, Lake County Courthouse, Lakeview, OR. The author requested a photocopy of circuit court case file #40, State of Oregon vs. R. B. Jackson, on June 4, 2009 and paid a research fee. A careful search by court personnel failed to produce the file.

"In the Circuit Court," *Lake County Examiner,* October 20, 1910.

Harney County History Project, oral history interview #381, Shelby Petersen, August 4, 1991, p 56.

"Official Vote of Lake County," *Lake County Examiner,* November 17, 1910.

The Sociopath Next Door, The Ruthless Versus the Rest of Us, by Martha Stout, Ph.D., 2005, Broadway Books, New York, NY, p 91, 127, 156-162.

"W. Lair Thompson," *Oregonian,* August 7, 1940.

"W. Lair Thompson," *Oregonian,* editorial by Herbert P. Welch, August 18, 1940.

"W. Lair Thompson," advertisement, *Lake County Examiner,* August 27, 1908. States that Thompson's law office is "over Bank of Lakeview." In April of 1909 Thompson moved his office to the Umbach block of town.

"N. C. O. to Build at Once," *Lake County Examiner,* June 9, 1910.

Advertisement, *Lake County Examiner,* June 16, 1910. States that Thompson's office is in the "O. V. L. Co's building."

"Brief Mention," *Lake County Examiner,* November 17, 1910.

"Brief Mention," *Lake County Examiner,* April 6, 1911.

"Louis Veyssade is 'Not Guilty,'" *Lake County Examiner,* November 10, 1910. This case was a major coup for Lafe Conn and Lair Thompson as a court appointed defense team.

"Grim Reminder of 1904 Range War," *Lake County Examiner,* November 24, 1910. Story was picked up from the *Silver Lake Leader,* and described exhumation of Creed Conn.

"County Court Proceedings," *Lake County Examiner,* September 28, 1911. Jackson's resignation is accepted.

"Docket for May Term of Court," *Lake County Examiner,* May 4, 1911. Names Thompson as Jackson's defense attorney.

"Brief Mention," *Lake County Examiner,* May 4, 1911.

"Teachers Institute," *Lake County Examiner,* April 4, 1912

"Institute Held Worthy Session," *Lake County Examiner,* April 25, 1912

"Irrigate by Pump," *Lake County Examiner,* October 6, 1910.

"In the Circuit Court," *Lake County Examiner,* October 20, 1910. Reports that "R. B. Jackson, county school superintendent, was indicted for refusing to pay over public money at the time provided by statute."

Introducing Dr. Daly, by Forest E. Cooper, Lake County Historical Society, Maverick Publications: Bend, Oregon, 1986, p 6768.

"Official Vote of Lake County," *Lake County Examiner,* November 17, 1910. Payne ran uncontested for the post of County Clerk, and so was elected.

"Democrats are Shy on Ticket," *Lake County Examiner,* September 15, 1910.

"In the Matter of Claims Against Lake," *Lake County Examiner,* September 22, 1910. Shows salaries of Payne and Jackson.

"City and County Briefs," *Lake County Examiner,* March 10, 1910. This column carries information about Barnum's injury and also Payne employing additional help.

"Brief Mention," *Lake County Examiner,* July 14, 1910.

"Proceedings of Lake County Court for This Term," *Lake County Examiner,* March 10, 1910.

"County Court Proceedings," *Lake County Examiner,* May 19, 1910.

Twelfth Census of the United States, Oregon, Lake County, Lakeview, 1900.

"Russell and Mary Emery," Harney County Oral History Project, AV-Oral History #382, side A, August 16, 1991, Bend, OR. p 4.

Advertisement, Mammoth Livery, *Lake County Examiner,* March 3, 1910.

Thirteenth Census of the United States, Oregon, Lake County, Lakeview, 1910.

"Brief Mention," *Lake County Examiner,* October 6, 1910.

"Docket for May Court," *Lake County Examiner,* May 4, 1911. Florence Payne's suit for divorce against Frank W. Payne.

"Barnum-Simpson," *Lake County Examiner,* September 6, 1900.

"Seeks Peace in Great Unknown," *Lake County Examiner,* December 8, 1910.

"Card of Thanks," *Lake County Examiner,* December 15, 1910.

"Last Sad Rites Over Eli Barnum," *Lake County Examiner,* December 15, 1910.

"Observations and Statistics Relating to Suicide Weapons," by I. C. Stone, Chief, Physical Evidence Section, Institute of Forensic Sciences, Texas. *Journal of Forensic Sciences,* vol 32, issue 3 (May 1987). Abstract.

The Sandy Knoll Murder, Legacy of the Sheepshooters, by Melany Tupper, 2010, Central Oregon Books LLC, Christmas Valley, Oregon. Details the murders of John Creed Conn and Harold Bradley.

"Marriage Records, vol. 3, 19091920, County of Lake, Lakeview, Oregon," 1995, Oregon Youth Conservation Corps, Lakeview, Oregon, p 16.

"Popular Clerk Weds," *Lake County Examiner,* November 16, 1911.

The Iceman and the Psychiatrist, The Iceman Interviews, 1991, Gaby Monet producer, Arthur Ginsburg director, America Undercover special, HBO/Time Warner.

Chapter Four

The Road to Altamont

In the summer of 1910, Jackson was delighted to make the acquaintance of Lambert R. Jones, who would become the new editor and publisher of the *Chewaucan Press* at Paisley. Jackson was delighted, because seeing his name in print was the thing that he loved almost as much as he loved money. Jackson even went so far as to put his money where his mouth was, and invested financially in Jones' fledgling newspaper, launched some time in early 1911.

At the time of that big stock sale to Alex Davis in 1910, the *Examiner* described Jackson in such glowing terms that the account was actually picked up by the *Oregonian*. That piece was clearly a product of Jackson's superficial charm and grandiosity, and a great example of his ability to influence others. It made a case for his expertise with cattle, and also firmly established his mastery of "bull."

How Men Thrive Here

R. B. Jackson has sold to A. A. Davis, Klamath Marsh about $33,000 worth of cattle to be delivered at Williams River, April 15th. He also retains about 500 head of yearlings from his herd. The exact price paid per head for these cattle is not known but is considerably in advance of anything sold before in the county.

Mr. Jackson embarked in the cattle business about eight years ago in northern Lake county. At that time he was a school teacher, having a capital of $40 in money, a hard hat and a pair of red socks. This development in so short a time again shows the resources of Lake County.

The line about a pair of red socks was probably a reference to Jackson having some unknown good luck charm, and the hard hat could be a reference to some sort of alleged pioneer toughness and grit.

Around the first of May in 1911, editor Lambert R. Jones of the *Chewaucan Post* at Paisley, obligingly printed a boastful claim by Jackson that the pump and pipe for the Ana River Irrigation Company were en route from Alturas, California, and that "President Jackson assures us that inside of 30 days the pump will be throwing a stream of three thousand inches of water." Later that week was when Jackson was found guilty on that bothersome embezzlement charge, and was asked to resign his position as school superintendent.

Jackson and Virgil Conn accompanied Governor Oswald West on a tour of the Ana River irrigation plant, and of Silver Lake after a luncheon at the Hotel Paisley in July of 1911. Although the chief aim of the trip north seems to have been to gripe about the inaction of the Portland Irrigation Company that, "had not done a thing toward fulfilling their contract with the state" to develop and irrigate lands around Paisley, Jackson took advantage of the tour to show off the Ana River project. The *Examiner* article describing the visit to Paisley and parts north originally appeared in the *Chewaucan Press,* and was probably written by Jones.

In the summer of 1911, Jackson and Jones decided to become bankers. In order to do that, they would need to come up with a bunch of money, and of course, a bank to put it in. The banking idea, like so many of Jackson's other schemes, came to Jackson by association. In the first week of August, C. S. Hudson, cashier of the First National Bank of Bend, and Paul H. Van Winkle, cashier of the First Bank of Fallis, Oklahoma, traveled by car from Bend to Silver Lake and Paisley. And, according to a short account in the *Silver Lake Leader,* the men were "looking over the banking possibilities of this part of the country."

The following, 'puff piece,' seems to have been a byproduct of Jackson and Jones' fevered imaginations. It was (very poorly) written around the middle of September.

Bank for Paisley
Chewaucan Press:

It is possible to asset (sic) positively that Paisley is to have a bank. The Press has known for several weeks that plans were afoot for the establishment of such an institution in our midst, but hesitated to make the matter public until it was finaly (sic) assured. This is now the case and we may congratulate ourselves un (sic) on securing an addition to the business institutoins (sic) of the town that will not only facilitate the transaction of business here but will mean that Paisley will be the depositary (sic) of the wealth of our adjacent valleys, instead of towns far distant.

Capitalists from Bend and even from Oklahoma were instrumental in promoting the bank and local money is also enlisted in the enterprise. A site has been secured upon which it is intended to erect a substantial and handsome stone building, one that will be a credit to the town. The president and cashier of the bank will also live in Paisley and will probably erect handsome residences.

Had we entertained any doubt that Paisley had a great future this news would settle the question to our mind beyond dispute. When capital begins to come in, we may rest assured that the other desirable things will follow in its wake. So get your money out of that old sock and get it in the bank.

The next week, Jackson and Jones secured an automobile and headed off to Bend to try to raise the aforementioned capital. Both men were well-endowed with the gift of gab, so were under the misimpression that merely talking big and loud about a thing would make it happen. "R. B. Jackson and L. R. Jones made a trip to Bend Monday by auto, returning Tuesday. While in that busy town, they made final arrangements that mean the coming of a strong bank to Paisley. It is expected that construction work on the building will begin next week. The site to be occupied by the bank is next to the Mercantile Company's store," wrote Jones, referring to Jackson's Chewaucan Mercantile.

Then, Jackson's great plans began to dissolve before his very eyes. By the time of the October 1911 annual meeting of the irrigation company, he was no longer president, and was probably asked to resign that position, or was voted out.

In the middle of October, he was arrested for violation of the local option law, along with his drinking pal, George Ranney, and fined four hundred dollars. "Local option" is a general term for laws that allow voters to decide if or how alcohol will be sold in their communities, and Oregon passed such a law in June of 1904. In the county election of June 1, 1908 the precincts of Silver Lake, Summer Lake, and Paisley voted in favor of prohibiting the sale of intoxicating liquor within their boundaries. Since Jackson was fined for two counts of violation of the law, it can probably be assumed that he illegally sold alcohol to two men.

Not only had Jackson lost his job with the county, but all of the money he made on the big cattle sale seemed to have evaporated as well, because he made the delinquent tax list that fall. In spite of all that recent 'bad press,' Ray Jackson did manage to get himself elected to the city council of Paisley in October of 1911. He had only lasted with the irrigation company for about a year.

By the end of 1911, Jackson's association with Frank W. Payne seems to have dissolved as well, and they were never again mentioned together in politics, irrigation, ranching, or the mercantile trade. Payne had become county clerk in 1908, and was reelected in 1910. It would have been very natural for Payne, as an elected official, to have cut financial ties with Jackson after the embezzlement scandal. At the end of 1911, on December 14, Jackson's other cattle ranching partner, Frank Dobkins, married Frank Payne's ex-wife, Florence L. Martin Payne, further straining the friendship between Payne and Jackson.

By the middle of November, 1911, it became obvious that Jackson and Jones were out of their depth in the realm of banking, and a short article in the *Examiner* named stockholders in the project as the First National Bank of Bend, the Deschutes Savings Bank, and Northwest Townsite Company. The later being the same organization that owned the Portland Irrigation Company, much reviled by Jackson, Jones, and most of the population of Paisley. Paul Van Winkle was mentioned again, this time as president of the new concern.

When articles of incorporation for the Chewaucan State Bank were filed in Lake County in January of 1912, incorporators J. M. Lawrence, F. F. Smith, and R. F. Averill, all of Bend, had raised fifteen thousand dollars in capital stock, and the names of Jackson and Jones were conspicuously absent. In November of 1912, Governor West and Senators Bourne and Chamberlain recommended that the Controller of the Currency at Washington grant a charter to the new bank, with George M. Bailey of Northwest Townsite Company as president. But, the firm did not actually open its doors until April of 1913, and under a new name, the Paisley National Bank.

The partnership of Jones and Jackson was abruptly terminated on June 10, 1912, when Jones was shot to death in the woodshed of B. F. Cannon after "Frank" caught the editor with his wife for the last time. Jackson himself was a lady's man, and that was probably another reason why he and Jones had hit it off so well. Jackson's reputation preceeded him to such an extent that many of the residents of Harney County, where he lived for the last 20 years of his life, knew him only as "Tomcat." Around 1910, Jones lived on the Wagontire ranch of Anton Egli as his hired hand, and probably became acquainted with Jackson through the Egli family. The Eglis had a stock ranch east of Wagontire Mountain, and Jackson had a ranching relationship with them dating back to about 1902, when he registered his cattle brand in Harney County.

Anyone who reads through old newspapers from the years that Jackson lived in Lake County will realize that the man made a deliberate effort to get his name into print, and can gain some important insight into his character. In May of 1909, Jackson took advantage of a front page article, that was supposed to have been about the school system, to 'bash' the Portland Irrigation Company:

Mr. Jackson says the northern part of the county is receiving many new settlers. In this respect the country about Paisley is receiving a fair share, but not so many as would be the case were it not for the fact of a great part of that section being tied up by Portland people under the pretext of improving same with water from the Chewaucan river under the Carey act.

In 1909, Jackson spent about a month touring the county at taxpayers' expense, for the ostensible purpose of polling the population on their feelings about the construction of two new high schools. One in Lakeview, and one in the north end of the county, possibly at Paisley because that was where he was living at the time. His grand vision included "a manual training course for young men, and a course in domestic science for the young ladies," with a small farm attached to each school for agricultural studies, "that heart, brain and hand would be so trained that they would be fitted as first class citizens. Graduates from such schools would be sought after, and in this way Lake County would win a place in educational matters second to none in the state." Critics of Jackson's scheme were unhappy about the prospect of increased taxes, and wrote that the citizens of Lakeview should pay for their own school, and that parents around the county should pay tuition in order to send their kids there.

Soon after he was elected, readers of the *Examiner* had to endure a piece titled, "Superintendent of our Schools, Teaches School, Runs a Big Farm, and Has 1,000 Head of Cattle." The piece was so indulgent, it could have been written by Jackson himself.

R. B. Jackson, of Paisley, the new county school superintendent of schools (sic) is in town this week in attendance at the county examination.

Mr. Jackson is a very pleasant gentleman to meet. He intends making a regular trip each week to Lakeview to look after his official duties. In addition to being Lake County superin-

tendent Mr. Jackson is also the principal of the Paisley schools. He also is the owner of a 1000 acre farm adjoining Paisley, and is the owner of 1000 head of cattle, a number of which he is now pasturing on the Klamath flats, getting them ready for market at either Ashland, Ore., or Yreka, California.

It will be seen that with his manifold duties and property interests that Mr. Jackson is a very busy man.

The area of "Klamath Flats" named in the article was and is not in Klamath County at all, but in northern California at the foot of Mt. Shasta, and contained a historic mining camp that dated back to the early 1850s. The area was also known as "Thompson's Dry Diggins," and "Little Klamath" back in the gold rush era. Jackson's ranching friends, the Eglis, also had ranching operations in the area around Yreka and Mt. Shasta, and the road that Jackson would have traveled to reach his herd at Klamath Flats in California passed through Klamath Falls, via the small town of Altamont.

SOURCES:

"Paisley Press Items," *Lake County Examiner,* May 11, 1911.

"Brief Mention," *Lake County Examiner,* October 5, 1911. Lists the officers of the irrigation company. Jackson is not named.

"Judge Benson is Busy," *Lake County Examiner,* October 19, 1911.

"Big Archie is Acquitted by Jury," *Lake County Examiner,* October 26, 1911. Article is a summary of the term of circuit court.

"Liquor Control, Temperance, and the Call for Prohibition," web site of the Oregon State Archives, http://arcweb.sos.state. or.us/pages/exhibits/50th/prohibition1/temper ance.html

"In the county court of the state of Oregon, for the county of Lake." Order declaring result of election and prohibiting the sale of intoxicating liquors in Silver Lake, precinct no. 1, Summer Lake, precinct no. 2, and Paisley, precinct no. 3 of Lake County, Oregon," *Lake County Examiner,* June 25, 1908.

"Brief Mention," *Lake County Examiner,* December 15, 1910. Short item stating that the newspaper to be established at Paisley is being backed by R. B. Jackson.

"Delinquent Tax List, 1910" *Lake County Examiner*, October 26, 1911.

"Silver Lake Items," *Lake County Examiner,* August 10, 1911. News items picked up from the *Silver Lake Leader.*

"Paisley PickUps," *Lake County Examiner,* September 28, 1911. News items picked up from the *Chewaucan Press.*

"Brief Mention," *Lake County Examiner,* November 16, 1911.

"Bank For Paisley," *Lake County Examiner,* September 21, 1911. Picked up from the *Chewaucan Press.*

Marriage Records, volume three, 1909 1920, County of Lake, Lakeview, Oregon, compiled by Oregon Youth Conservation Corps, 1995, Lana J. Morrison, p 17. Frank Dobkins married Florence L. (Martin) Payne on December 14, 1911.

"Charter Granted for Paisley Bank," *Lake County Examiner,* November 7, 1912.

"Local News Items" *Bend Bulletin,* April 30, 1913. Short article names Earl H. Conser of Bend as cashier of the new Paisley National Bank.

"Finding Editor in Home, Paisley Man Kills Him," *Bend Bulletin,* June 12, 1912.

Search results for Lambert Russell Jones on the web site of Find A Grave. A photograph of his grave stone gives his date of death as June 10, 1912. http://www.findagrave.com /cgibin/fg.cgi?page=gr&GSln=Jones&GSfn=Lambert& GSbyrel=all&GSdyrel=all&GSst=39&GScntry=4&GSob=n&GRid=30335574&df=all&

Thirteenth Census of the United States, Oregon, Harney County, Curry Precinct. Shows Lambert R. Jones as the hired hand on the stock farm of Anton Egli on April 29, 1910.

"Spokane Son Honors Pioneer Father," *Spokesman-Review,* June 19, 1948.

"Lake County High Schools," *Lake County Examiner,* June 10, 1909.

"North End of the County Frowns on High Schools," *Lake County Examiner,* June 24, 1909.

"How Men Thrive Here," *Lake County Examiner,* February 24, 1910. Article was picked up by the *Oregonian* for their March 8 issue, under the headline "Getting Along."

"Supt. Jackson Talks of Schools," *Lake County Examiner,* May 6, 1909.

"Superintendent of Our Schools," *Lake County Examiner,* August 13, 1908.

The 'real' Bridge of Sighs in Venice. Supposedly, the bridge in Klamath Falls was named after this one, because it provided a connection between a brothel on Oak Avenue and the city jail, rather than connecting a historic palace to a prison, like the original.

Chapter Five

The Bridge of Sighs

The brutal murder of Charles D. Lyons on the morning of August 19, 1911 had several features that made it similar to some of Ray Jackson's early murders. The man had been bludgeoned, and like the Wallende and Conn murders, the killer had left no trace, tracks, or blood evidence at the scene. The body was found in water, a canal, and near a small bridge. The bridge being a prominent feature of both the Conn and Wallende murders that seemed to be a theme during the early period of Jackson's 'career.' Lyons was believed to have been killed, like Wallende, at night and after collecting his pay and leaving a lodging house, which, in this case was actually a house of ill-fame. The murder occurred in Klamath Falls during a period of time when Jackson was known to frequent that town.

A fragment of information about Jackson's whereabouts around the time of the murder was found in the gossip column of the county paper. Every week, the *Lake County Examiner,* and papers like it all over the country, would publish a wide variety of personal news tidbits, each about one sentence long. They were a sort of 'chatter,' not unlike the social networking web sites of today, and were just as popular, and a fabulous source of information. Sometimes, they were divided by town or region, with titles like "Paisley Items," or "City Briefs." There you could find who went where and when, who they traveled with, births of children, sickness, accidents, and who had checked into the hotels during a particular week. Plus, business startups and dissolutions, and a variety of facts from the minutiae of everyday life. Those news items were the 'grasslands,' a fertile hunting ground for both the criminal and the investigator.

In the "Brief Mention" column of the *Examiner* of August 31, 1911 we find that, "R. B. Jackson, the well known Paisley merchant and one of the 'livewires' of central Lake County paid a visit here last week." "Here," in this case, meaning the town of Lakeview. Like any short blurb, it offers incomplete information, but it shows that Jackson was away from home, and possibly passing through Lakeview on his way to or from somewhere else.

Jackson was known to travel to and from Klamath County on livestock related business. In 1907, he and Frank Payne and William B. Owsley delivered some beef cattle to a buyer 20 miles east of Klamath Falls. Since at least 1908, Jackson had kept a herd of cattle at Klamath Flats in northern California, at the foot of Mt. Shasta, and would have probably traveled by stage between Lakeview and Klamath Falls any time he wanted to visit northern California on cattle business. In the spring of 1910, Jackson delivered cattle to the Davis ranch on Williamson River in northern Klamath County. In the 1920's, Jackson had a relationship with a woman who he referred to as his wife, although no record of that marriage has ever been found. She may have been a common law partner, and Jackson apparently kept her at Klamath Falls, and even wrote to the U.S. Land Office from that town concerning his homestead claim in northern Klamath County, saying that his wife could not tolerate the altitude at the homestead. Then, there was Jackson's friendship and association in the Ana River Irrigation Company with the Barnes brothers, Billy and Frank. Billy was the sheriff of Klamath County from 1908 through 1912, and lived in Klamath Falls.

Charles Lyons had been struck twice in the head with the sharp end of a hatchet or a similar instrument, which could have been the same weapon that was used in the Wallende murder. It will be remembered that Wallende was killed with the blunt end of some heavy instrument, and his body was deposited in Silver Creek. The fatal wound in Lyons' case was delivered to the fragile right side of the skull, and that wound location matched that of some of Jackson's other victims. Could there be a connection between all of those victims? Could they all be attributed to a malicious psychopath who killed with a hatchet?

Other victims of Jackson's, either definitely or probably, had some association with him. So, would Jackson lash out and kill a man who he did not know? Lyons was basically a logger and a teamster, and had worked around the mills and logging camps of Klamath County for several years. Around 1911, Jackson was known to be interested in ranching, education, irrigation, the mercantile trade, and banking. He had dabbled in the timber industry in 1907 as a locator, but the chances are slim that he would have known Lyons, who was employed at an obscure logging camp in the south end of Klamath County at the time of his death. In other murders that the author has attributed to Jackson, namely the Conn, Wallende, and Bradley murders, it was apparent that Jackson loved to toy with investigators. He mailed anonymous letters, involved himself in the investigations so that he could misdirect them, and elaborately staged the crime scenes. Jackson dearly loved to think of himself as highly intelligent, and he wanted to outsmart the investigators, to beat them at their own game.

In the case of the Lyons murder, investigators were confounded by a set of puzzling circumstances. The man had no known enemies, and no motive could be discovered for the crime. No witnesses to the killing could be found. If any trace or clue as to the identity of the killer existed around the crime scene, it was not discovered. They could not even find the murder weapon, and Lyons had not been robbed. His murder seemed so inexplicably random and savage at the same time, some thought it was the work of a madman.

Charles D. Lyons was 38 years old when he died in the restricted district of Klamath Falls. He was born in Ireland, and his parents still lived in Limerick. He had served in the Philippine War, then lived in Petaluma, California before coming to Klamath County. Lyons worked for several years around the sawmills, and in 1910 the census found him working as a teamster for a logging camp on the Odessa to Fort Klamath Road. Just before he died, he was employed in the logging camp of Lost River Lumber Company near Stukel Mountain, southeast of Klamath Falls.

At the time of the Lyons murder, August 19 of 1911, Ray B. Jackson was associated with Billy Barnes and his brother, James F. "Frank" Barnes, in the Ana River Irrigation Company. Frank's homestead contained the four valuable springs that were the source of the whole enterprise, and Frank was also on the board of directors. Billy's homestead claim was next to Frank's, and in 1911 he told a reporter for the *Klamath Chronicle* that the brothers had been trying to irrigate their land around Ana River for 15 years, or since about 1896. Lyons was killed just a couple of days after Sheriff Barnes returned from a visit of more than one week to the Summer Lake country where he and his family had gone to see relatives and friends, and he no doubt checked up on the condition of the irrigation works while he was there.

That Friday morning, August 18, Lyons and a logging buddy, Ben Robbs, traveled from the camp at Stukel Mountain to the little town of Altamont, about six miles away, and cashed their paychecks. From there, they traveled with their driver, J. A. Gordon, to the Livermore Hotel on East Main in Klamath Falls. Robbs and Lyons must have planned on spending the night at the Livermore, because Lyons left half of his $80 in wages at the hotel for safekeeping.

Around 4 p.m., Lyons and Robbs traveled again by car to a drinking establishment known as the Road House at Sixth and Main, and remained there several hours. Lyons got a shave from the barber at the Road House, and around 7 p.m. Lyons and Robbs, with James Crowley and William Langell, rode to the restricted district on West Oak Avenue. The last person to have spoken to Lyons was Ben Robbs, who talked to him around midnight and tried to get Lyons to leave the Red House brothel with him. According to Robbs, the two men had made plans for the weekend to meet a friend at Upper Klamath Lake. On Saturday morning, Robbs looked for Lyons, but was unable to find him.

The murder of Charles D. Lyons occurred at Klamath Falls on August 19, 1911, and was sufficiently similar to the rest of the murders the author has attributed to Ray Jackson to make it worthy of close inspection. The following articles were copied exactly and in their entirety. The first story contains an error about the location of the fatal wound that should be noted. The wound was, in fact, on the *right* side of the head, as described by the examining physicians.

Klamath Republican
August 24, 1911

FLOATING CORPSE POINTS TO CRIME

BODY OF CHARLES LYONS, HIS SKULL CRUSHED AS THOUGH BY AN AXE, FOUND TODAY IN OAK STREET CANAL

Was Charles Lyons murdered and his body thrown in the Oak street canal? Could he possibly, in an intoxicated condition, have fallen from the Bridge of Sighs in such a manner as to so badly cut his head that death resulted either from the wound or from drowning?

The above are two of the many questions which are bothering the officers of the law, both city and county, as a result of the finding of a man floating in the Oak street canal, opposite the city jail Monday afternoon by Jesse Hunsaker. The body was floating with the left side down.

After Coroner Earl Whitlock had been summoned, the body was taken from the water, and evidence of death by violence rather than drowning was disclosed in a horrible gash on the left side of the head. This extended from the middle of the skull to a point just in front of the left ear. As the man's hair was closely cropped the wound was easily discernible. It has the appearance of having been made with an axe, grubbing hoe or some similar instrument.

After the body was removed to the morgue a search of the pockets brought to light a purse containing $15.85, so robbery was hardly the motive for the man's death. J. A. Gordon, of the Southern Oregon Automobile company, seeing the body at the morgue, identified it as Charles Lyons who of late has been employed by the Lost River mill. Gordon says that he brought Lyons and some companions to this city Saturday evening from the Altamont Tavern.

Lyons was pretty well acquainted in Klamath Falls, and was for some time in the employ of Charles Willson. He came to this city from

~83~

Petaluma, Calif., but told several people that he was originally from Limerick county, Ireland, where his parents are said to reside. He was about 32 years of age. Until a short time ago Lyons wore a mustache, and it was owing to the fact that he recently shaved it that many did not recognize him.

Klamath Falls Express
August 8, 1911

MURDERER OF LYONS IS STILL ENJOYING HIS LIBERTY

It is now preety (sic) certain that Lyons was not murdered on the spur of the moment. It is very sure that he was killed with eitehr (sic) an ax or some heavy tool, either an ax or hatchet, (sic) although a broken ax handle was found by Harry Galarneaux, Jr., near where the body was found in the canal with a stain on it indicating blood. This stain was decided to be something else, however, besides it would have been absolutely impossible for the dead man to have been cut up the way he was with an ax handle. It was argued by some that the ax used in killing Lyons had been on this and the handle was broken by the murderer. This theory is hardly tenable at (sic) this piece of handle had not been freshly broken off and had been whittled which showed it had been done some weeks ago.

The belief that the object, with which Lyons was killed is in the canal where it was thrown after the brutal murder. An effort has been made to find this tool, the canal having been raked by the order of the district attorney's office with a big fine toothed rake and when anything was struck that felt like metal or a heavy object, Harry Galarneaux, who was assisting in the work, would dive to the bottom and bring this to the top.

The belief that Lyons was not killed on the spur of the moment is strengthened by the fact that it would just be a chance circumstance for the murderer to have found such a weapon as the ax that he was slain with at hand unless it had been placed there intentionally. This strengthens the belief that when Lyons left the Oak street houses Friday night some one was waiting for him with his weapon ready to pounce upon the man from the rear as he was evidently struck on the back of the head first.

It is suggested that Lyons met his death at some other place than near these houses and there is but one chance, apparently, that such can be the case. He may have not been so stupefied with drink when he left the places taht (sic) he wandered off in another direction than up town. He may have gone to some point along the water front where he was slain and possibly dragged into the canal. But had this been the case, he was towed through the water, for had the body been taken overland and thrown in near the spot where (sic) was found some bloodstains would have been left.

The officers have run down every possible clue. Each of these takes them back to the red light district where the dead man was last seen alive. While they are still in hopes of being able to land the dastardly criminal he has had ample time to get out of the country ere this and many miles from here (sic).

In the far away city of Venice, in northern Italy, there stands a historic bridge known as, the Bridge of Sighs. It crosses the Rio di Palazzo canal and connects an old prison to a historic palace. About 100 years ago, Klamath Falls had its own version of the Bridge of Sighs. It crossed the canal on Oak Avenue near the city jail. But, despite its rather elegant name, the Klamath Bridge of Sighs was not located in a very nice neighborhood.

The open canal on Oak Avenue carried raw sewage into Lake Euwana. In place of a royal palace, was the Red House brothel. The only watercraft on the canal were not gondolas, but the occasional small barge or steam launch. And those crossing the bridge were not suntanned tourists, but inebriated loggers, ranchers, and railroad laborers going back and forth from the Red House and the other three houses of ill fame on Oak Avenue. The neighborhood was known as the "restricted district" or the "red light district." Lyons' body was found on August 21 in the Oak Avenue canal, and so close to the Bridge of Sighs that it was speculated at first that he might have fallen from the bridge and drowned.

The restricted district was "restricted" because, in 1910, Mayor Fred T. Sanderson and the town council set aside a parcel of land in what was known as the First Hot Springs Addition for brothels. Mayor Sanderson also appointed a new police chief that year, Edward C. Townsend, previously stage carpenter for the Pocatello Opera House. Townsend shared police duties with a patrolman by the name of Samuel L. Walker, who interestingly enough, did double duty as a deputy under Klamath County Sheriff William B. "Billy" Barnes. Walker worked for Barnes since the election of 1908, and would continue to work for both agencies through 1911. Barnes was a Californian, who first settled in Lake County at Ana River, and then moved to Klamath Falls in 1904. In 1908 Barnes had begun working as a deputy under Sheriff Silas Obenchain.

Policeman and deputy sheriff Sam Walker became "acting chief of police" for Klamath Falls some time in September of 1911 because chief Townsend came down with a serious case of typhoid fever. The illness turned to pneumonia that took Townsend's life, and on October 16, Walker was appointed chief of police by Mayor Sanderson. At the time of his appointment, two members of the town council spoke out against the problem of whiskey being sold without a license in the restricted district brothels, and asked Walker and Sanderson for enforcement of the liquor laws, implying by their comments that the mayor and his police department were a part of the problem. So, in October and November, by order of the mayor, Walker went through the motions of investigating the brothels, and closing them. But, not really. The four lady proprietors were brought in on charges of selling liquor and operating bawdy houses, fined, and let out on bail, making it a rather profitable effort on the part of the city. Police Judge T. F. Nicholas reported to the town council that, during the six month period between June and November of 1911, he had turned in $1,236 in fines, all of which went into the town's road improvement fund.

In December of 1911, the *Evening Herald* printed an amusing story of the goings-on at the Comet Lodging House during that time when the brothels were supposedly no longer in operation.

> *Several nights ago in the Comet lodging house old man Haley, the same who when peeved at being refused a drink endeavored to let atmosphere in the Du Fault saloon by shattering the plate glass windows thereof was making Rome howl. He was yelling and carrying on in a very unseemly manner, according to the story. He was disrobed, in bed, full, and waving a $10 bill in his hand.*

> *When Patrolman William Hall entered the sacred portals of the lodging house and later the inner recess in which old man Haley, who is a civil war veteran over three score and ten, was lodging, there was Haley as described above.*

> *Just why he was yelling, the police cannot say, unless it be that he had a skinful of joyful oil which made him feel like exulting aloud. As to the cause of his waving the $10 bill there is also some doubt, although the motive may have been*

a financial one. Just whether he wished to sub-
sidize the police or buy a bottle of wine, or pay
the first installment on a lot, could not be
learned this morning. At any rate Patrolman
Hall determined to arrest Haley $10 and all.

It is important to note that ten dollars was the going rate, at the time, charged by certain women in Klamath Falls for the pleasure of their company and a bottle of wine. At the end of December 1911, Walker was terminated as a deputy sheriff by Barnes, although the sheriff would cite no particular reason for the dismissal. The well-publicized fuss that Walker had made about pretending to shut down the brothels may very well have been due to his intention of running for sheriff. And, he did announce himself as a candidate for that office four months later.

1912 dawned in Klamath Falls with the sensational Faye Melbourne trial. The four brothels in the neighborhood employed about 20 prostitutes, and the Red House at Sixth and Oak was constructed and owned by 26 year-old Faye Melbourne. Despite its surroundings, the Red House was rather stately on the inside. As described by Chief of Police Samuel L. Walker in 1911, it was outfitted with a wine parlor, dance hall, and pianos. The 1910 census for the Linkville Precinct showed that Melbourne's establishment employed three women, Ollie Sheldon, Addie Nichols, and Maude "Belle" Evans. Faye Melbourne's Red House seems to have been the most prominent establishment of its type at the time, and according to the *Evening Herald,* when her case went to trial in January of 1912, the courtroom was packed.

> *"The only woman present was the defendant,*
> *who sat with her wraps on, occasionally turn-*
> *ing around to smile at someone with whom she*
> *was evidently acquainted,"*

Melbourne's attorney, C. M. O'Neill, based his case for the defense on the culpability of the city police department in maintaining the profitable prostitution trade in Klamath Falls. The August murder of Lyons, who had been a customer at the Red

House, and other crimes, helped draw attention to the problem of the brothels.

The *Evening Herald* covered the trial with an article headlined "Tenderloin Case Draws Big Crowd." And, for the meaning of that particular metaphor, we must turn to another district of infamy existing around the turn of the century, the one below Forty-Second Street and west of Broadway in New York City, known for its vice and corruption. It was called the "Tenderloin District" because it was regarded as a choice assignment for police grafters, and the name was subsequently applied to similar districts in other towns. Gambling and prostitution flourished in the Tenderloin, giving police officers luscious opportunities for graft. According to *The Encyclopedia of New York City*, police Captain Andrew S. "Clubber" Williams gave the area its name in 1876 when he was transferred to a police precinct in the heart of the district. Referring to the increased payoffs he would get for police protection of both legitimate and illegitimate businesses there, especially the many brothels, Williams said, "I've been having chuck steak ever since I've been on the force, and now I'm going to have a bit of tenderloin."

One of the most shocking moments of the Melbourne trial came when her attorney accused Chief Walker of having shielded "certain houses of ill-fame in this city." At first, Walker tried to give the impression that he had only remote and hearsay knowledge of the Red House, but then revealed that he had discussed the construction of the establishment with Melbourne.

> *"She said to me that she was going to put it up for that purpose, for the running of a house of illfame. She wanted to know where to put up a house, and asked me my opinion on it said she wanted to have it where she would not be bothered. I told her I couldn't promise her any protection from the consequence of such a thing."*

> *Chief of Police Samuel L. Walker*

The jury in the Melbourne trial could not agree as to her guilt and, with an eight to four split, Faye Melbourne was let out on two hundred dollars bail to await a new trial. But, Melbourne skipped town in early February, before her case went back to court and without paying her attorney, and was never heard of again.

1912 also saw the enactment of a new city charter that gave exclusive control of the bawdy houses to the city council. Under "Powers of Council," the April 23 charter declared that the city council "shall have exclusive control on behalf of the city, to prevent and suppress bawdy houses or places where fornication is practiced, and to punish any inmate, keeper, or frequenter thereof." By August, just one year after the Lyons murder, the Women's Christian Temperance Union petitioned the city council to obey their own charter, and begged for enforcement.

The request was tabled under a motion by councilman Doty, who expounded upon the benefits of keeping the brothels together in one place, and said that he himself had installed some houses of ill fame in the restricted district. Mr. Doty was in the rather unique business of relocating structures from one part of town to another.

> *I went to the late mayor, Mr. Sanderson, to get a permit to move some houses in there. The mayor said I did not need a permit, as the land had been set aside for them.*
>
> *Councilman M. R. Doty*

Doty was of the opinion that keeping the brothels inside of the restricted district kept the rest of the town 'clean,' and there can be little doubt as to the convenience of such an arrangement. The city officials of the period, like Mayor Sanderson and various chiefs of police, seemed content enough to ignore the houses of ill fame. After all, they drew traffic and business into the town from the far corners of the county, and the constant arrests for prostitution, liquor law violations, and other petty crimes channeled money into the city coffers. And, Mayor Sanderson was much more concerned with the 'upbuilding of the town.' Improvements to the roads, sidewalks, sewer, and water systems, and construction of a new city hall all happened during his administration.

The three other brothels, often referred to as "sporting houses," were also on Oak Avenue, and the proprietors of them paid rent at the extortive rate of $150 to $300 per month. Maud "Belle" Evans, Dorothy Ward, and Stella Seedgrass were proprietors of the other three houses, and another woman, Rosette Murray, may have been associated with Faye Melbourne because they shared the same attorney. The names of all of those women came before the public eye in 1912 when they were tried in the circuit court by Judge Henry L. Benson and fined $125 each. Despite a stern warning from Benson that future violators would be sentenced to the county jail, rather than fined, brothels continued to operate in Klamath Falls until at least 1920.

For years, the citizenry of Klamath Falls was forced to endure the problems of the brothels, with all of their attendant violence, late night drinking, and crime. In 1915, the police chief and mayor again went through the motions of ordering the women out of town. In July of 1920, the *Evening Herald* published an editorial with the ghastly accusation that the city council was in the business of licensing bawdy houses under the guise of "lodging houses," and that the councilmen pretended to be "blind" to the enterprises operating under the protection of the city government.

> *When the present council licensed bawdy houses, we thought that it had reached the limit of insult to the decent people of this community. But we were mistaken. It had to go further, and it is fair to assume that it did so under the same orders that directed it to issue the license. It had to assure a supply of "roomers" for the "rooming houses" to which it guaranteed official protection and to do so it had to step from the gutter down into the cesspool of the tinhorn, the pimp and makareau.*

Doctors Hamilton and Chilton, who examined Lyons' body in 1911, found no water in the lungs, and were certain the man was dead before his body was cast into the channel. John W. Hunsaker was the man who first spotted the body around 2 p.m.

on Monday when he was driving by the canal. Bodies cast into water that is relatively warm, like that of the Oak Avenue Canal, will remain submerged for a couple of days, and that explains why the body was not found before Monday. It was hauled ashore by a launch passing toward Upper Klamath Lake, and when Coroner Whitlock arrived it was removed from the water.

The murder of Charles Lyons certainly seems like it could be attributed to Ray Jackson. But, because the murder of Lyons occurred many years ago, there are several holes in the story. Some of those holes can be filled in if we base our reasoning on the facts of the case, a process that was obviously not adhered to by the police department of Klamath Falls, or the coroner's jury.

For example, the jury, in their official verdict of the case, gave the date of Lyons death as "on or about the 18th day of August." That was despite the sworn statement of Lyon's friend, Ben Robbs, that he had last seen Lyons alive at midnight on the 18th. If the man was alive at midnight on the 18th, then surely his was killed on the 19th, and that was the date that should have appeared in the verdict, that read as follows:

> *That the deceased's name is Charles Lyons; that he came to his death at Klamath Falls, Oregon, on or about the 18th day of August, 1911; that the cause of his death was a wound inflicted upon the right side of the head by some sharp instrument in the hands of a person to this jury unknown.*
>
> > *Geo. B. Snyder*
> > *J. A. Uerling*
> > *K. North*
> > *M. G. Wilkins*
> > *L. H. Bath*
> > *S. B. Low*

The investigation, such as it was, and as described by the newspapers, centered around the canal and the bridge, the area where the body was found. Investigators were looking for clues as to the identity of the killer, and the spot where the murder happened. An important fact to keep in mind is that no blood evidence was found anywhere in the vicinity of the canal or bridge.

Because any man struck twice in the head with a sharp instrument bleeds profusely, especially when one of those blows severs the temporal artery, the possibility that Lyons was killed on the bank of the canal must be ruled out. Furthermore, when we rely once again on the testimony of witnesses, Lyons was last seen alive inside of the Red House. Of all the many people interviewed for the inquest, no one stated that they had seen Lyons outside of the Red House after midnight. How, then, did the police conclude that Lyons had left the Red House and was killed outside of it?

Not only did the police fail to find any blood evidence around the canal, they did not find any drag marks or signs of a struggle, or anything that might point to the spot where the body was put into the water. Unless the body was somehow thrown through the air over a great distance, it seems probable that it was carried to the water, by either one large person or two small people, and dropped in. If it had been dropped from the hard surface of the Bridge of Sighs in the wee hours of Saturday morning, the killer or killers could have avoided leaving any trace or eye witnesses to tell about it. The body must have been deposited in the canal after it had bled out, and some time early Saturday morning, because one of the examining doctors, Dr. Hamilton, stated that "the body had lain in the water probably two or three days." And the statement of the second doctor, Dr. Chilton, agreed. "The man was dead when he struck the water. He must have been dead about three days."

The police searched in vain for the murder weapon, putting forth a great effort and expense. They brought in a diver, and raked the entire canal for some distance with a fine-toothed rake, yet were unable to locate anything that may have been used to commit the crime. Surely, the canal would have been a likely place to have thrown the weapon if Lyons had been killed on the bank. But, the possibility of that should have been ruled out before the search of the canal drained the resources of the department.

The instrument believed by the examining doctors to have been an axe, hatchet, or similar tool was an interesting choice for a murder weapon. It was not the sort of thing that most people would carry around town with them, like a gun or a knife. That particular tool could suggest that the killing was not premeditated, but was done in anger, and that the hatchet just happened to be nearby, a weapon of opportunity that was snatched up. Either that, or the killer was a psychopath with a particular attachment to a hatchet, and actually did lug it around with him.

"The belief that Lyons was not killed on the spur of the moment is strengthened by the fact that it would just be a chance circumstance for the murderer to have found such a weapon as the axe he was slain with unless it had been placed there intentionally," stated the *Klamath Falls Express*. "This strengthens the belief that when Lyons left the Oak street houses Friday night someone was waiting for him with his weapon ready to pounce upon the man from the rear as he was evidently struck on the back of the head first."

It is regrettable that the coroner's jury, six men who gathered to examine the facts of the case, wasted a great deal of time on the subject of Lyon's money. How much he had, how much he spent, and how much was found on the body. Those men were, no doubt, exploring the possibility of robbery as a motive. The testimony of men who were with Lyons the night of the murder showed that he started the evening with $40. By the time he got to the Red House around 7 p.m. he still had about $20. Lyons and his friend, Robbs, were at that establishment until at least midnight, and it does not take a lot of imagination to conclude how they had spent their time and money while they were there. Robbs said he borrowed $10 from Lyons which, again, was the going rate for the pleasure of the company of a lady of a certain disposition. By then, Lyons had spent about $40, including the money he loaned his friend. He then returned to the Livermore Hotel and withdrew another $20 of his pay and went back to the Red House, where he continued drinking, spending about another $5, by midnight when Robbs left. That would leave about $15 still unspent, and that amount matched what was found on the body. The working of that little mathematical story problem, combined with the quizzical fact that the attacker completely overlooked the money, forces us to conclude that robbery should never have been considered as a possible motive.

Brothels, with all of their inherent crime, corruption, violence, and late night drinking, posed a nagging social problem for the town of Linkville from it's inception in 1867, through at least 1920. The entrepreneurial, young, Miss Faye Melbourne, however, was nobody's fool, and capitalized on the situation. The town was originally named for Link River, but the name was changed to Klamath Falls in 1892.

Turning again to the statement of Ben Robbs, we are reminded that Robbs tried to get Lyons to leave the Red House at midnight, but that Lyons refused to leave with him. What ads interest to that statement is the fact that midnight was, by law, the exact time when the houses were supposed to stop selling alcohol. We know that Lyons was a strong man, a logger by trade, and probably a rather imposing figure, and that he had been drinking all day. The men who were with Lyons that night described his behavior as "drunk, but sensible." Could such a man, under those conditions, have grown belligerent when he was refused a drink or was asked to leave the establishment?

A study of the news articles of the day about the goings on in the restricted district proves instructive as we try to imagine the chain of events leading up to Lyons' death. About one month before the Lyons murder, a young man by the name of White, who was a stranger to the town, fetched the police to the Red House with a complaint that he had been "robbed" of ten dollars. He claimed that he had paid one of the girls in advance for the pleasure of her company, and then she had broken their date by leaving the establishment in an automobile with another patron. Faye Melbourne and the girl had both refused to refund Mr. White's money.

Even more interesting was the case of J. W. Rosler, a middle-aged man who was fished out of the Oak Avenue canal around 2 a.m. on November 9, 1911, about three months after the Lyons murder. Two of the women of a nearby house heard his cries for help. The women fetched officers Hall and Messner, who were in the area. Rosler, probably greatly embarrassed by the whole ordeal, would not say any more about how he ended up in the canal other than, that he had been refused admittance to a house in the district. The wet, cold, drunk, and shivering man was taken to the city jail to sober up and, despite his reticence, Mr. Rosler did leave us with the lasting impression that men refused service at a brothel after hours could end up in the Oak Avenue canal.

We know that Ray Jackson had a tendency to bludgeon his victims. But, was there anyone else in and about Klamath Falls who had the same nasty habit? The first blow to Lyons' head was struck from one side and glanced off, possibly as Lyons ducked to avoid it. It left a circular, C-shaped gash in his scalp at the back of his head. The second blow, probably inflicted while Lyons was down on the ground, struck the right temple, penetrating the skull and causing death. It was struck with "a very violent force," according to Dr. W. L. Chilton, and extended downward in front of the right ear. That fatal wound, because of the amount of force involved, was probably inflicted by a man. The amount of force exerted also serves to steer us away from the motive of robbery, when a minor blow, sufficient to knock the man out, would have been all that was necessary.

One of the men who liked to hit people over the head in Klamath Falls in 1911 was night Patrolman William Hall, who had the habit of clubbing rowdies and others when his temper became aroused. He had clubbed a man during the fracas with old man Haley at the Comet Lodging House, and made a well publicized attack on newspaper reporter, R. Vance Hutchins, in 1912. Hall could have been the man who struck Lyons, in the commission of his duties, enforcing the liquor law shortly after midnight on the 19th of August. But, if Hall had been the attacker, wouldn't he have used the billy club that he always carried with him on his belt?

> *"Crime is common. Logic is rare. Therefore, it is upon logic, rather than upon crime, that you should dwell."*
>
> Sir Arthur Conan Doyle
> The Copper Beeches

Another man known to frequent the restricted district in the year 1911 was one Charles Freeman, an African American. His wife, Faith, described as "a comely mulatto," was a cook in one of the "houses" there. Freeman was notorious for being an angry drunk, and about one year after the Lyons murder made the headlines of the *Evening Herald* for swinging an axe at his wife. "Every time this man gets drunk he starts abusing me," said Mrs. Freeman. "He gets it into his noodle that I am mixing up with white men, and then he tries to beat me up."

Freeman had been employed as a porter in more than one of the saloons in town, "but his inability to refrain from looking upon the wine when it is available resulted in his being without work," reported the *Herald*. The references to wine, to "mixing it up with white men" and a house in the restricted district all point to the likelihood that Mr. Freeman was employed at one of the brothels at the time of the Lyons murder.

Freeman was jailed on a charge of assault with intent to kill in 1912, but his wife had a change of heart a couple of days later and refused to prosecute. He was released from jail, and the couple seems to have left Klamath County shortly afterward.

The murder of Lyons was probably not premeditated, because if it had been, a more easily concealed weapon would have been used. It was a crime of passion or anger. Lyons was drunk. He was killed by a man at about the time that he would have been refused service at the Red House. He was probably killed inside of the Red House and, a short time later, his body was carried, not dragged, to the Bridge of Sighs and cast into the water by persons to whom money was not a concern. They dumped the body, and did not even bother to search Lyons' pockets. They were more concerned with covering up the crime.

When the facts of the Lyons murder case are combed through as carefully as the Oak Avenue canal was raked at that time, a likely scenario of what transpired on the morning of August 19, 1911 is revealed. And, reasoning based upon those facts demonstrates how a murder with some of the features of Ray Jackson's other killings can be eliminated from his list of crimes. The Lyons case has been intentionally detailed here to demonstrate the means by which many similar cases were reviewed, explored, and eliminated in search of Jackson's likely victims.

If Lyons really was killed inside of the Red House, then the proprietress of the Red House, Miss Faye Melbourne, would have been considered an accessory to the murder. She would have had knowledge of the crime, may have encouraged the killer, failed to report the murder, and probably helped to conceal it by removing evidence. She would have been tried alongside of the killer, probably a patron or a male employee. Consider her behavior after her first trial, and the way that she suddenly disappeared. Did she get word that something was brewing from one of her friends inside of the police department? Perhaps it was the possibility of a charge more serious than prostitution that made her take to her heels?

Charles D. Lyons was buried at the Klamath Falls I.O.O.F. cemetery, although his name does not appear in the current index of that place.

SOURCES:

"Stock and Land Sales," *Lake County Examiner*, October 17, 1907.

"Superintendent of Our Schools," *Lake County Examiner*, August 13, 1908.

"How Men Thrive Here," *Lake County Examiner*, February 24, 1910.

Letter, Roy B. Jackson, La Pine, Ore. Aug. 14, 1929, to U.S. Land Office, Lakeview and Washington D.C., Homestead patent application file of Roy B. Jackson, serial #1032174, Bureau of Land Management, records of the General Land Office, National Archives and Records Administration, Washington, D.C., township 23 south, range 9 east, sections 25 and 26. Patented November 18, 1929.

"W. B. Barnes is Out For Sheriff," *Evening Herald*, February 18, 1914.

Settlers in Summer Lake Valley, by Teressa Foster, 1989, Maverick, Bend, Oregon, Errata and Appendix, p 2, 16-20.

"Murder Verdict of the Jury," *Lake County Examiner*, March 18, 1908.

"Verdict of Coroner's Jury," *Klamath Chronicle*, August 23, 1911.

"Murder at Klamath," *Lake County Examiner*, August 24, 1911.

"Murderer of Lyons is Still Enjoying His Liberty," *Klamath Falls Express*, August 24, 1911.

"Canal Holds Man's Body," *Oregonian*, August 23, 1911.

"Floating Corpse Points to Crime," *Klamath Republican*, August 24, 1911.

"Major Worden Offers $1,000 Reward for Lyons Murderer," *Klamath Falls Express*, August 31, 1911.

"A public Spirited Citizen," editorial, *Klamath Falls Express*, August 31, 1911.

Thirteenth Census of the United States, Klamath County, Oregon, Klamath Lake precinct.

"Barnes Bros. Have Irrigation," *Klamath Chronicle,* August 16, 1911.

"Irrigate by Pump," *Lake County Examiner,* October 6, 1910.

"Paisley Press Items," *Lake County Examiner,* May 11, 1911. Mentions Jackson as president of the "Anna River irrigation project."

"Red Light Folk May Stay Quiet," *Evening Herald,* August 20, 1912.

"Townsend Gone to Last Reward," *Evening Herald,* October 9, 1911.

Julius Cahn's Official Theatrical Guide, 19061907, vol. 11, Julius Cahn, New York, N. Y., 1906, p 361.

"Barnes Returns from Portland," *Evening Herald,* January 26, 1912.

"No Successor to Townsend Named and Body Leaves for Missouri," *Evening Herald,* October 12, 1911.

"Social Evil to Be Looked Into," *Evening Herald,* October 17, 1911.

"Disorderly Resort Women are Fined Heavily for Breaking Liquor Law," *Evening Herald,* October 21, 1911.

"Women Ordered to Leave City," *Evening Herald,* November 15, 1911.

"Women's Exodus Almost Complete," *Evening Herald,* November 22, 1911.

"Overdrawn Fund for Street Work," *Evening Herald,* November 23, 1911.

"Drink Maddened; Breaks Windows," *Evening Herald,* November 7, 1911.

"Redshirt Man Ordered Hence," *Evening Herald,* December 22, 1911.

"For Sheriff," political advertisement, *Evening Herald,* April 17, 1912.

Thirteenth Census of the United States, Oregon, Klamath County, Linkville Precinct.

"Tenderloin Case Draws Big Crowd," *Evening Herald,* January 9, 1912.

The Encyclopedia of New York City, "Tenderloin" by Lisa Elsroad, Kenneth T. Jackson, editor, 1995). New Haven: Yale University Press. ISBN 0300055366. , p.1161

"Bench Warrant Out for Meldourne (sic) Woman, Believed To Have Skipped," *Evening Herald,* February 5, 1912."

"Attorney Sues For Fee Balance," *Evening Herald,* April 17, 1912.

"Motion to Quash Indictment is Cause of Delay," *Evening Herald,* September 23, 1912.

"M. R. Doty," advertisement, *Evening Herald,* November 29, 1909.

"Frederick T. Sanderson," biography. *The Centennial History of Oregon 1811-1912,* by Joseph Gaston, 1912, The S. J. Clarke publishing company, Chicago, IL. p 531-532.

"Bawdy Houses Will Not Be Tolerated in This Community," *Evening Herald*, September 30, 1912.

"Oak St. Women Are Ordered Out," *Evening Herald*, August 7, 1915.

"The Council and Gambling," *Evening Herald*, July 21, 1920.

"Investigation into the death of Chas Lyons," Coroner Earl Whitlock, *Record of Coroner's Investigations, 19061916* (1 volume), p 17-18, Clerk's basement storage, Klamath Government Center, Klamath Falls, Oregon.

"Rescued from Canal, His Money and Watch Missing, Man Makes Mystery," *Evening Herald*, November 9, 1911.

"Policeman and Reporter Engage in Fistic Encounter on Street," *Evening Herald*, October 10, 1912.

"Trouble Among Colored Folks," *Evening Herald*, July 10, 1912.

"Wife Pleads for Release of Man Who Struck Her," *Evening Herald*, July 12, 1912

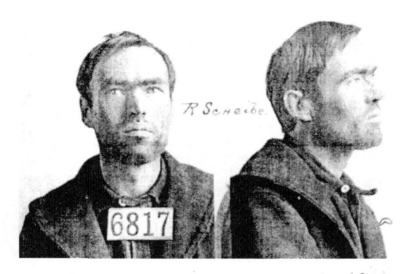

Mug shots of Robert Scheibe, taken when he was incarcerated in 1913 for the murder of George Webster in Harney County. Bertillon card of Robert Scheibe from the archives of the Oregon Department of Justice is one of the few shreds of information that has survived him.

Chapter Six

Death Follows Him

In January of 1913, two crimes occurred in Harney County that were so close together in space and time that it was assumed from the first that they must have been the work of one man. There happened to be, also in that neighborhood and at that same time, a stranger, Robert Scheibe, who gave every indication of being a drifter. A man without means, on foot and traveling from ranch to farm and looking for employment. The investigators, so-called, nabbed Scheibe and labeled him as an arsonist and murderer.

One crime was the sadistic killing of George Webster, age 62, and a trapper by profession. Webster was found inside of his camp wagon one and a half miles from the Double O's Warm Springs ranch. He had died of multiple gunshot wounds, so the crime seemed like an ordinary murder case, at least on the surface of it. But, the killer had not simply shot Webster and departed. Nor did he steal any of the cash, valuable furs, or gold nuggets that the victim had in his possession. The killer first shot Webster in one leg, at close range, deliberately aiming for the bone so as to break it. Then, he did the same to the other leg. Two other shots were fired into the upper body. One shot seemed to have passed through both the arm and chest, leaving a total of three bullet holes in the upper body and suggesting that Webster was still alive when the third shot was fired and attempted to block it with his arm. Webster was found slumped forward and more or less seated on the edge of his bed, suggesting that he may have been killed at night or in the early morning. His head and one arm came to rest on a box, also suggesting that the arm was raised in an attempt to block one of the later shots.

The trapper seems to have only just arrived at the spot, and could not have been there for more than a few days. It was the middle of the trapping season, but he had not set out any of his coyote or wildcat traps. About 50 of them were found among his possessions, and he had a number of unsold furs at his camp from his last location. It had snowed for several days before his body was found, leaving an unusually deep snow cover that was commented on several times in the newspapers during the weeks prior to and after the crime. So, Webster may have pulled over along the main road and waited for the weather to clear. When the botched investigation of the crime began, no one in the area knew even the first thing about Mr. Webster. No one knew where he was from, knew anything about his family, his past, or his age. They didn't even know his first name, "George," that was only discovered after the coroner sifted through the man's effects and papers. All of those things suggest that Webster had only just arrived in the Warm Springs area, and had spoken to no one. The fact that Webster was so unknown in the community more or less ruled out a crime of vengeance or passion.

Along with the valuable traps, several guns, furs, and $137 in cash, that were gold nuggets, and documents among Webster's effects suggesting that, sometime during the past three years, he had come from California where he had worked as a prospector. The fact that all of those things were left behind by the killer, combined with the time that was taken in terrorizing Mr. Webster, allows us to eliminate robbery as a motive. Although theft may have crossed the mind of the killer, what he was there for and what he was mainly focused on, was torturing George Webster. The coroner estimated that Webster was killed on either the 21st or 22nd of January, and his body was found by chance when the other crime called attention to the area early on the morning of January 23.

The large barn of August C. Vollmer, located on the east slope of Iron Mountain, mysteriously caught fire while the family slept and burned to the ground. Inside the barn were seven valuable work horses, all burned alive, plus a large quantity of hay, farm tools and implements, harnesses, and two wagons. Mr. Vollmer was one of the most successful farmers in the area. He owned about 400 acres in township 27 south and ranges 27 and 28 east, about four miles from the scene of the Webster murder. During the county fair of 1911, the Vollmer family carried away several premiums and prizes for their exceptional farm produce.

To the great misfortune of all involved, including Robert Scheibe, both the sheriff of Harney County and the town marshall of Burns, were out of the country during the month of January 1913. Marshall R. L. Haines took a leave of absence for one month, leaving Ernest E. Owsley to substitute for him in his absence. Haines had come down with a case of typhoid fever, and was receiving medical treatment in Portland. Owsley, as only an 'acting' town marshall, had no jurisdiction whatsoever over either crime scene, both located over 30 miles outside of Burns.

Harney County Sheriff Richardson had traveled to Portland "on official business" on January 9, and did not return until the evening of January 25, the day after Scheibe was "arrested." The true reason for Richardson's absence was to attend a big irrigation congress in Portland, a sort of convention, with Judge Levens, Judge Miller, William Hanley of the Double O ranch, and county Assessor Donegan. Why the other four men were incapable of representing the irrigation interests of Harney County without the help of Sheriff Richardson is a question that begs an answer. But, not so much as the question of why Richardson failed to deputize or find a replacement to watch over the county as a whole in his absence.

A few men were named as having responded to the fire, as having found Webster's body, and in apprehending Robert Scheibe. It would be a mistake to call them investigators, or even "officials" because it is an absolute fact that local and inexperienced laymen acted in an official capacity in the case. Most notable among them was Owsley, who seems to have put himself in charge of the investigation of both crimes. Owsley was not a policeman, a sheriff, or even a deputy. He was a teamster by trade, who later earned a rather unsavory reputation for himself around Burns. In 1914, a man who worked for Owsley as a driver was jailed for selling liquor without a license along the route from Burns to Bend. That same year, Owsley was charged with assault with a dangerous weapon. In 1915, Owsley "accidentally" shot a different man in the chest.

Another interesting person named in connection with the apprehension of Scheibe was James E. Sizemore. "Scheibe was trailed by a posse of neighbors to a cabin where he had taken refuge," reported the *Oregonian*. "The cabin was surrounded and Scheibe commanded to surrender. He refused, and when the pursuers attempted to push the door of the cabin open, they were met by a shot from the fugitive's rifle, which narrowly missed J. E. Sizemore, who was in the lead. Sizemore seized the gun and wrested it from Scheibe's hand, and then the other men in the posse rushed in and overpowered Scheibe."

James Sizemore owned a large ranch on the west side of Harney Lake, in the same general area as the Double O ranch, the Webster murder scene, and the cabin where Scheibe was found. His main claim to fame was that he was the older brother of George S. Sizemore, County Attorney and Director of the Burns School Board. Brother George seems to have been rather chummy with Harney County Sheriff, Alonzo K. Richardson, in addition to being connected to Richardson in an official capacity. George was also the local attorney for the big Pacific Livestock Company, and represented them in an important water rights case involving the Silvies River. George Sizemore and Sheriff Richardson were frequently mentioned together in the local paper as they traveled about on legal business. And, occasionally George Sizemore would travel over to Salem with some of the sheriff's deputies to deliver Harney County prisoners to the penitentiary.

The prominent attorney's older brother, James, seems to have wanted more out of life than cattle ranching. During the year before the Webster murder, he ran for the office of county commissioner, but was defeated in the election. Exactly how he came to be "in the lead" of the posse that captured Scheibe is not known, although it is apparent that he knew the sheriff through his brother. It is highly unlikely that James Sizemore had any official authority to act for the sheriff at the time he overpowered Scheibe. If Richardson had deputized any man to fill in for him during his January absence, he probably would have selected someone from around Burns, not the far-off community of Warm Springs, located over 30 miles distant. In May of 1913, James Sizemore and Joe Thompson traveled with Sheriff Richardson to deliver Scheibe to the Oregon State Penitentiary. And, although Sizemore may have been temporarily deputized on that later occasion, there was no evidence that he was deputized or acting in an official capacity when Scheibe was caught.

There was some disagreement between the two news accounts of Scheibe's arrest. The January 25 version printed in the Burns Times-Herald, and the January 27 version printed in the Oregonian. As quoted above, the local correspondent for the

Portland paper reported that Scheibe shot through the door of the cabin where he was apprehended, just before the mob broke in. But, the *Times-Herald* seems to have confused facts with hearsay, reporting that Scheibe "admits having served time in the Illinois penitentiary for shooting at a man through a door." The parallel between the two accounts cannot be overlooked, leaving us to wonder if Scheibe ever really did shoot through a door in the state of Illinois. Indeed, the details of that crime from the Illinois Department of Corrections make no mention of a door.

The *Times-Herald* version did not credit Sizemore with apprehending Scheibe, but two other men as having moved in while Coroner Clevenger and Owsley were on their way to Warm Springs. "In the meantime, it seems Gus Bardwell and S. S. Smith had gone to the cabin and succeeded in getting the man from the cabin and brought him to the Double O ranch." There was no mention of gunfire in that second account, but apparently Sizemore, Bardwell, and Smith were all members of the unsanctioned, so-called "posse" that grabbed Scheibe, and Owsley and Clevenger arrived later.

What seems most likely is that, on January 26, the day after his return, Sheriff Richardson spoke to the *Oregonian* correspondent about the crimes. None of the other men involved, like Smith and Bardwell, felt it necessary to brag about the encounter to the local paper, so the account of the shot narrowly missing James Sizemore can probably be put down to Sizemore describing his own valor to the sheriff.

Seth S. Smith, known to his friends as "Tubby," had a farm at Warm Springs where he lived with his brothers, Russel K. and Neil T. Smith. The only other salient fact about Seth Smith, aside from his apparent friendship with Bardwell, was that his brother Russel was one of the members of the jury that would later determine Scheibe was sane enough to stand trial. Was Russel Smith also in the gang that captured Robert Scheibe? And, how did his conversations with his brother, Tubby, influence his conduct on that jury?

Harney County's newly elected coroner, George W. Clevenger, was a man of unimpressive credentials and no medical training, a carpenter who decided that there would be more money in the undertaking business and began selling caskets around 1906. He also signed his name in the "undertaker" box of Mr. Webster's death certificate. On Friday, January 24, the day after the fire, Clevenger impanelled a coroner's jury from among the neighboring ranches, whose job it was to report on the facts surrounding the case and to determine the manner of death: suicide, natural causes, accident, or homicide. That was to be the very first murder investigation, so-called, that Clevenger was involved in, because he had only recently taken the job of county coroner, and the inquest was probably held at the Double O ranch house. Another glaring example of Clevenger's lack of expertise came one year later when an inquest under his direction made the astonishing ruling that the death of Silver Creek homesteader, Otto Hirsch, was a suicide that warranted no investigation whatsoever, although Hirsch had been shot twice, once in the chest and once in the head.

The official Harney County Physician, Tillson L. Harrison, was a true medical doctor, but did not put in an appearance at the crime scene. Furthermore, the *Burns Times-Herald* reported that, just prior to the murder, Harrison had refused to attend to a patient in an outlying district due to the needs of his patients in town. The attending physician in the Webster murder, the man who determined that the means or physical cause of death was "gunshot wounds," and who signed in the "M. D." box on the death certificate, was John W. Geery, physician and surgeon, and also the former county coroner. It is doubtful that Geery took part in the inquest because he did not sign the certificate until January 30 and was not named in any of the news articles about the crimes. What that all meant was that the poorly qualified Mr. Clevenger was the lone 'expert' at the crime scene.

Clevenger, in his official capacity as the new coroner, did fill out the death certificate, but only partially and not very well. The place of death space was left blank, although a legal description of the place could have easily been obtained. Several other spaces were left blank, such as marital status, date and place of birth, and the names of Webster's parents, probably because Webster was a relative stranger. Although, Clevenger could certainly have exerted a bit more effort in determining the identity of the deceased before he filed the certificate on January 31. An examination of current genealogy records for the immediate family of

George R. Webster shows that they were never notified that he had died, nor when, where, and how, and had no knowledge of his burial at Burns. To this day, the family knows nothing of what became of George.

Clevenger did jot down a couple of helpful notes on the certificate. He had obtained Webster's name, age, and occupation of "trapper and prospector" from *"papers found on body,"* presumably including the man's trapping license. A note that the body was found about 30 miles southwest of Burns was jotted in the "date of death" box. Webster was, in fact, a former gold prospector, having given his occupation as "quartz miner" in the California census of 1910.

Perhaps the biggest mistake and most inappropriate thing that Clevenger did during the course of the whole sloppy affair was to make a declaration of willful murder in the "cause of death box." It was not the place or right of the county coroner to make any statement beyond the simple manner of death in that box. Information that described the caliber of the shells used or the number of gunshot wounds, or describing contributory wounds to other parts of the body, would have been truly useful information. Instead, Clevenger wrote, "Gunshot wounds by someone with intent to murder." That statement was not only vague, but was completely inappropriate and beyond the coroner's purview. The coroner's jury was supposed to determine the manner of death, and their choices were either accident, natural causes, suicide, or homicide. The determination of willful murder, versus homicide, could only be decided in court. There is plenty of room for speculation about how effective Clevenger was in his management of the coroner's jury, and the inquest, that ultimately fell short of its goals.

Details about the life and character of Robert Scheibe, the accused, are very sketchy. When he was "arrested" by Owsley, the *Burns Times-Herald* reported "it was thought that he was demented," and the paper made the highly irresponsible statement that "it was rumored the man had admitted setting fire to the barn and had also said he killed the old trapper, but this seams to have been only rumored as it is now said the man denies any knowledge of the murder or the fire." There are few newspapers today that would risk such incriminating statements. The same article contained the slanderous claim that, "Some are of the impression that the man is not demented at all, but is rather a bad one." As if the subjective perception of nameless parties had anything whatever to do with the question of guilt.

The doubts about Scheibe's sanity seem to have grown out of the very flimsy reasoning that no logical motive, such as theft, could be found for the killing of George Webster. But, instead of trying to come up with a viable motive, the men involved jumped to the conclusion that Scheibe must have been insane. "Motive for the killing of Webster, also, is lacking as yet," reported the *Oregonian* correspondent on January 27. When found the dead man had $150 on his person, and the authorities therefore are convinced that the crime was committed by an insane man."

The unfortunate declarations of Scheibe's guilt made by the *Times-Herald* were read by almost everyone in Harney County, the population from which the jury for Scheibe's trial was drawn. The jury selected for the April term of circuit court that year consisted of T. J. Shields, Ben Brown, Charles Wilson, Charles Laborence, T. J. Baker, Frank Dunn, and Russell Smith. "Robert Scheibe, who had been indicted for murder in the second degree, being accused of killing G. R. Webster, an aged trapper, last January, was tried before a jury yesterday morning to determine his sanity," reported the *Times-Herald*. "The question to decide, according to the court, was whether the accused man was mentally capable of going to trial on the charge or not.... The jury decided that he should go to trial."

We can see how investigative reasoning completely broke down in the case when Scheibe was found to be sane. If the murder of Webster was committed by an insane man because there was no motive, then Scheibe, who had just been declared sane, could not have been Webster's killer.

Scheibe's arrest seems to have been purely coincidental. The correspondent for the *Oregonian* reported that Scheibe "denies that he committed the crimes, although circumstantial evidence against him is strong. Scheibe professes friendship for Vollmers (sic), and says that he stopped at the latter's cabin for several nights and had no reason to feel ill toward him. Motive for the killing of Webster, also, is lacking as yet."

When Vollmer's barn burned to the ground, the men who responded to the scene probably asked the farmer if he had seen anyone hanging around the property or had noticed any strangers in the area. Would it not have been perfectly natural for Mr. Vollmer to mention Robert Scheibe, the drifter who had just spent a few days there, probably working on the farm?

Maybe the neighbors who "investigated" the crime would have found better advantage in treating Robert Scheibe as a material witness, instead of presuming that he was guilty. The *Times-Herald* told its readers "While the evidence is all circumstantial respecting the murder, it seems the charge of arson is more strongly fixed on the accused man, as he was tracked from the scene of the fire to the cabin in which he was found." Of course, there were tracks leading from the Vollmer place to the cabin that Scheibe removed to after he left the farm, but that was hardly proof that he set the fire or murdered someone. Consider the possibility that Webster was killed for a reason, shortly after the fire was started, early on the morning of the 23rd, and about 12 hours before his body was found inside that frozen wagon.

The *Lake County Examiner* reported that the temperature hovered around zero on the night of January 22, and the early morning of January 23. Although the town of Lakeview is about 85 miles from the scene of the crime, it is common knowledge that temperatures at Burns and Lakeview are often quite similar. The fact that Coroner Clevenger got information about Webster from *"papers found on body"* could mean that Webster was fully dressed and had his wallet and trapping license on his person when he was shot. If Webster was fully clothed, that opens the possibility that he had ventured outside of his wagon before he was shot.

The way that he was killed, slowly and by multiple gunshots at close range, indicates coercion. That the shooter was trying to force an issue, to get information from Webster, or was trying to frighten him into compliance of some kind. The pattern of bullet wounds tells us that Webster was sitting and raised one arm halfway through the encounter, also suggesting a verbal exchange.

What if the Vollmers were the true, original target of the criminal, and the fire was set out of vengeance, as is so often true in cases of arson?

Another explanation for the lack of theft could be that, just after the shooting, the killer realized he was in immediate peril of being found out. If he was familiar with the neighborhood, he realized that the scene of the murder was in a visible spot along the main road to the Double O ranch, and that the fire was visible for several miles to the east, as indeed it was. Webster's wagon was in the marshy low country, four miles to the east of Vollmer's farm. And Vollmer's farm was on the east slope of Iron Mountain.

The men who responded to the fire, Gus Bardwell, Tubby Smith, and James Sizemore, all lived to the east in the vicinity of the Double O ranch and Warm Springs. Seeing that Webster still had not sold his pile of furs, the killer may have assumed that the old man had no cash. Not taking the time to search the wagon would have been the logical act of an arsonist and killer, not an act of insanity.

Webster, if he was an early riser, could easily have seen or heard the flight of the arsonist as he traveled the road going east, with the big blaze lighting up the sky behind him. Did Webster stop the horseman and ask about the fire? Did he think the man was riding out from the scene in search of help?

The date of Webster's death, recorded on the certificate by Coroner Clevenger as the 21st or 22nd of January, has to be interpreted as simple guesswork. Considering Clevenger's complete lack of medical knowledge, the condition of the body, and that no expert opinion was extracted from the crime scene, how could it be anything else? Determination of date and time of death has always been an inexact science. Crime scene investigators believe to this very day that the only certain way to determine the time of death is to be there when it happens.

The dates of January 21 and 22 placed the death of Webster two or three days before the January 24 inquest. But, how did Clevenger arrive at that conclusion? Rigor mortis *usually* occurs within a couple of hours of death, and then dissipates in two or three days, under *normal* conditions. However, the conditions at the time of Webster's death were far from normal. Clevenger had worked as an undertaker, not a coroner, for at least six years prior to the Webster murder, and certainly would have encountered rigor mortis many times. But, rigor mortis can be delayed under extraordinary conditions, and it seems unlikely that Clevenger had ever experienced anything to compare. When the body of George Webster thawed before the inquest at the Double O ranch, the lack of rigor mortis could have led Clevenger to assume that the man had been dead for two or three days.

The intense cold that occurred at the time would have caused the body to have cooled very rapidly, and delayed the onset of rigor mortis. Also, the rapid exsanguination of the body via the two leg wounds, that probably lacerated the femoral arteries or veins, would have delayed the onset of rigor mortis even further. Clevenger, thinking that it would have taken two or three days for rigor to dissipate, may have concluded that Webster was killed two or three days prior, or on the 21st or 22nd. But, if Webster had, in fact, died very early on the morning of the day prior to the inquest, then bled out and cooled quickly, rigor mortis would have been greatly delayed, and no stiffening would have occurred until some time after the inquest.

Another possibility was that the coroner's jury reasoned that Webster must have been killed two or three days before the inquest because that was the very time when Scheibe left the Vollmer farm and was known to be on that road. The *Times-Herald* reported that Scheibe "was seen in the vicinity of the place where the old man was murdered on the day he was supposed to have been killed, but there is no direct evidence that he committed the deed." *Supposed to have been killed* being the operative phrase. Instead of building their theory to match the facts, did those men manipulate the facts to match their theory?

When Scheibe's court date arrived, seven men together agreed that he was not crazy. That he was not totally off of his rocker, nor was he "demented." Yet, the self-styled criminologists hovering about the case expected the public to believe that Scheibe, a sane man,, committed a sadistic and unmotivated murder on Tuesday evening, remained in the immediate area for two days, set fire to a large barn in order to draw attention to himself, walked back to the immediate vicinity of the murder scene, entered a nearby shack, and intentionally left a clear trail in the snow.

Even though Scheibe did have a rifle in his possession, the question of the murder weapon remained unanswered. If Scheibe had the murder weapon in his possession when he was apprehended, then that would have provided material evidence of his guilt. But Scheibe's rifle was never identified as the murder weapon. Did the true killer carry the weapon away with him? Was Scheibe just in the wrong place at the wrong time? Did firing a shot at an armed mob of men who took the law into their own hands unduly incriminate Scheibe? He was later indicted for arson on Vollmer's barn, and murder in the second degree.

Scheibe's attorney, Patrick J. Gallagher, seems to have taken a gamble on a defense of innocent by means of insanity. Maybe he thought that, since everyone in the county had already read in the newspaper that Scheibe was nuts, that the insanity tactic could save his client from the death penalty. And, to Gallagher's credit, he did ultimately succeed in saving Scheibe 's life.

Scheibe's fate seems to have been the result of a plea bargain arrangement. In a second attempt to avoid trial, the defense attorney had Scheibe enter a plea of guilty to the charge of second degree murder. That meant that his client would be, and was, automatically sentenced to life in the Oregon State Penitentiary. Scheibe was, indeed, incarcerated on April 17, 1913. If Gallagher believed that the feeling against Scheibe was strong, or that proof of his innocence was weak, then he might have thought that going to trial was too risky. That, if the case went to trial, Scheibe would get the death penalty. Harney County District Attorney William H. Brooke might have offered Gallagher the chance to avoid trial if he could get Scheibe to agree to plea guilty to the lesser charge of murder in the second degree. In other words, Scheibe may not have plead guilty because he was guilty, but because he wanted to avoid hanging, and because Gallagher did not want the man's blood on his hands.

The question of whether or not Robert Scheibe got a fair shake in the court proceedings is a good one. Various shortcomings in the so-called investigation of his alleged crimes have already been pointed out. Turning our attention to the qualifications of Scheibe's defense attorney also leaves us with plenty of room for concern as to whether or not justice was served. Patrick J. Gallagher, the young attorney who had passed the bar only two years prior, had barely hit town when he took charge of Scheibe's case. He had arrived in Burns in January, and opened his law office in late March, only a couple of weeks before Scheibe's court date. Given the fact that Scheibe's financial circumstances were very strained at the time of his arrest, it is likely that Gallagher, being the new young attorney in town and more or less the low man on the totem pole, was appointed by the court to defend Scheibe. It is doubtful that Gallagher had very much time at all to prepare, and he seems to have set aside his duty to test the weak reasoning and equally weak case of the prosecution.

Gallagher's law practice did not exactly thrive in east Oregon. He practiced law in Burns for less than four months, then relocated to the new startup town of Juntura in Malheur County. While in that vicinity, he pursued several other endeavors, including starting a newspaper, the *Juntura Times*, of which he was the editor. He filed on a homestead and tried to raise grain and orchard fruits. He was secretary of the Juntura Commercial Club, and tried to convince Harney and Malheur counties that they should give up land for the creation of a new county called "Davis." Despite his zeal, Pat Gallagher was not able to make a go of it in Juntura, and moved his family into Vale after only seven months. In the fall of 1915, he relocated again, this time into Ontario, where he remained until about 1925 and continued in his practice of law which, prior to that time, seems to have been only a sideline. A review of the newspapers of Harney and Malheur counties from 1913 and 1914 reveals that Gallagher was not a defense attorney, but worked mostly on civil cases, such as equity and divorce. His defense, so-called, of Scheibe may very well have been his first and only experience in defending a man accused of murder.

Given the botched inquest; the condition of Webster's death certificate; the unsavory character of the teamster who played cop for the investigation; the total absence at the murder scene of anyone having even the slightest idea of what they were doing; the chaotic state of the neighborhood in the wake of the Vollmer fire; the failure to establish any motive whatsoever for the crimes; the absence of a murder weapon; the poor quality of

Scheibe's legal representation; the fact that Scheibe was never actually tried for the crimes; and the circumstantial character of the evidence, we must consider the possibility that the killer of George R. Webster was someone other than Robert Scheibe, who was ultimately railroaded off to the state penitentiary.

But, who was Robert Scheibe, and what information about him survives? The best journalistic detail, as usual, was printed in the *Oregonian*, and was the product of an interview with the accused man. "Scheibe betrays no evidence of any mental defection. He says that he is 34 years old and a native of Germany, coming to America when four years old. He says that his relatives lived at Batavia, Ill., the last he knew. Scheibe acknowledges that he served two years in the Illinois state prison for shooting at a man."

Official government documents related to the case contain contradictory information about Scheibe. Those source documents are usually much more reliable than newspapers and hearsay. But, in Scheibe's case, we find that when he was sentenced to prison, the circuit court spelled his name "Schiebe." The Oregon State Penitentiary spelled his name "Scheibe," and gave his age as 34, placing his year of birth at 1879. But, when the census of 1920 was taken, Scheibe's age was given as 35 years old, meaning a birth date of 1884. That census said that Scheibe and his parents were all born in the United States, not Germany, although the names of the states were not provided.

Some time after he was incarcerated, Scheibe was examined by the prison psychologist, then was sent to the Oregon State Insane Asylum in July of 1914. He was still there when the census of 1920 was taken, and lived in that place for about 14 years. It seems like the staff of the asylum would have known a little bit more about him, and would have learned something about his history or attempted to contact his family but, they apparently did not, because his census information in 1920 was all wrong. In the summer of 1927 Scheibe became ill, then died over a year later, on September 10, 1928 at the age of 49.

Scheibe's death certificate, while basically matching the 1913 account of his age and nationality, was terribly incomplete, without any information about his family, or even providing his middle initial. The only bit of helpful information on the death certificate was the cause of death, described as "cerebral arteriosclerosis." His place of death was the state asylum, which had recently been renamed "Oregon State Hospital." The institution's complete lack of information about a man that they had housed for fourteen years could mean only one of two things. Either they made no effort to contact Scheibe's family; or Scheibe communicated almost nothing about his background when asked. It might be helpful to note that English was Scheibe's second language, and that he never graduated from high school.

Little detail about the nature of Scheibe's mental disturbance has survived him. It is possible that the cerebral arteriosclerosis could have shown itself in 1913, affecting his memory, speech, and emotional highs and lows, and giving the impression that he was not sane, at least to inexperienced laymen. We have only the hearsay information from the newspaper that he was "irrational at times," was frightened when he was apprehended, and the speculation that, "it was thought that he was demented." Whatever the nature of his impairment was, the finding of the jury that Scheibe was sane enough to stand trial, and the interview experience of the *Oregonian* correspondent, both suggest that he was sensible and intelligent, at least at times.

As bad luck would have it, "Robert" and "Scheibe" are both fairly common names among Germanic people, as is the name "Schiebe," although not to such a great extent. The United States censuses for the years 1900 and 1910, as well as many genealogy databases and resources, were thoroughly sifted through in order to learn something about his family, with some success.

Robert Scheibe was born somewhere in Germany in 1879. He arrived in New York Harbor with his mother and some of his siblings on the ship, Rhaetia, on April 30, 1884 at the age of five. His father, Henry, born in 1834, and oldest brother, Henry Jr., had apparently arrived in this country in 1873. His mother, Auguste Benz Scheibe, born in 1837, traveled across the ocean with Robert, Laura 23, Emilie 19, Auguste 17, Helene 7, Bertha 6, and another son, age 8, whose name was not legible.

In 1896, at the age of 17, Scheibe moved out of the family home, but was still living in or near Batavia, Illinois and working as a "machinist's helper" when he was arrested in 1903 and convicted of "assault to kill," meaning assault with the intent to kill.

In other words, an assault occurred during an alleged attempt to kill someone.

His prison record from the state reformatory at Pontiac, Illinois gave the details of the crime as, "Convicted while drunk. He shot at one Eugene Otis to whom the mother and sister of the defendant had fled for protection from his threatened assault." The Eugene Otis referred to was the next door neighbor of Scheibe's parents. Further detail about his abuse of alcohol came from profile details in the record. In terms of drink, his use was considered "moderate," and his general reputation was given as "saloon habituate of late." Those details leave the impression that Scheibe, at the age of 24, went on a 'bender' that frightened his family, and fired a gun on the property of a neighbor.

Robert Scheibe paid dearly for his first offense. The reformatory at Pontiac was, ostensibly, a less harsh place than Joliet prison, supposed to serve the needs of young and first time offenders. Scheibe was immediately put in a chain gang, in which he worked for about a year, then was hospitalized with an unknown condition for three months, then put back in the chain gang for another five months.

In a special session of the parole board in March of 1905, Scheibe was ordered to be released into the custody of one Peter Klein, who was a bit of big shot in Aurora, a town near Batavia. Klein was director of the German American National Bank, and publisher and editor of the *Aurora Volksfreund*, a German language newspaper. Klein himself was a native German, and it would have made sense for him to have hired another native German for his language skills. Scheibe had only worked for Klein's newspaper for five days when Klein wrote to the reformatory to say that his new worker had "skipped" out of town.

The 1910 census captured Scheibe's parents living on East Wilson Street in Batavia, Kane County, Illinois. None of the children remained in the household at that time, although Auguste reported that she still had five living children, and the couple lived near their daughter, Emilie, and her husband, Karl or "Charles" Groener. Both of Robert Scheibe's parents died in 1917, and were buried at East Batavia Cemetery. Their children, Henry Jr., Bertha, and Emilie were eventually buried at the same place. Members of the Scheibe family seem to have remained in the

Batavia area from about 1886 until at least 1917, when the parents passed away.

Another item out of the murky past of Robert Scheibe was published in the *Times-Herald* on February 1, 1913. The brief article stated that, "He has admitted spending six months in jail over in Washington and asked that the sheriff of the county be notified he is here. It is possible he is wanted there but he has not said so." When Scheibe was delivered to the state penitentiary in April of 1913, James E. Sizemore made a side trip to Seattle, presumably to have a chat with the sheriff who had some knowledge of the young man's past. The author found no other information about Scheibe's activities from 1905 through 1912.

A few fragments of information from the brief time that Scheibe spent at the Oregon penitentiary have survived in the form of a Bertillon card, another document describing his sentencing at Harney County, and his fingerprints. His mug shots show a man who appears to be in his mid-thirties, with a hairline that was beginning to recede, and facial features drooping slightly on the left side.

If we take a second look at the crimes of January 1913, and return to the observation that they occurred close together in both space and time, we have to consider the neighborhood where they happened in order to put them in their proper context. In chapter two, Ray Jackson's early days in east Oregon were recounted, and it will be remembered that he had several important ties to the area described in the Webster and Vollmer crimes. After he got out of prison in 1898, Jackson went to work for the Double O ranch in Harney County, probably at Warm Springs, because that was where his childhood friend from Linn County, Willis G. Bardwell, relocated with his family around 1899. Bardwell and Jackson seem to have remained friends throughout their lives because, in one of the articles about Jackson's 1938 suicide, Bardwell described himself as a "boyhood friend" of Jackson's, and he was a member of the coroner's jury in that case.

In July of 1901, Willis Bardwell and Anna Hurlburt acquired water rights along Big Stick Creek near Iron Mountain, in sections 5, 8, 9, 10 and 11 in township 26 south, range 26 east, and Bardwell patented a homestead in the same township in 1906.

That was the same ranch where Jackson was raising cattle in 1902 when his brother William sued him to recover the money he had loaned to Ray. That same year, Jackson gave his address as "Narrows," Harney County when he mortgaged his cattle to the First National Bank of Burns, that being the nearest post office and located just to the east of the Double O ranch at Warm Springs. He registered his circle 7 brand with the Harney County Clerk on the same date that he took out that loan. When his cattle were auctioned off to pay some of his debts at the end of 1902, the auction took place at the Hurlburt ranch, and they were sold to Bill Hanley, owner of the Double O.

To better describe the neighborhood, there was and is to this day a main road that connects the Egli Ridge area northeast of Wagontire Mountain, where Jackson had important connections from at least 1910 forward, to The Narrows. In 1913 it was known as the "Narrows Wagontire Road." The road starts just north of the Egli ranch, runs east for about six miles, then turns to the southeast, passes the Bardwell homestead, follows Big Stick Creek, runs along the north side of Iron Mountain and the Vollmer farm as it straightens out to run east again through the Webster murder scene, to the Double O ranch at Warm Springs, then comes within two miles of the old Hurlburt place on the west side of Harney Lake.

In 1929, Jackson bought out the 1,600 acre Egli holdings at Wagontire, and continued ranching there until the time of his death. Lambert R. Jones, who became a close friend and business associate of Jackson's in 1910, worked on the Egli's Wagontire ranch as their hired hand that same year. Jackson may even have known the Eglis since his years at Silver Lake, from 1902 through 1905, because Henry Egli lived in Silver Lake during that same period.

But, what was Jackson's connection to those people and that neighborhood in late 1912 and early 1913? There can be no doubt that he was friendly with the Hurlburts during that time period, after he had worn out his welcome in Lake County, lost his job, and was looking to relocate. In mid-October of 1913, the *Burns Times-Herald* carried a short news item saying that "Ray Jackson, a former teacher of this county, but late of California, is here on a visit with the Hurlburt family." Corroboration of that visit was contained in the next issue of the *Lake County Examiner* with a similar news item describing Jackson's return from Harney County.

Jackson was connected to the Hurlburts through his lifelong friend, Willis G. Bardwell, who was the brother of Augustus Hurlburt's wife, Annie Bardwell Hurlburt. The brother and sister water rights of Annie Hurlburt and Willis Bardwell at Big Stick Creek were believed to have been shared with Ray Jackson in 1902. The son of Willis G. Bardwell, Gus Bardwell, was about 21 years old in 1913, and was one of the men who helped to extract Scheibe from that cabin where he was found. Ray Jackson had plenty of connections to the area. He knew the neighborhood, and he knew the people there. He may even have renewed ranching interests with the Bardwells and Hurlburts in 1912 after his partnership with Frank Payne dissolved.

In 1991, writer Edward Gray interviewed Mr. Shelby Petersen, a longtime resident of Harney County who had known Jackson in the 1920s. Petersen stated that he believed Ray Jackson had taught school at "what they call the Petersen Schoolhouse" during the late teens, and also described that schoolhouse as being located at the Double O ranch. Petersen, however, did not have firsthand knowledge of Jackson's Harney County teaching experience because Petersen attended school in Burns. In mid-December of 1914, Ray Jackson did take and pass the teacher's exams given at Burns, so he probably had already begun teaching under a temporary certificate in Harney County by the fall of 1914.

From Jackson's history, we know that he was an essentially sadistic and malicious man, and just the kind of person who could have killed George Webster slowly and with multiple gunshots. He was also the author's main suspect in the 1904 arson on the barn in Silver Lake where Creed Conn stored his freight wagons, and in the poisoning of Conn's freight team. Those actions against Creed Conn seem to have been done out of spite when Jackson felt that Conn had shortchanged him in a timber land deal that Jackson had arranged.

The difference between a sociopath and a psychopath, generally speaking, is that a psychopath preys upon people, maliciously, in one way or another. Most psychopaths are malicious toward animals as well, and from an early age. They do things far worse than lighting a barn on fire with several horses trapped inside of it.

Arson is very often an act of revenge, and there is one suggestion that Jackson could have held a grudge against the Vollmers, whereas Robert Scheibe held none and considered the Vollmers his friends. A lesson can be taken here from the FBI's research into arsonists and how to identify them. The FBI approach to the study of arson caused fires is "victimology," a study of the victim of the crime. In other words, the life of the victim often points to the motive of the arsonist. Mrs. Della Vollmer was involved in local school matters and probably had a position on the school board for District 43 in 1913. She held the position of School Clerk in that same district in 1914. The district encompassed the neighborhood of Big Stick Creek and Iron Mountain. According to the school laws of Oregon, the district's board of directors was a body that had "entire control of the public schools of their district, and the teachers employed therein."

When Jackson went off to Harney County in search of a teaching position, he had plenty of ill repute to try to live down. His embezzlement from the Lake County school system was well known and much gossiped about among teachers all over the region. And, despite the apparent efforts of the county government to keep that matter quiet, it had appeared in the newspaper. Moreover, the Vollmers were neighbors of the Bardwells, who were intimately familiar with Ray Jackson's earlier forgeries against another school system and the crime spree that followed. In 1895, Jackson forged two pay vouchers, stole a horse, fled to California, and evaded arrest a couple of times, seduced a lady school superintendent, and finally was captured in Jackson County. The Bardwells had known Jackson back when those sensational and well-publicized crimes were taking place.

A revenge arsonist usually has a history of professional or interpersonal conflict with the victim. He is responding to some injustice, perceived or real, is usually an adult male, in a blue-collar category with low socioeconomic status (such as a deposed school superintendent). He has a record of other crimes like burglary, vandalism and theft. A criminal versatility, just like Ray Jackson. He has no stable or long-term relationships, just like

~122~

Mr. Jackson. He often lives in or is familiar with the community and its residents, just as Jackson was. After the fire is set, he will focus his attention on establishing an alibi, and it was very typical of Jackson to work to pin his crimes on someone else during the course of an investigation. He likes to make a fast getaway from the scene, and in 1913 would have meant the use of a horse or car, more likely a horse, given the condition of the roads during the week of the Vollmer fire and the murder of the trapper, George Webster.

The camp wagon that George Webster used for his high desert trapping of coyotes, wildcats, and other fur-bearing animals, was probably very similar to this sheepherder's arc. The wagons were a common sight on the high desert of Oregon around the turn of the last century.

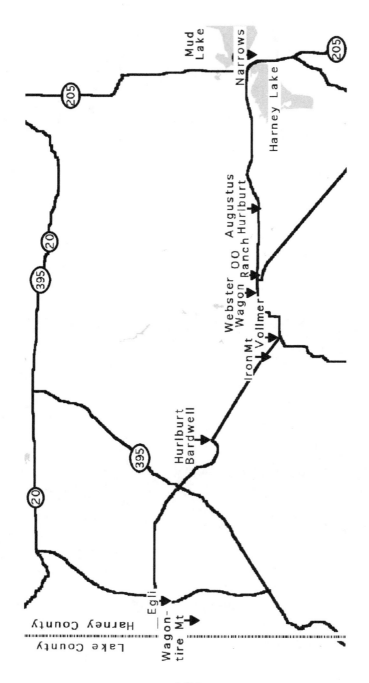

SOURCES:

"Murder and Arson Denied by Suspect," *The Oregonian* January 27, 1913.

"Man Charged with Murder and Arson," *Burns Times-Herald* January 25, 1913.

"Trapper Murdered," *Lake County Examiner,* January 30, 1913.

"Local News," *Burns Times-Herald,* February 1, 1913.

Death Certificate of George R. Webster, Harney County registered No. 080.

"Local News," *Burns Times-Herald,* January 18, January 25, February 1, 1913.

U.S. Department of the Interior, General Land Office Records, online databasehttp://www.glorecords.blm.gov /search/default. aspx. August C. Vollmer obtained federal patents on 392 acres is 1922 in township 27 south, range 27 east, section 1 and township 27 south, range 28 east, section 6. BLM serial numbers ORB 0005584 and ORB 0005585.

"Local News," *Burns Times-Herald,* August 17, 1912.

"Local News," *Burns Times-Herald,* January 4, 1913.

"Local News," *Burns Times-Herald,* January 11, 1913.

"Good Prospects for Harney County," *Burns Times-Herald,* February 1, 1913.

"Circuit Court," *Burns Times-Herald,* October 3, 1914.

"Local News" *Burns Times-Herald,* January 10, 1914.

"Man Accidentally Shot," *Burns Times-Herald,* February 13, 1915.

Obituary of Rebecca E. Johnson Sizemore, *Burns Times-Herald,* May 10, 1919

U.S. Department of the Interior, General Land Office Records, online database http://www.glorecords.blm. gov/search/default. aspx. James, Otus, and Rebecca Sizemore all patented land claims in the same general area on the west side of Harney Lake near Warm Springs, township 27 south, range 29 east, sections 2, 9, 10, 14, and 15, between 1914 and 1922.

Thirteenth Census of the United States, Oregon, Harney County, Warm Springs precinct.

Thirteenth Census of the United States, Oregon, Harney County, Burns.

"Foley Sough Suit is Compromised," *Burns Times-Herald*, July 20, 1912.

"Local News," *Burns Times-Herald*, May 3, 1913.

Political Advertisement of James E. Sizemore, *Burns Times-Herald*, March 23, 1912.

Find A Grave listing for Seth S. "Tubby" Smith, Burns Cemetery, Harney County, OR. http://www.findagrave .com/cgibin/fg.cgi? page=gr&GSln=smith&GSfn =seth&GSbyrel=all&GSdyrel= all&GSst=39&GScntry=4&GSob=n&GRid=46105673&df=all&

"The Circuit Court is Now in Session," *Burns Times-Herald*, April 12, 1913.

"G. W. Clevenger & Co.," Advertisement, *Burns Times-Herald*, January 13, 1906. This is the first mention of Clevenger in this paper, and seems to approximate the time he began his under-taking business.

"Young Man Commits Suicide," *Burns Times-Herald*, January 10, 1914.

"Local News," *Burns Times-Herald*, January 25, 1913.

"Brief Mention," *Lake County Examiner*, January 23, 1913. Reports an ambient temperature "hovering around the zero mark" on the morning of the Vollmer fire.

"Postmortem Changes and Determination of Time of Death," from the web site of the J. M. Tawes Technology and Career Center, Westover, MD. Author unknown.www.somerset.k12 .md.us/JMT/postmortem_changes.htm

"Harney County is Busy," *Oregonian*, April 19, 1913.

"Journal Entry on Sentence," The State of Oregon vs. Robert Schiebe, State of Oregon Circuit Court for the County of Harney, Burns, April 14, 1913.

"P. J. Gallagher," *Oregon Voter,* January 4, 1919, Vol. 16, No. 1, page 44. Biography.

"P. J. Gallagher," *History of the Columbia River Valley from The Dalles to the Sea,* Vol. III, 1928, S. J. Clarke Publishing Company, p 441442.

"Brooke & Gallagher is New Legal Firm," *Ontario Argus,* May 31, 1917.

"Local News," *Burns Times-Herald,* January 18, 1913.

"Local News," *Burns Times-Herald,* March 15, 1913.

"Local News," *Burns Times-Herald,* July 12, 1913, July 19, 1913. Gallagher and family departed Burns on July 17, 1913.

Untitled article, *Malheur Enterprise,* February 28, 1914.

"New York Passenger Lists, 1820-1925." Available online at Ancestry.com: http://search.ancestry.com/browse/view.aspx?dbid=7488&iid=NYM237_4750821&pid =10425206&ssrc=&fn=Robert&ln=Scheibe&st=g

Fourteenth Census of the United States, Oregon, Marion County, Salem.

Web site of Oregon State Archives, Oregon Historical Records Index, detail information for inmate record of Robert Scheibe, case 6817. Incarcerated April 17, 1913 from Harney County. Remarks state "transferred to OSIA July 1914 died there 9/10/1928. http://genealogy.state.or.us/ detail.php?id=228279

"Oregon State Hospital, formerly the State Insane Asylum," Salem Oregon Online History Project. Article available online at: arcweb.sos.state.or.us/doc/tour/2009 00020shadov.pdf

Inmate Record of Robert Scheibe, #6817, Oregon State Penitentiary. Oregon State Archives, Salem, OR.

Thirteenth Census of the United States, Illinois, Kane County, Batavia.

Listings for Henry Scheibe, b 1834; Augusta Benz Scheibe, b 1839; Henry Scheibe Jr., b 1872; Bertha Scheibe, b unknown; Emilie Scheibe Groener, b 1864. East Batavia Cemetery, Batavia, Kane County, Illinois. Web site of Find A Grave, http://www.findagrave.com/cgibin/fg.cgi?page =gsr&GSfn=& G S m n = & G S l n = S c h e i b e & G S b y r e l = a l l & G S b y =&GSdyrel=all&GSdy=&GScntry=4&GSst=16&GScnty=734&GS grid=&df=all&GSob=n

"Pioneer Rancher Takes Own Life," *Harney County American,* February 4, 1938.

Harney County Oral History Project, AV-Oral History #274, "Jessie Williams Discusses Bill Brown," Burns, Oregon, 1980, by Richard Cowan, p 19.

Twelfth Census of the United States, Oregon, Harney County

"Suicide is Verdict of Coroner's Jury in Jackson Death," *Burns Times-Herald,* February 2, 1938.

W. L. Jackson Vs. R. V. Jackson, circuit court of the state of Oregon for the county of Harney: undertaking, affidavit, and complaint for attachment, October 27, 1902; journal entry on default and order for sale of attached property, April 20, 1903. Harney Circuit Court, Harney County Courthouse, Burns, OR.

Record of Marks and Brands, of R. B. Jackson, residing in Harney County, OR, September 10, 1902. Harney County Clerk's Office, Harney County Courthouse, , Burns, Oregon.

Indenture, R. B. Jackson to First National Bank of Burns, September 10, 1902.

"William 'Bill' W. Brown 18551941: Legend of Oregon's High Desert," by Edward Gray, Your Town Press, Salem, OR, 1993, p 166.

Thirteenth Census of the United States, Oregon, Harney County, Curry precinct.

"Brief Mention," *Lake County Examiner,* December 15, 1910.

Twelfth Census of the United States, Oregon, Lake County, Silver Lake.

"Local News," *Burns Times-Herald,* October 18, 1913.

"Brief Mention," *Lake County Examiner,* October 23, 1913.

Harney County Oral History Project, AV-Oral History #381, "Shelby Petersen," Burns, Oregon, 1991, by Edward Gray, p 16.

"Teachers Receiving Passing Grades," *Burns Times-Herald,* January 30, 1915.

The Sandy Knoll Murder, Legacy of the Sheepshooters, by Melany Tupper, Central Oregon Books, LLC, Christmas Valley, OR, 2010.

Crime Classification Manual, a Standard System for Investigating and Classifying Violent Crimes, by John E. Douglas, Ann W. Burgess, Allen G. Burgess, and Robert K. Ressler, second edition, Jossey-Bass, San Francisco, 2006, p 263-264, 267-274.

"April Apportionment County School Funds," *Burns Times-Herald,* May 9, 1914.

The Oregon School Laws, with Rules and Regulations of the State Board of Education, by J. H. Ackerman, Oregon State Printing Office, Salem, 1909, p 36.

Tenth Census of the United States, Oregon, Linn County, Center Precinct.

Ed Logan's cabin at Little Lava Lake, where three men were murdered in 1924, was probably located near the present day site of the Little Lava Lake Campground.

Chapter Seven

Also Known As

The first connection between Ray Jackson and another criminal, named Charles Hyde Kimzey, can be drawn before Charles, or "Charley" was even born, with the birth of another member of that family, Mary Jane Kimsey, at Yamhill County in 1849. She was the daughter of Alvis Kimsey.

Charley's father, about half way through his life, started to spell the family name with a "z" instead of an "s." Probably the best proof that Charley Kimzey was a member of the Kimsey family was contained in a handwritten letter from Charley's nephew, Charles Grover Kimsey, to the Oregon penitentiary, dated December 5, 1964, in which he wrote, "I would like to make a few inquires (sic) of my uncle, former inmate, Charles Kimzey." The letter was clearly signed "Charles G. Kimsey."

When Mary Jane Kimsey was born, Charley Kimzey's father, James, lived next door, and would continue to do so until about 1857, or for about eight years. James was a first cousin of little Mary Jane, because their fathers, Alvis and John, were brothers. James lived with his widowed mother, Susan Kimsey, who would later marry Henry H. Hyde in Yamhill County in 1850. Later on, little Mary Jane became the mother of the woman that William Jackson, Ray's only brother, would marry.

About 1857, James, Susan, and her second husband, Henry Hyde, moved to California, and the 1860 census found James still at home with his mother and stepfather in Yreka at the age of 24.

In December of 1869, Ray Van Buren Jackson was born at Saline County, Missouri, in the town of Grand Pass, to Martin Van Buren and Callie Jackson.

By 1870, James Kimzey had moved to Boise City in Idaho and was working as a butcher for William Ryan. That was a fact that Charley would recall much later in life. When he was 71 years old and serving out his sentence in Oregon, he told prison officials that he remembered his father working as a wheelwright and butcher. It was about 1870 that James broke with tradition, and began spelling his last name with a "z." In 1876, James married Mary Basil Peasley after she divorced her first husband, Stephen

L. Peasley. It was a second marriage for James as well, because he had previously been married to the rather colorful Pernecia Edonia Young Taylor, who was said to have been a "dance hall girl," and would later become the live-in companion of Felix Duncan at Silver Lake, Oregon.

By the time of the 1880 census, James and Mary Kimzey were living in Union in Grant County, Oregon and James was working as a teamster. They had two sons, John B. and Earl. Around 1881 the family moved to Idaho, where their daughter, Mary E., was born in 1882. By that time, a brother of James, William T. Kimsey, and family had arrived and settled in Lake County, Oregon. On October 12, 1885, Charles Hyde Kimzey was born in Caldwell, Idaho.

In 1892, a great disruption occurred in the life of Charley Kimzey that may have eventually played a part in his criminal mentality. When he was only seven years old, his parents divorced. In the book, *Bad Men Do What Good Men Dream*, Robert Simon described the potential affect of the absentee father, citing an important FBI study of 36 incarcerated psychopathic killers. Almost half of the killers had fathers who left home before the boys were twelve years old. "The absence of a solid male role model is a significant fact in their development as killers," Simon wrote. "But the presence of a father in the house is no guarantee of normality. For these boys, the presence in the house of a cruel, insensitive father may be worse for them than having an absent father. The general fact is that in the midst of a caring, loving family, it is unlikely that a child will consistently prefer fantasy to real life."

Just after Charley Kimzey's parents split up in Idaho, over in Oregon in 1893, Minnie Peery, daughter of Mary Jane Kimsey and Hiram W. Peery, Jr., married William L. Jackson at Albany.

Charley Kimzey would later tell prison officials that he dropped out of school in 1901, or the 9th grade, and the 1900 census found him still at home and in school at Caldwell, Idaho. In 1902, an aunt of Charley's, Mary E. Chandler Kimsey, filed on a homestead in Lake County in township 37 south, range 21 east, about thirteen miles northeast of Lakeview.

In the summer of 1914, Kimzey committed grand larceny by stealing some grain in Blaine County, Idaho and was sentenced to three years in prison. In June of 1915, he was incarcerated, but in October of that same year escaped from the Homedale Work Farm with a stolen farm horse. After parking his stolen steed at his brother Jim's house, Kimzey went to work, under the alias of Bob Dales, for the Fall Creek Sheep Company in Idaho. The authorities lost all trace of Kimzey at that time, but he seems to have managed to stay out of sight and out of trouble for several years, and made his way to Oregon.

Kimzey's comprehensive prison records from Oregon and Idaho reveal that "Collins" was one of his preferred aliases. Many sociopaths use several aliases as they weave a continuous web of lies throughout their lifetimes, and Kimzey was proven to have used the aliases "Lee Collins" and "Tom Collins" in Idaho, central Oregon, and Montana. He also worked as a sheep herder in central Oregon between 1915 and 1921.

In the spring and summer of 1922, Kimzey worked for Carin H. Degermark at her Elk Lake summer camp, located on the present day Cascades Lakes Highway about 25 miles west of Bend. Degermark knew him as Lee Collins and, in a 1955 letter she told the warden of the Oregon State Penitentiary that Kimzey "was the best worker we ever had." Degermark asked the warden for information on Kimzey, and was interested in writing an article about him and his connection to an unsolved murder case, the Lava Lakes triple murder of 1924.

It wasn't until 1923 that Charles Kimzey, alias Lee Collins, became notorious in central Oregon for a short crime spree and assault with a deadly weapon, committed on August 21. That was when Deschutes County Sheriff Samuel Elbert "Bert" Roberts became interested enough in Collins to learn his true identity. In 1933, Kimzey was finally apprehended and brought back to Oregon for questioning about his involvement in the Lava Lakes murders, and was tried for that 1923 assault with a deadly weapon and robbery of a man named William Harrison. Although the subject of that trial was the attack on Harrison, practically everyone in Bend, and the Bend officials, were much more interested in Kimzey's connection to the Lava Lakes case.

Even Kimzey's defense attorney, Ross Farnham, dwelt on the subject of the triple murder as he questioned prospective jurors. "Each prospective juror was questioned regarding his or her attitude toward Kimzey on the assault charge and how it might be affected by the linking of his name with the Lava Lake case," reported the *Bulletin*. Indeed, most of the jurors were found to know very little at all about the Harrison matter.

"The court room was so crowded with spectators when court opened that there was no room for jurors. Early arrivals who had occupied the best seats in front of the court room were ordered out and jurors were brought in through a front door and given the front seats," reported the *Bulletin* of April 20, 1933. "The early arrivals among the spectators objected to leaving and crowded into the aisles already 'filled like a sardine can' as Bailiff Sam Newell worked vainly to clear seats for jurors. It was estimated there were at least 150 persons in the court room seated, standing in the aisles, on benches and other projections."

Harrison took the stand on the first day of the trial, and identified Kimzey, known to him as Lee Collins, as the man who had paid him to drive his jitney, or taxi, to the Last Chance ranch about 60 miles southeast of Bend on the morning of August 21, 1923. Kimzey had stated the purpose of his trip was to buy some pack and saddle horses to use at Lava Lakes. Harrison drove Kimzey to a point a few miles beyond the Last Chance Ranch, to Frederick's Butte and some deserted buildings in township 22 south, range 19 east, section 32. While stopping at that place, Kimzey pulled a revolver and demanded that Harrison turn over the car. But, instead of shooting Harrison, Kimzey hit him on the head with the gun. When Harrison began to regain consciousness, Kimzey forced him to drink a drug that made him pass out, then took the man's shoes, coat, and $17 in cash, dragged him by the feet to a cistern, then stole the jitney to make his getaway.

When Harrison awoke, he was resting on his head and shoulders at the bottom of the cistern, and his hands and feet were tied with bailing wire. He managed to work himself loose and crawl out, then walked in a sickened and bruised condition back to the Last Chance ranch for help.

When the sheriff went to investigate the scene, he found the license plates from the stolen car hidden in the brush nearby, and the wire that was used to tie Harrison was in the bottom of the cistern. Tracks of the car were followed as far as Millican.

After the Harrison crime, Kimzey was not only pursued by the sheriff and his deputies, but also by Joe Keller, an automobile insurance agent for Pacific Coast Underwriters. Keller wanted to recover that stolen car, and interviewed several people who knew the theif.

"At Boise I talked with a woman who was intimate with Kimsey (sic) and from her I learned the real reason for this crime," Keller told the *Oregonian* in reference to the Lava Lakes murders. "Kimsey had trouble with Nichols (sic) and told the woman that he was going back to Bend to 'clean out that bunch.' I believe that he sneaked back into the Lava Lake country for the express purpose of murdering the three men."

Despite his criminal history, Kimzey was described by those who knew him as pleasant and likable, with the ability to gain the confidence of others, and he made friends with several people in central Oregon during the 1920s.

He befriended one of the Lava Lakes victims, Ed Nickols (frequently misspelled in the papers as "Nichols"). In 1922 and 1923, the two men ran a pack string around the Cascade Lakes for tourists and campers in the spring and summer, and made moonshine and trapped around the lakes in the fall and winter. Kimzey and Nickols also cared for several fur foxes of considerable value that belonged to Ed Logan.

Another friend of Kimzey's who bears close examination is Allen W. Willcoxon, who Kimzey trusted to such a degree that, when he went before the parole board of the Oregon State Penitentiary in 1940, he named Willcoxon as a character witness. Willcoxon was burdened with a last name that was misspelled by practically everyone, but it is probably safe to say that, when the man himself spoke to the census agent in 1910, and mourned the death of his little son in 1912, he used the correct spelling of his own name. It can be found in old articles and records as Wilcoxen, Willcoxen, Willcoxson, and Wilcoxson, but Allen himself spelled it "Willcoxon."

Allen Willcoxon was born in Alabama in 1883, son of George and Lucy B. Willcoxon. By 1908, Allen was living on his homestead farm at Powell Butte in Crook County. He had married Arba Roe, daughter of George H. and Lou W. Roe in 1907. The couple had a daughter, Harriet, born in Oregon in 1908. A boy,

George Reeves Willcoxon was born in August of 1910, but died in January of 1912. It is not known what brought Allen Willcoxon to central Oregon, but a man by the name of Reeves A. "Willcoxen," who lived in Redmond during the period, seems to have been a brother or close relative of his. Allen may have met his wife, Arba Roe, in Pasco, Washington where her parents operated a boarding house until at least 1910.

Four years prior to the triple homicide at Lava Lakes, when the 1920 census was taken, Allen Willcoxon was divorced and living at the sawmill of William R. McKinley on Tumalo Creek and worked as a teamster, probably hauling logs to the mill, or delivering lumber to customers. Interestingly enough, during the period when Willcoxon befriended Kimzey, he was also closely associated with Claude L. McCauley, who may not have joined the Sheriff's Department until after the murders, but became actively interested in the investigation when he was elected sheriff in 1928. McCauley was the manager of the McKinley sawmill in 1920. Also at the mill was Stella Shearer, a divorced lady and cook for the camp who became Willcoxon's second wife around 1920.

It was probably during his employment at the mill that Willcoxon learned about brewing beer and distilling moonshine. In central Oregon during the prohibition days, small sawmills were notorious for producing moonshine. They were usually remote locations with fresh cold water, and the process gave the mill men a source of income in the winter months.

In 1924, *Pine Echoes*, the employee newsletter of the Brooks-Scanlon Lumber Company, described how the Elk Lake camp was owned by the Forest Service, but operated by Willcoxon. Carin Degermark leased and operated the camp via a Forest Service permit around 1923, so we might presume that Willcoxon took over the operation of the camp in 1924. In her article *Elk Lake Remembrances,* Carol Blackwell described how Willcoxon built trails and cabins, and campers would walk in from Snow Creek Road, several miles to the south. Blackwell believed that Willcoxon worked at Elk Lake as early as 1921, so it seems that he transitioned from Degermark's employee to manager of the camp around 1923.

In April of 1924, Paul Hosmer, editor of *Pine Echoes*, praised the quality of Willcoxon's home brew, manufactured at the Elk Lake Resort, and described it as the best place for Saturday night parties. "Editor of Pine Echoes has probably said more nice things about Elk Lake and received fewer invitations to sample homebrew than any other agency," quipped Hosmer. "Will try once more and if nothing happens this time we'll start boosting Lava River cave. Elk Lake owned jointly by U.S. government and Allen Wilcoxen (sic), the latter doing all the work."

Willcoxon was a central character in the Lava Lakes murder case, not just because of his concurrent close associations with the notorious Mr. Kimzey, and Claude L. McCauley. A 1941 report to the parole board by Deschutes County District Attorney Bert Boylan summarized the Lava Lakes crimes, and described how, on January 15, 1924, Willcoxon stopped at Lava Lakes and spent the evening with the three victims, and it was believed that the murders occurred shortly after that visit. "A woodsman and neighboring trapper, Allen Willcoxen (sic), had stayed at the cabin the night of January 15, 1924, and testified that all were well and in excellent spirits," wrote Wayne Negus in 1990. "Willcoxen (sic), however, was never a suspect in the case. He was the last person, as far as is known, to have seen the three men alive, with the exception of the murderers, of course."

"The calendar showed the January leaf untouched," reported the *Oregonian* of April 25, 1924. "It was established that a fresh supply of food for the five foxes, which Nichols (sic) had cared for at Logan's fur farm, had been brought in on or about January 13," and that delivery May have been made by Logan himself. "It was apparent that only about two day's rations had been given the animals and their last ration remained in the feed pans." Given that information about the fox food, the investigators seem to have extrapolated that the killings happened right after Willcoxon's visit.

Another element of timing that the investigators must have considered was the later appearance of Kimzey and his accomplice at Portland on January 22, and the number of days it would have taken them to travel that distance. The Lava Lakes investigation began as a search for missing persons, because what was initially found was nothing more than blood evidence at a deserted cabin. So, when the search began on April 13, the date of the men's mysterious disappearance was fixed at January 15, the date of Willcoxon's visit.

It was mentioned earlier that Kimzey had been a trapping partner of victim, Ed Nickols, in the 1922-1923 season, and so had been intimately connected with Nickols' operation at Little Lava Lake. It was during that time that Kimzey also befriended Ed Logan, the owner of the fur foxes that Nickols and Kimzey, and later Nickols and two other men, cared for.

Surprisingly enough, there were four "Ed Logans" living in central Oregon in 1924, so it is important not to confuse them. Wayne Negus, who seems to have been a distant cousin of one of the victims, described fox owner Ed Logan as, "a Bend logging contractor," and that detail helps to identify him as Edward Fields Logan. In 1920 Edward F. Logan was a 49 year-old railroad contractor from Minnesota, who worked in a railroad camp and lived in Bend on Franklin Street with his wife Catherine Hayes Logan.

At the end of the trapping season, in the spring of 1923, Nickols and Kimzey turned over their catch of furs to Logan to sell for them. "Later Logan reported that he had not or could not sell them, and had them at his home in Bend," wrote Deschutes District Attorney Boylan. Kimzey told the sheriff and Boylan that "Nickols and Logan were trying to beat Kimzey out of his share of the furs and that Kimzey did not get his share of the packhorse money." When Kimzey decided that he had been cheated, he stole $500 that Nickols had hidden in the woods near their cabin at little lava lake.

On August 20, 1923, just before Kimzey's attack on the driver, Harrison, Kimzey rode into Bend in the morning with Logan, then arranged to make the trip back to Little Lava Lake with Logan later the same day, an appointment that he did not keep. Kimzey attended a picture show at Bend with a friend, and when Logan made the trip back to the lake that afternoon, Kimzey broke into Logan's house in Bend and stole a trunk containing his wife's beaver coat and a diamond ring.

Those accounts make it apparent that Kimzey held a grudge against both Logan and Nickols, and so had stolen Nickols money and Logan's possessions, then left the country after attacking Harrison. About ten days later, when the authorities pursued Kimzey into Idaho, they found his tan traveling bag at a Boise rooming house containing several letters he had received in April of 1923 at Ed Logan's post office box in Bend. That finding reinforced the idea that Kimzey and Logan were friends, and also suggests that Logan delivered mail to Little Lava Lake on a regular basis.

Another man who was apparently a good friend of Kimzey's in the 1920s, and was close to the events at Lava Lakes, was Grover H. Caldwell. "In the fall of 1923, Ed Nickols told Grover Caldwell that Collins (Kimzey) was angry at him when he left in August, and had threatened to come back and kill Nickols," wrote district attorney Boylan. "Nickols said he was afraid he would. Nickols got two other men, Morris and Wilson, to stay with him at Lava Lake that winter, '23-24.'"

Grover Caldwell was also the friend who Kimzey went to the movies with on August 20, right before he broke into Logan's house. "During the evening of August 20th, defendant and Grover Caldwell attended picture show in Bend. After the show, Kimzey told Caldwell he wanted to make a trip out to Last Chance ranch, and wanted Ace Dobson, who regularly carried large sums of money on his person, to take him out. He asked Caldwell to be sure to contact Dobson and have him ready to go at six in the morning," wrote Boylan.

"At six in the morning of August 21st, Kimzey met Caldwell on Bond Street, Bend, and Caldwell told him Dobson would not go. Kimzey was angry and refused Caldwell's offer to get another jitney driver, saying he would get one himself. He then stopped at the Downing Restaurant and ordered his breakfast telling Kline, the waiter, he wanted a jitney driver to take him out about sixty on the desert. Kline called Harrison and they left together."

Grover Caldwell, who knew Kimzey as "Lee Collins," had a bit of an unsavory reputation himself. He was a house carpenter who lived in Bend with his wife, Jessie Pearl Andrews Caldwell, and children, Nora and Wenzel. From about 1920 through 1940 Grover and his brother Lee Caldwell trapped coyotes to collect a bounty from Deschutes County in the La Pine area, and that may be where and how Kimzey became acquainted with him. The Caldwells also had a homestead on Paulina Prairie, about three miles north of La Pine, and a house in Bend so that their children could attend school in town.

In 1915, Caldwell accused a man named David Dunn of having stolen one of his horses. Dunn was acquitted of the horse theft charge on the grounds that the horse was a stray, but reported that Caldwell had threatened his life on several occasions. Dunn also said that Caldwell had hired a lynch mob out of Pendleton in retaliation for the alleged horse theft.

On March 20 of 1918, Caldwell confronted Dunn on a Bend street and asked about his missing horse. "Caldwell struck him a glancing blow on the head and shoulder," reported the *Bulletin,* and Dunn pulled a knife and stabbed Caldwell several times. Dunn was later found guilty of attempted murder.

By the summer 1923, Kimzey had definite knowledge that Ed Logan kept five valuable fur foxes at Little Lava Lake, because he had been there and seen them for himself, and he and Nickols had cared for the animals the previous winter.

On September 4, 1923, Sheriff Roberts and Deputy George Stokoe returned to Bend from Boise with the stolen touring car. The *Bulletin* reported that the thief, one Lee Collins, had eluded arrest, and was also suspected in the theft of a fur coat and diamond ring from the home of Ed Logan of Bend, and was "thought by officers to be implicated in the loss of $500 in cash reported by William Nichols (sic) of Lava Lake." The officers did manage to recover the trunk that Kimzey used to ship the coat to his brother at Barber, Idaho.

When the story of the murder of the three trappers broke in 1924, Kimzey was immediately identified by both the sheriff and the newspapers as the prime suspect. "Reports are current that Kimzey had sworn to have revenge on the men at the lake for giving information to the authorities which nearly resulted in his capture in Boise," reported the *Bulletin* of April 25, 1924. When Kimzey stole that car from Harrison and fled, both the sheriff and insurance man Keller questioned Nickols and Logan, who told what they knew about the man from Idaho, known to them as Lee Collins. "Kimzey, who had previously been employed at the fox farm, was suspected for several reasons. He had escaped from the Idaho State Penitentiary, where he was serving a 14-year sentence, and while employed at the lake, had robbed

Nichols (sic) and Logan of several valuable articles," reported the *Bulletin* in January of 1925. "It was reported that he had promised to get revenge on the men at the lake for giving information which nearly resulted in his recapture."

The Harrison case was a very telling one in terms of Kimzey's criminal 'style.' Nothing about it was very well planned out, and Kimzey seems to have been just improvising and making things up as he went along. As they drove, Kimzey looked for an isolated spot to steal the car. When they stopped at the abandoned ranch, he used some old wire he found to tie Harrison, and came up with the idea that the cistern would be a good way to hold the driver temporarily. Taking off the license plates was probably thought of before hand, because he replaced the taxi plates with a set of plates that he had stolen from Ed Logan earlier that day. Putting Logan's plates on the stolen car was not a very smart idea, because those plates could easily identify Kimzey. At some point he decided that removing Harrison's shoes might slow him down as he went for help, so he took the shoes and quickly buried them under one edge of an abandoned ranch house.

Kimzey's record is full of examples of his clumsy criminal style. It was rather 'dense' of him to tell his friends in Oregon, Logan and Nickols, that he was from Idaho, during the same period that he was wanted in Idaho as an escaped convict. When Kimzey was arrested in 1932 in Montana on a forgery charge, he failed to relocate after his release, even though he knew that he was wanted at the time in Oregon for both the Lava Lakes and Harrison crimes. He also chose to use an alias that was similar to "Lee Collins" when he told the arresting officers that his name was "Tom Collins."

Kimzey thought that name was a clever choice, because Tom Collins was the old alias that he had used in Colorado just prior to Lava Lakes murders. He thought that use of that name would provide him with an alibi, because it would be found on payroll records from the Moffat Tunnel construction site. But, he was not smart enough to realize that, by evoking his old alias, he was further incriminating himself. It was just like waving a red flag that said, "I know I am guilty of those murders, and now I am trying to manufacture a cover story."

Another small insight into Kimzey's makeup came from an examination of his possessions when he was finally arrested and returned to Oregon in 1932. He was carrying several medicines with him during the time when he was wanted in several states, and wanted for the trapper murders. He changed identities and moved around a lot, doing seasonal work. He was an escaped convict. His situation might have called for 'traveling light,' and most people would have only carried the items that they considered essential. Sociopaths are usually profoundly self-concerned to the point of hypochondria, and Kimzey carried "blue ointment," which was a 20 percent mercury salve traditionally used for lice, primarily crabs; also Cascara, one of the first laxatives; and Mercurochrome, a mercury antiseptic solution.

Note how, in his work with Nickols, trapping, guiding, bootlegging and the like, Kimzey did not play a leadership role, and left the management of the business and the handling of money up to his partner. Although the author believes that Kimzey was a dangerous man and a sociopath, there were several indications that Kimzey played a secondary role in the Lava Lakes murders. And, when the bodies were located in that crime, it was decided that the murders had been the work of two men. It was that other man, the accomplice, the organized one, the 'talker and the thinker,' the one who killed without compunction, upon whom the investigation should have focused, instead of the clumsy Mr. Kimzey.

Kimzey seems to have gone to Idaho about one year after selling the furs from the Lava Lakes murders. By the spring of 1926 the William J. Burns International Detective Agency was hired by the Citizen's Bank and Trust Company to track him down for a forgery of $715, committed the prior year at Pocatello.

In December of 1925, Kimzey arrived in Salt Lake City and answered an advertisement placed by a draftsman named William R. Howard, who was looking for a companion to help him drive a car cross country to Tampa, Florida. The car belonged to Mr. A. O. Treganza, an architect and Howard's employer who had recently moved to Florida. Howard told a friend, contractor S. W. Farrer at Salt Lake, that he was very nervous about making the trip. "Mr. Howard was extremely nervous the day before he left," said Farrer, "and said he was very anxious to have more company on his contemplated trip to Tampa." That was obviously after Howard had met Kimzey, alias William Becker, and made arrangements to travel with him, so Howard already had a bad feeling about Kimzey. The two men stayed at the Arrowhead Hotel in St. George, Utah on December 8th.

W. H. Ingersoll, who managed the Burns agency office in Salt Lake, wrote a letter to the warden of the Idaho State Penitentiary on April 23, 1926 in which he surmised that Kimzey and Howard had first traveled to Las Vegas, and that Kimzey had killed Howard on the day that they checked out of the Overland Hotel there, December 9, 1925. The two men were driving south, probably because they wanted to cross the country by a southern route to avoid bad weather.

Howard's remains, described as "a skeleton," were discovered by an Indian known as "Baboon" on December 7, 1927 on a small side road about 19 miles south of Las Vegas. From an examination of the clothing and the blood evidence on the front seat of the car, Sheriff Sam Gay and District Attorney Harley Harmon determined that Howard had been stabbed in his right side, just above his belt line, as he sat behind the wheel. The car also had a broken turn signal indicator, that was thought to have been snapped off during Howard's struggle with Kimzey, who pulled Howard out of the car and left him to die in the desert. Dental records were later used to identify the remains.

A sheepman, J. W. Imlay, reported that he saw Kimzey in the Treganza automobile on December 10 near Yermo, California, en route to Victorville. Because the investigation would have to cover several states, and because the crimes of kidnapping and murder seemed to have happened outside of his jurisdiction, Salt Lake County Sheriff Benjamin R. Harries turned the case over to the Burns agency in January of 1926, after traveling with their agents through southern California. According to a November 1927 report by agent Ingersoll, the Burns detective agency was paid to investigate the case by Howard's father, William H. Howard, and the American Bankers Association, who still wanted Kimzey on the Pocatello forgery charge.

Kimzey vacationed the last half of December 1925 in the San Diego area, spending Howard's travelers checks and, rather stupidly, signing them "W. R. Howe." It is interesting to note that, after stabbing Howard, Kimzey assumed the victim's identity to a certain extent by using an adaptation of his name, and by driving his car. He also mimicked Howard in his next move, which was to place an advertisement in the newspaper to find a companion to travel east with him to Florida. W. O. Hurd answered the ad saying that he would go as far as Louisiana, and the two left San Diego around the first of the year. Kimzey and Hurd picked up a woman and a cowboy, who were never named, at different places in Arizona. The woman parted company with them at El Paso, where the three travelers held up a party of motorists and robbed them.

Upon reaching San Antonio, the unnamed cowboy and Kimzey robbed Hurd and left him tied to a tree, then parted company. At San Antonio, Kimzey seems to have conveyed the stolen Treganza car to James F. and William Holmes, who used it in a robbery of their own. The Holmes brothers were stopped and taken into custody when they attempted to cross the Rio Grande at Eagle Pass into Mexico with the bloodstained and badly damaged car. Accounts differ as to what exactly transpired between Kimzey and the Holmes boys, but they told authorities that they had been given the car by a man who paid them seventy-five dollars to dispose of it in Mexico.

On April 28, 1926, the Salt Lake County Sheriff's Department issued a warrant for Kimzey's arrest for murder and robbery in the Howard case. But, at the end of 1926, the Burns agency and the sheriff's of Utah and Nevada closed their books on the Howard disappearance after all efforts had failed to recover Howard's body.

In November of 1927, Burns agent Ingersoll at Salt Lake once again picked up the trail, and wrote a report stating that Kimzey was believed to be living in the vicinity of Lyman and Fort Bridger, Wyoming. Ingersoll got his information from Deputy Arthur S. Nichols of the Salt Lake County Sheriff's Department, who told him that a year before, in November of 1926, Nichols saw Kimzey at the Johnston Hotel in Lyman, Wyoming. During that encounter, Kimzey had the 'cheek' to ask deputy Nichols if he remembered the Howard murder of 1925, and asked if the body of Howard had ever been found. Luckily, Deputy Nichols recognized Kimzey from his prison photos.

In December of 1927, about two years after he left Las Vegas with Kimzey, Howard's body was recovered from the desert south of town, and the Burns men at Salt Lake appealed to their headquarters in New York for permission to reopen the case, although the private detectives seem to have not pursued the matter much further.

On June 5, 1928, Burns agent Charles E. Love of the Salt Lake office wrote a special report implicating Kimzey in yet another murder. Love had traveled to Boise on other matters, and met with the captain of the police department there. "I was informed that they had found a man murdered about two weeks ago and floating on a small lake just west of Boise; that he, the captain, and the community as a whole, suspected one Charles Kimzey who lives with his two brothers, one of whom is a hunchback, on the other side of this lake where the body was found," wrote Love.

"It is generally known that Kimzey is a fugitive from justice, but that the people in that vicinity and the authorities are afraid to arrest him. He stated the only directly accessible way to Kimzey's house is across the lake, his house being the only one on that side of the lake," continued Love. "When either Kimzey or his brothers see anyone approaching they either hide in the nearby hills or stand them off with a gun until they determine their business; and that they have several large dogs, eight or ten, for the purpose of warning them when anyone is approaching across or around the lake.... The captain stated that owing to the reputation of Kimzey as a notorious 'bad man,' he has been unable to get a posse together and surround Kimzey's place."

The lake referred to was certainly Lake Lowell, the only lake immediately west of Boise. It was actually a natural reservoir, filled by manmade means for irrigation, and completed in 1900. The area was colloquially known as Deer Flat, and the nearest town to the lake was Nampa, about five miles to the northeast, although the community near the lake where the Kimzey brothers lived was known as Moore's Creek.

Burns agent Love reported having seen Kimzey and another man near Fort Bridger, in late June of 1928, trying to sell some wool that was believed to be stolen property. Love was also able to identify Kimzey from a photo, and his report of the encounter was forwarded to the warden at Idaho. He was, incidentally, arrested in Great Falls the previous fall for writing bad checks as "Tom Rose."

Kimzey's next brush with the law came in September of 1932 when he and an unnamed boy stole some clothing and a rifle from a store in Valier, Montana and made their getaway in a stolen truck. J. H. Williams, a policeman in Butte, forwarded information about that crime to the warden at Idaho. Also in 1932, Kimzey's name found its way into the files of J. Edgar Hoover and the FBI when he was charged with manufacturing liquor in March in Great Falls, Montana.

In January of 1933, John Duggan, acting chief of police at Butte, received a tip from a woman in Forney, Idaho about a man known to her as both "Kimberly" and "Lee Collins" living in the area. Kimzey and an accomplice also knocked over a still at Arrowrock, Idaho in early February of 1933 and went to Butte, then back to Salmon City, Idaho. Those crimes in Montana led to Kimzey's eventual capture, return to Oregon to be tried in the Harrison case, and sentencing to life in prison.

On March 9, 1933, Kimzey was arrested at Kalispell and brought back to Oregon by Sheriff McCauley, and Art Tuck of the Oregon State Police, for questioning about the attack on Harrison and the Lava Lakes murders. When he was arrested near Great Falls, officials in Portland, identified him as the man also known as Lee Collins by studying his fingerprints.

In April 1933, Kimzey was only tried for the attack on Harrison, having been charged with "assault and robbery while armed with a dangerous weapon," and the court room was crowded with approximately 150 people. Although the matter at hand was the attack on Harrison, the public's attention was clearly focused on the Lava Lakes murders. Kimzey's name was so widely associated with that sensational case, that his attorney, Ross Farnham, dismissed many prospective jurors because they had a definite opinion about Kimzey's guilt in the trapper murders. The prosecutor was not able to find cause to charge Kimzey with attempted murder in the Harrison case, probably because Kimzey had a clear opportunity to kill, but chose not to. Before Kimzey dumped him into that cistern, he told the taxi driver that he wanted time to get away before Harrison could report the theft of the car, and that showed a clear intention to spare Harrison. Although Kimzey had a pistol, he did not use it.

To this day, there is a common misconception around Bend, Oregon that Kimzey was tried for the Lava Lakes murders, and on March 22 of 1933 the *Bulletin* even stated that Kimzey was currently "bound over to the grand jury this week on a murder charge growing out of the death of three trappers nine years ago." In fact, Kimzey was questioned about the Lava Lakes murders, but was only tried for his crimes against Harrison. In April of 1933, Kimzey was found guilty of assault and robbery while armed with a dangerous weapon in the Harrison case, and sentenced to life in the Oregon State Penitentiary by Circuit Judge Timothy E. J. Duffy, who chose to administer the maximum sentence. Also, contrary to popular belief, Kimzey did not die in prison, however his incarceration did put an end to his life of crime.

It is interesting to note that, over the course of Kimzey's 'career' he had entered into many brief, ad hoc partnerships with others, usually shortly before the commission of some felony. In the theft of grain at Idaho, he had a partner, Henry Brown; in the robbery of the store and auto theft in Valier an unnamed boy was with him; at Lava Lakes he definitely had a partner; one of his brothers may have had a hand in the Lake Lowell murder in 1928; he and a partner robbed a still at Arrowrock; Kimzey, Hurd, and the cowboy held up a group of motorists; later Kimzey and the cowboy held up Hurd; and Kimzey had a partner with him as he tried to sell stolen wool in Wyoming.

His hearing before the Oregon parole board in April of 1940 brought forth the remark, "from my understanding of this man's case, no lives were lost as a result of his crime," meaning the attack on Harrison. "Therefore I feel that it is possible that his sentence is too severe and would recommend that his sentence be commuted to a term more in keeping with the crime."

In November of 1944, Kimzey was assigned to a labor gang under the charge of a guard named Tilton, and he escaped on August 5, 1945 near Mehama, Oregon, but was apprehended by another guard named Johnson and sent back to prison. Despite that black mark on his record, parole was ordered for Kimzey in June of 1957, and he was released from the Oregon penitentiary on August 5, 1957 at the age of 72. He went back to Idaho, where he lived out the remaining few years of his life without incident, and died in 1976. He was buried northwest of Boise at the Dry Creek Cemetery.

These photos of Charles Hyde Kimzey were printed in the Oregonian in 1933 when he was apprehended in Montana. The photo at left was taken when Kimzey was incarcerated in Idaho at the age of 30. Photo at right was how Kimzey appeared when he was brought back to Oregon at the age of 48, nine years after the triple murder at Lava Lakes.

SOURCES:

Cecil Houk's Family Tree on WorldConnect Project (Kimsey family)http://wc.rootsweb.ancestry.com/cgibin/ igm.cgi? op=GET&db=cchouk&id=I04779

The Lone Pine Ranch, by Maurice Graves Emery, 2003, IUniverse, New York, NY, p 4.

Thirteenth Census of the United States, Oregon, Lake County, Silver Lake

Find A Grave, memorial page for Pernecia Young Taylor, available online at: http://www.findagrave.com/cgibin/ fg.cgi?page= gr&GSln=Taylor&GSbyrel=all&GSdyrel=all&GSst=39&GScnty= 2223&GScntry=4&GSob=n&GRid=38300802&df=all&

Bad Men Do What Good Men Dream, by Robert I. Simon, 1996, American Psychiatric Press, Washington D.C., p 297

"Jury Acquits in Dunn Case," *Bend Bulletin,* October 18, 1917.

"Two More Stock Men Arrested," *Bend Bulletin,* March 7, 1918.

"Verdict Rendered Against D. Dunn," *Bend Bulletin,* April 18, 1918.

"Dunn Testifies on Own Behalf," *Bend Bulletin,* April 18, 1918.

"Second Guilty Verdict Found," *Bend Bulletin,* April 18, 1918.

"Kimzey Case Opens Today," *Bend Bulletin,* April 20, 1933.

"Harrison Tells of Journey Into Desert," *Bend Bulletin,* April 21, 1933.

"Kimzey Waives Extradition to Face Trial," *Bend Bulletin,* March 3, 1933.

"Charles Kimzey Held, Federal Man States," *Bend Bulletin,* March 10, 1933.

"Stolen Auto Recovered," *Oregonian,* September 5, 1923.

"Signs Found of Attack on Jitney Driver," *Bend Bulletin,* August 28, 1923.

"Trappers Shot; Bodies in Lake," *Oregonian,* April 24, 1924.

"Slain Trappers Shot to Pieces," *Oregonian,* April 25, 1924.

"Trail of Murderer Ends at Fur Store," *Oregonian,* April 25, 1924

"3 Slain Trappers Buried at Bend," *Oregonian,* April 26, 1924.

"Friends Pay Honor to Slain Trappers," *Oregonian,* April 27, 1924

"Kimzey Given Life Term in State Prison," *Bend Bulletin,* April 4, 1933.

"No Trace Found of 3 Bend Trappers," *Silver Lake Leader,* "April 24, 1924.

Editorial, *Deschutes Pine Echoes,* Brooks-Scanlon Lumber Company, Bend, OR, Vol. 5, No. 12, April 1924, p 56, 12.

"Captive Taken in Death Case Not Identified," *Bulletin,* January 22, 1925.

"The Little Lava Lake Murders," by Don Burgderfer, *Little Known Tales From Oregon History,* Vol. III, No. 61, *Cascades East Magazine,* Bend, OR, p 27-33.

Wilderness Tales and Trails, by Wayne Negus, Maverick, Bend, OR, 1990, p 63-67, 157-162.

"Howard Feared Attack During Trip, Declared," *Salt Lake Telegraph,* January 7, 1926.

Inmate record of Charles Kimzey #12582, Department of Corrections, OISC, Wilsonville, OR. Contains information about where Kimzey attended school and his father's occupation.

"Elk Lake Remembrances," by Carol Blackwell, *Little Known Tales from Oregon History,* No. 117, Cascades East Magazine, Winter 2003-04, p 56-61.

W. H. Ingersoll, manager of Salt Lake City office of the William J. Burns International Detective Agency, to Warden, State Penitentiary, Boise, Idaho. Letter dated April 23, 1926. The warden at this time was J. W. Wheeler. Convict Record of Charles Hyde Kimzey #2316, Idaho State Penitentiary. Idaho State Archives, Division of the Idaho State Historical Society, Boise, ID.

"Nationwide Search For Alleged Slayer Of Howard Planned," *Salt Lake Telegraph*, December 9, 1927.

"Howard Last Seen in Mohave Desert, Belief," *Salt Lake Telegraph*, January 12, 1926.

"Salt Lake City Office Manager W. H. Ingersoll Reports," Special Report, November 18, 1927, William J. Burns International Detective Agency, Salt Lake, UT. Convict Record of Charles Hyde Kimzey #2316, Idaho State Penitentiary. Idaho State Archives, Division of the Idaho State Historical Society, Boise, ID.

"Howard Hired Holmes Pair, Newest Story," *Salt Lake Telegram*, January 6, 1926.

"Sheriff Finds No Trace of Howard," *Salt Lake Telegraph*, January 20, 1926.

Find A Grave memorial page for William Roberts Howard, available online at: http://www.findagrave.com/cgibin/ fg.cgi?page=gr&GSln=Howard&GSfn=William&GSmn=Roberts&GSbyrel=all&GSdyrel=all&GScntry=4&GSob=n&GRid=175137&df=all&

J. H. Williams to Warden, Idaho State Penitentiary, March 12, 1933. Convict Record of Charles Hyde Kimzey #2316, Idaho State Penitentiary. Idaho State Archives, Division of the Idaho State Historical Society, Boise, ID.

John Duggan, Acting Chief of Police, Butte, Montana to Salt Lake County Sheriff's Department, January 24, 1933. Convict Record of Charles Hyde Kimzey #2316, Idaho State Penitentiary. Idaho State Archives, Division of the Idaho State Historical Society, Boise, ID.

J. J. Murphy, Chief of Police, Butte, Montana to warden, Idaho State Penitentiary, February 11, 1933. Convict Record of Charles Hyde Kimzey #2316, Idaho State Penitentiary. Idaho State Archives, Division of the Idaho State Historical Society, Boise, ID.

Special Report, C. E. Love, Salt Lake City Investigator, William J. Burns International Detective Agency, June 5, 1928, Salt Lake City, Utah. Convict Record of Charles Hyde Kimzey #2316, Idaho State Penitentiary. Idaho State Archives, Division of the Idaho State Historical Society, Boise, ID.

U.S. Department of the Interior, Bureau of Land Management, General Land Office Records. Homestead patent of James F.

Kimzey, Canyon County, Idaho. Township 5 north, Range 2 west, section 17, patented 1913. This homestead was located on the southeast end of Lake Lowell. Available online at: http://www. glorecords.blm.gov/ details/patent/default.aspx?accession =326394&docClass=SER&sid=hgldln45.ovz

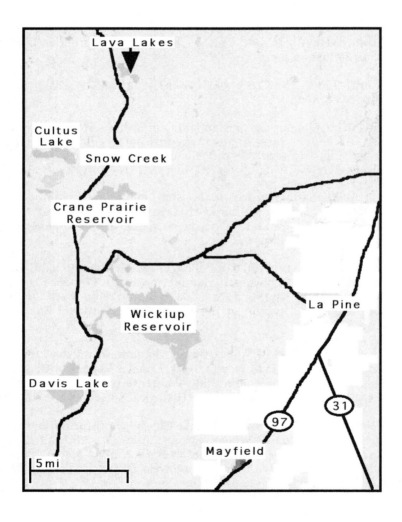

Chapter Eight

A Definite Materiality

A comparison of the criminal behaviors of Ray Jackson and Charles Kimzey can be helped along when we remember that Jackson was very organized in his handling of the Conn murder. By contrast, Kimzey can only be described as disorganized. The authorities, including the sheriff of Deschutes County, and the media, falsely imbued Kimzey with the qualities of a criminal mastermind to such a degree that they never realized that his more dominant partner was the reason for the brilliance reflected in the Lava Lakes murders..

Deschutes County Sheriff McCauley and District Attorney Boylan told the Oregon State Parole Board that they believed Kimzey acted as "a leader" when he worked with an accomplice. George Costello, an agent for the U.S. Department of Justice, said Kimzey was "one of the most dangerous criminals in the nation." And, when he was sentenced to prison that same year, Judge Duffy of Bend described him as "absolutely without moral responsibility." The Oregon State Parole Board reported, "Kimzey is a very intelligent man, much above the average criminal." Yet, when Kimzey's I. Q. was tested in the Oregon State Penitentiary in 1957, he only scored an 81, showing an intelligence that was no better than average.

Psychopaths do not make very good friends. That was the reason why, when the author set out to find the murderer of Creed Conn, she looked for someone who Conn had known for only a short time. Psychopaths have a broad criminal versatility and other behaviors that really rub people the wrong way. Mr. Ray Van Buren Jackson, for example, was known to have committed assault, robbery, forgery, petty theft, embezzlement, arson, murder, attempted murder, and poisoning. He was also a horse thief. And those were just the crimes that were documented. He was egocentric, selfish, demanding, sexually aggressive and callous, with no conscience or sense of fair play. So, although the average citizen would soon have had enough of Jackson's attitude and behavior, some other criminal could have formed an alliance with him, at least on a short term basis.

While Kimzey has often been pointed to as the man who killed the three trappers at Little Lava Lake in 1924, the fact that Kimzey had a partner in those murders has been mostly forgotten by history. Investigators found evidence at the scene that led them to believe that Kimzey had an accomplice, and Kimzey appeared at Portland with a partner a few days after the murders. That partner was never captured or identified.

> *The bloody trail which starts along the shore of isolated Big Lava lake in the foothills of the Cascades, where Dewey Morris, Ed Nichols (sic) and Roy Wilson, trappers, were murdered last January, ends here in Portland, at the store of the Shumacher (sic) Fur company, Third and Main streets.*
> *Oregonian, April 25, 1924*

If we go back to the year 1919, we find another likely connection between Charles Hyde Kimzey and Ray Van Buren Jackson, aside from their family ties. In 1919, a Lake County man, Archie A. Warner, married Neva Schroder. The wedding took place on January 1 at the home of Neva's father, Augustus B. "Gus" Schroder, in Silver Lake. During that time period, Warner was a friend and business partner of Reub Long's in a Silver Lake pool hall called The Pastime. Long's name may be recognized as the coauthor of the popular book, *The Oregon Desert*.

Later in his life, in April of 1933, when Kimzey was on trial for robbery and assault on William Harrison, he specifically named Archie Warner of Silver Lake as someone who could testify as to his true identity, who could recognize him on sight. Warner was born in Idaho and was the same age as Kimzey, so it is possible that the two men knew each other for many years. And, it seems likely that Kimzey knew Warner during the period from 1915 through 1923 when Kimzey was known to have worked around central Oregon. He told prison officials that he had worked as a sheep herder during that period, and Warner was a sheep rancher as well as a business owner.

Also present at the Warner wedding in 1919, and named as a witness in the marriage record, was Frank Dobkins, who was probably Warner's best man. Frank Dobkins was, of course, the longtime friend and ranching partner of Ray Van Buren Jackson. According to government land patent records, Jackson and Dobkins became acquainted in 1902. They were well-known as ranching partners by 1912, and through 1917, and remained friends until Jackson's death in 1938. All of that information taken together, means that Jackson and Kimzey were mutual friends of Archie Warner's during the same time period, and may have both been present at Warner's wedding. Furthermore, the 1920 census shows a man matching Kimzey's age and using the name "Lee Collins" living in Silver Lake, Oregon and working as a sheepman for Charles W. Pitcher.

Another friend of Kimzey's in central Oregon was a prominent rancher by the name of Ted Carson, who owned the Alvord Ranch in the vicinity of Andrews in Harney County. Kimzey named Carson as a character witness to the Oregon Parole Board during his incarceration, and described him as a "friend" in a 1943 list of people that he would like to correspond with. That information, from Kimzey himself, demonstrated that Kimzey and Jackson lived in the same county at one time.

Kimzey was definitely a diverse criminal in his own right, and gained considerable notoriety as one of Oregon's most wanted criminals when he became the key suspect in the shocking triple murder that occurred at the Lava Lakes west of Bend in January of 1924. That terrible crime, like the Conn murder, was never solved. The Deschutes County Sheriff's Department first realized two men were involved in the killings at Lava Lakes when they examined the crime scene. There was a large hat found inside the cabin that seemed out of place and that could not be identified as belonging to any of the victims. It was believed to have been left by one of the killers. Empty shells found at the scene showed that two or three guns were used in the crimes.

There was also the shear difficulty of one man taking the lives of three, one of them an ex-marine, who resided in a log cabin well-stocked with guns and ammunition. Surely Kimzey, who seems to have been a bit of a bungler, could not have acted alone and come out of a confrontation like that in one piece.

A wanted poster, created by Sheriff Bert Roberts on May 7, 1924, offered a $1500 reward for Charles Kimzey, alias Lee

Collins, and his unknown partner, or for any person arrested and convicted of the Lava Lakes murders of January 1924. The poster contained a description of the mysterious partner that was probably a composite taken from the memories of people at the fur shop and the policeman who had seen the two men in Portland a few days after the killings. "Unidentified man wore khaki suit, beaver hat, leather puttees," wrote Roberts. "Weight 150 pounds, sandy complexion. Armed with .32 Colt's automatic, with two chips out of lower left handle, underneath."

Presuming that the accomplice changed clothes at least once between January and May, the clothing description was of little use as the investigation began, with the exception of the beaver hat, which was believed to have been taken from the victims' cabin at the same time that the strange large hat had been left there. The sandy complexion might have been a helpful detail, if it weren't so open to interpretation. Some would take it to mean that the man had a light tan. Others might say his hair was graying or blondish. Or, that he was freckled. Perhaps the most useful bits of information were contained in the details about the gun.

The wanted poster said the man carried a .32 caliber Colt's automatic. But, what about the detail of the chipped handle? Even if that suspect carried the weapon on his hip when he talked to the men at the fur shop and the traffic cop in Portland, what were the chances that those witnesses, who knew nothing of the murders at the time, would have noticed two chips in the handle?

Indeed. That detail about "two chips" could have come from an entirely different source, from the coroner, as he examined the wounds of the victims, and the wounds of Dewey Morris in particular. If Sheriff Roberts was working off of the supposition that Morris was struck in the head with the butt end of a revolver, then he might have presumed that said weapon had two chips in the handle that would match two small marks found in more than one of the wounds on Dewey Morris' face and head. Roberts may have fallen into the trap of ignoring or reshaping the facts of a crime to match his theory about the gun, even though coroner Niswonger insisted at the time that Morris had been killed with a hammer of some sort. It must not have occurred to either man that the raised periods in the butt end of a

"U. S." marking hatchet could have been responsible for that wound pattern of two small marks.

One rather sketchy eyewitness account of the appearance of a mysterious stranger contained a detail that could point to Ray Jackson as Kimzey's partner. "About the time that the men were believed to have disappeared, a horseback rider visited La Pine, the nearest town to the Lava Lake camp," reported the *Oregonian* on April 24, 1924, one day after the bodies were found. "It was recalled that he asked for a likely trapping location. He was a stranger in the community and has not been seen since that time." Although many people owned cars by 1924, Ray Jackson does not seem to have been one of them, and the people around Wagontire who knew him said that he normally traveled on horseback.

The previous chapter described the connections between Jackson and Charley Kimzey. Jackson's family, including his brother, and the Kimseys, did not have very warm feelings toward Ray. Wiley A. Kimsey, an uncle of Charley's, played a major role in the auctioning off of Jackson's cattle at the end of 1902 to satisfy some of his bad debts.

Even if Kimzey and Jackson didn't have an awareness of one another prior to the period in question, Jackson and practically everyone else in the region became acutely aware of Kimzey's presence in central Oregon in the summer of 1923. That was when Jackson, who loved to read newspapers, read about Kimzey's robbing of Nickols and Logan and the auto theft. He already knew Kimzey, and the crime spree of his younger relative definitely created a media stir.

When Kimzey was finally apprehended in 1933, and brought to Oregon for questioning in connection with the Lava Lakes triple homicide, he was taken to Portland and put into a police lineup. A Portland traffic cop who had directed two men with a bag of furs to the Schumacher Fur Company on January 22, 1924 failed to identify Kimzey in 1933. And, the owners of the fur shop failed to identify Kimzey as one of the men who sold them a parcel of fox pelts and displayed the trapping permit of Ed Nickols. Could it have been that the face of Jackson, the talker, was more fixed in their minds because Kimzey played a passive role, remaining in the background during those transactions?

The annals of crime offer several examples of partnerships in which at least one of the pair is a psychopath. Most psychopaths cannot get along with other psychopaths because they are completely abrasive and intolerable, even to each other. Lying, self-centered control freaks can sometimes form partnerships when a dominant psychopath teams up with a more passive criminal who may or may not be a true psychopath himself. As long as the two have a shared or complimentary interest, the partnership can exist, at least temporarily.

"Generally, one member of the pair is a 'talker' who gets his or her way through charm, deceit, and manipulation, whereas the other is a 'doer' who prefers direct action, intimidation and force," wrote Robert D. Hare in his book, *Without Conscience, The Disturbing World of the Psychopaths Among Us*.

To his neighbors around Wagontire Mountain in east Oregon, Jackson was known as a "fast-talker," and their oral histories have preserved their impressions of him. In 1895, when Jackson was wanted on charges of forgery and horse theft, he secured teaching positions for himself and his young wife, and charmed a female school superintendent into helping him evade arrest. His braggadocio has also been documented, and during his short acquaintance with Creed Conn, he would introduce himself as "Professor Jackson," although he was not a teacher of higher education and had never taught anything above the eighth grade level. Despite his past crimes and prison record, Jackson was able to achieve political success with his election as school superintendent of Lake County. All that is known about Jackson's personality points to him as "the talker" in his supposed partnership with Kimzey.

Considering Kimzey's moderate intelligence, preference to work as a laborer, petty crimes, and clumsy handling of the truly disorganized Harrison robbery, he was hardly the "smooth" type, and plainly employed intimidation and force in his treatment of Harrison. Another example of his preferred role as "the doer" came from his deeds in Montana. "A short time before he was arrested, Kimzey, it is said, had some difficulties with sheepmen over wages and had 'beat up' on the son of his employer," reported the *Bulletin* in March of 1933. "When he was arrested,

Kimzey supposed it was on an assault charge growing out of the attack."

In another partnership, the packing job he had with Nickols, Kimzey obviously did not play a leadership role. His criminal past shows a man more comfortable with relying on assault and robbery, rather than wit and charm to get what he wanted. His past behavior, coupled with his being about 16 years younger than Jackson, make it seem likely that he was not the dominant partner.

In a 1940 hearing at the Oregon State Penitentiary, Gerald W. Mason of the parole board asked, "Where did you live in the interim of 10 years after you left the Idaho penitentiary?" To which Kimzey gave the roundabout answer, "Well, I was in Colorado part of the time and in northern Montana." An answer that did not admit or deny that he had also been in Oregon. In the same hearing he also denied having assaulted Harrison. But, in his final statement, Kimzey named Allen Willcoxon of Bend, Oregon as a character reference. "I am not a criminal. I never was a criminal. I worked hard all my life. There is two recommendations I could give you, people that is got pretty good influence," he said. Certainly, if he knew Willcoxon well, Kimzey must have lived in central Oregon.

The *Bulletin* at Bend continued to follow the investigation of the horrible Lava Lakes murders well into 1925. In January they noted that, "it was the theory of the Deschutes county officers that two men committed the triple murder. One lured the men from the cabin at Ed Logan's farm, and the other shot from ambush; but since two were shot with a shotgun and one died from a bullet wound, it was apparent that both of the men in the death plot had a hand in the actual killing."

Ed Logan began his fur farming enterprise at Little Lava Lake with Robert E. Lewellen, who was an experienced trapper, by February of 1919. In May of 1920, the *Bulletin* noted that the two men had begun raising marten and foxes. Bob Lewellen, a government trapper, came to the Cascade Lakes area from the Blue Mountains around 1914. He also worked off and on for the Brooks-Scanlon mill in Bend. Lewellen spent the winters of 1919 through 1922 trapping around the Cascade Lakes, with the Little Lava cabin as his headquarters.

In March of 1922, Lewellen was stricken with snow blindness that seems to have ended his partnership arrangement with Logan. By September of that year he was no longer living at Little Lava, and Cephas Gott became the new fur farming partner. That partnership also came to an untimely end when, that October, Gott was injured by the accidental discharge of a shotgun. It was at that time that Ed Nickols stepped into the role of fox care-taker, and was soon joined by Charles Kimzey. The arrangement with Nickols and Kimzey continued until the summer of 1923 when the two men had their 'falling out' over the question of Kimzey's pay.

Investigators believed that, even though Kimzey had stolen Nickols' hidden money and the Logans' fur coat and diamond ring in August of 1923 to satisfy a debt, he still held a grudge five months later. Maybe Kimzey used the details of his past troubles to gain Jackson's help and sympathy. Charley Kimzey's motive had a definite materiality about it, a promise of financial gain that Jackson would have found hard to resist. Kimzey's intention would have been to demand from Nickols any money that he felt was owed him, and also had designs on the fur foxes of Ed Logan, valued at about $1,800.

According to a report created for the Oregon State Parole Board, Kimzey collected his pay and left his job at the Moffat Tunnel in Colorado on January 7. One eye witness report of Kimzey's return to Oregon can be found in a document summa-rizing Kimzey's case history, created on April 18, 1940. "About January 12th, 1924, Kimzey was seen near Prineville, Oregon, by a trapper who knew him well. Kimzey was on horseback and said he was going to Cultus Lake trapping." It should be noted that Cultus Lake is about seven miles southwest of the Lava Lakes.

If the account out of Prineville was true, and Kimzey really was seen there on January 12, then he probably would have ar-rived in Bend on January 13. Allowing another day for Kimzey to ride his horse to the La Pine area and, assuming that he and his new partner traveled from La Pine to Little Lava Lake via Snow Creek, leaves Kimzey unaccounted for for about three days. That gave Kimzey ample time to learn from someone, like his friend, Grover Caldwell who had a home in Bend, that Nickols had com-pany out at the lake. During Kimzey's absence, Nickols told

Caldwell that he was afraid of Kimzey. In order to overcome three men, Kimzey would have realized that he needed the help of someone who would not be recognized. A partner who could approach the isolated cabin and do all of the talking, and he had at least three days to find such a man.

As we review the facts of this case, the importance of Allen Willcoxon is magnified. He is interesting because he was with the victims shortly before they were killed, and had a close association with Kimzey. But, what really made Willcoxon an important figure was not his activities and relationships around the time of the murders, but his ongoing friendship with law man, Claude McCauley.

It is possible that Deputy Sheriff McCauley never really considered Willcoxon a suspect because of their friendship, but Willcoxon's future influence over McCauley could be even more important to understanding one of the key aspects of the investigation. For many years to come, and after McCauley became Deschutes County Sheriff in 1928, he was committed to trying to solve the Lava Lakes murders. In an article for *Cascades East* magazine, writer Don Burgderfer wrote, "Sheriff McCauley brought Kimzey back from Montana, he had given hints to the media he knew who Kimzey's accomplice was. Nothing else was ever said, and that shadowy partner was never identified." McCauley was believed to have had some insight into the identity of the second suspect, Kimzey's partner, and that information probably came from Allen Willcoxon himself, and an encounter that he remembered from 1924.

That small detail in the case that is often overlooked, and appeared in a *Silver Lake Leader* article printed on April 24, the day after the bodies were found. The story had actually been picked up from a now extinct, early competitor of the *Bulletin,* a Bend paper called the *Central Oregon Press*. The original article had to have been written during the early phase of the investigation, some time between April 13 and April 24, and when it was still just a missing persons case. The story featured information provided by Allen Willcoxon. When Willcoxon told the sheriff's department that he had dinner with the three trappers on January 15, he also mentioned that he had "made arrangements for them to meet another party of trappers at Crane Prairie on

February 1." Willcoxon had obviously had contact with someone who was either in the area at the time, or was planning to be there. Could that have been another reference to the same shadowy character, the man on horseback, possibly Ray Jackson, who appeared near La Pine, looking for a trapping location? Were the two accounts one in the same, with Willcoxon as the source? Because of that information from Willcoxon, the crime scene was immediately expanded to include an area of about 12 miles to the south and Crane Prairie.

Sheriff Roberts definitely searched in that area, and even told the *Press* that he was investigating the possibility that the three missing men had attempted to cross the northeast arm of Crane Prairie Reservoir, to get to the Crane Prairie Campground, but had broken through the ice and died there. Robert's statements to the newspaper were very revealing in several ways, because they not only reframe the physical area of the investigation, they also provided insight into the character of Roberts as an investigator. We can see that, even when all three men were unaccounted for, even though Nickols did have a known criminal as an enemy, and even though there was blood evidence found at the victims' cabin, Roberts was not fully convinced of foul play. Was he having a hard time believing that all three men could have died all at once? Although the sheriff's heart was definitely in the right place, it was also rather amateurish of him to have revealed so much detail to the media so early in the investigation.

The *Oregonian* reported that a search of the 30 mile-long trap line of Roy Wilson and Dewey Morris was begun by deputy Clarence Adams around April 14. Morris and Wilson were known to have kept a food cache near the Crane Prairie Dam, and three cabins along the trap line were also searched.

During the course of their search, the sheriff's men came across something else that seemed suspicious. A report describing Kimzey's movements that January stated, "later a spot was found on Snow Creek about five miles from Lava Lake where a horse been (sic) tied to a tree during the winter for some time." It should be noted that Snow Creek was right on the way to Cultus Lake and in the same vicinity.

The Cascade Lakes west of Bend are notorious for being inaccessible in the winter, and in 1924, with fewer roads and rather primitive automobiles, the lakes were even harder to reach. A car would have been useless on those barely improved roads in deep snow. At the time, the only winter access route into Lava Lakes, used for the occasional delivery of supplies was, not coincidentally, from the south, from Crane Prairie and along Snow Creek.

How exactly had Roberts arrived at the idea that Wilson, Morris, and Nickols had broken through the ice of the reservoir and drowned? Did he come up with that all on his own? Did that thought come to him by letter, a letter that told him when and where to search, just as had happened in the Julius Wallende case? Or, did the idea come from Willcoxon, who got it from someone else who had made inquiries about trapping in the area, the man who appeared at La Pine? Did it come from the obsessive fantasy life of a predatory killer?

The area to the south of the Lava Lakes and around Crane Prairie figured prominently in the life of Ray Van Buren Jackson. It was where his ranching friends, the Mayfield family, had grazed their cattle since the late 1890s, and had Forest Service grazing permits from 1906 until at least 1945. In his book, *An Illustrated History of Early Northern Klamath County,* writer Edward Gray gave a detailed history of the Mayfield ranching enterprise, and of their seasonal cattle drives from another ranch north of Prineville on the Crooked River, along the Deschutes and past Lava Lakes, and on to Crane Prairie where they had a large spread of five miles of natural meadow. The Mayfields were also known to have wintered cattle at other points in Klamath County, like around Timothy Brown Spring, and Wild Billy Lake directly west of Paisley, and on Klamath Marsh. While Jackson was residing in Harney County during the last 20 years of his life, he and his cattle commonly spent about half of the year in Klamath County where feed was more abundant and the weather was less harsh. He would typically depart from Wagontire around October 1, and return around April 15.

The Mayfield family arrived in Clackamas County in 1867 via wagon train from Missouri, and the Jackson family arrived in the same place in the same manner from Missouri in 1877. The Jackson's lived with Mrs. Callie Jackson's family, the Blackburns, in a community known as Springwater, and the Mayfields settled in an area known as Cuttingville or Cutting precinct. Both communities were just outside of Highland, where the school for that part of Clackamas County was located. So, all of the Mayfield and Jackson children attended school at the same place. Michael S. "Mike," and William G. "Billy" Mayfield, who became stockmen in central Oregon, had a younger brother who was the same age as Ray Jackson, and whose name was, coincidentally, "Jackson." So, it seems very likely that Ray Jackson knew the Mayfields from the time that he was about eight years old.

The Highland School District was where Jackson received his first big conviction, in 1896, for forgery against his employer, the school system itself. More of the Mayfields, the family of Green W. Mayfield, had settled right in Highland, and the Mayfield brothers had a first cousin, Miss Tennessee Mayfield, who was a school teacher in the Highland District with Ray Jackson at the time of his scandalous forgeries.

It is possible that Jackson first become involved in ranching via the Mayfields, using summertime vaquero pay to supplement his school wages. The Mayfields first drove their cattle into Harney County in 1880. It should be remembered here that Jackson himself kept some cattle in Harney County as early as 1895, and registered a cattle brand there by 1902. Mike and Billy Mayfield both began working for the Double O ranch under the direction of Ike Foster, around 1881, when the outfit was known as "Foster and Riley," and Jackson was said to have been a book-keeper for the Double O in 1898.

About two years after the Lava Lakes murders, Jackson filed on a timber claim about 25 miles south of the Lava Lakes that adjoined the claims made by Mike and Billy Mayfield in 1904. Jackson told the government that he had established a residence on that claim in February of 1927, but he certainly would have been in the area before then It may have been the original inten- tion of Jackson to sell his claim to the Mayfields, who were al- ways looking to expand their holdings. According to Harney County folklore, Jackson and his friend, Frank Dobkins, were grazing their cattle in both Klamath and Harney counties at least as early as 1917. All of this historical detail makes it plain that both Ray Jackson and Charles Kimzey had an intimate knowl- edge of what winter was like in the Cascade Lakes region.

WANTED FOR MURDER
$1500 REWARD

$750 each for Charles Kimzey, alias Lee Collins, and his partner (unknown). The reward of $750 applies to any person arrested and convicted of the murder of three trappers at Lava lake, Deschutes County, Oregon, in January, 1924.

Charles Kimzey, ex-Idaho state penitentiary, No. 2316

DESCRIPTION

Height, 5 feet, 7 inches, weight 160 pounds, eyes blue; age, 38 years. Occupation, ranch hand, teamster, sheepherder, sheep shearer. Scars as follows: Scar on nose; scar on right cheek; scar on right wrist; scar on left shin. Dark spot back of left side. May be wearing heavy, sandy mustache.

Finger print classification {1 R 00 11; 1 R 00.

Kimzey talks rapidly, with teeth partly closed, and at the same time smiles, showing teeth. Is fast with a revolver, which is a .38 Colt's Special.

Photograph taken of Kimzey about 8 years ago. Face is now fuller, and hair much thinner on top than cut shows.

Kimzey and partner should be arrested on sight, and held incommunicado.

Brother officers, take no chances with these men, for they are desperate criminals, having killed three trappers at their cabin, without giving them a chance for their lives.

Unidentified man wore khaki suit, beaver hat, leather puttees. Weight 150 pounds, sandy complexion. Armed with .32 Colt's automatic, with two chips out of lower left handle, underneath.

Arrest and wire
S. E. ROBERTS, SHERIFF
Bend, Oregon

Bend, Oregon, May 7, 1924.

Photographic miniature of wanted poster for Charles Hyde Kimzey, that was printed when he became the chief suspect in a triple murder that occurred 25 miles southwest of Bend, Oregon in 1924 at Lava Lakes.

SOURCES:

The Sandy Knoll Murder, Legacy of the Sheepshooters, by Melany Tupper, 2010, Central Oregon Books, LLC, Christmas Valley, OR.

"Trappers Shot, Bodies in Lake," *Oregonian,* April 24, 1924.

Marriage Records, Volume Three, 1909-1920, compiled by Lana J. Morrison, 1995, Oregon Youth Conservation Corps, Lakeview, OR, p 61.

The Oregon Desert, by E. R. Jackman and R. A. Long, 1964, Caxton Printers, Caldwell, ID, p 251-253.

U. S. Department of the Interior, Bureau of Land Management, General Land Office Records, Timber and Stone patent of Frank Dobkins, T 33 S, R 14 E, Section 19, ORLAA 18152 patented October 5, 1908. National Archives and Records Administration, Washington, D. C. Jackson acted for Dobkins as a witness on his claim, and stated that they had known each other for about six years.

Fourteenth Census of the United States, Oregon, Lake County, Silver Lake.

"Slain Trappers Shot to Pieces," *Bend Bulletin,* April 25, 1924.

"3 Slain Trappers Buried at Bend," *Oregonian,* April 26, 1924.

"Wanted for Murder: Charles Kimzey, alias Lee Collins," image 2009.000.0068, Des Chutes Historical Museum, Bend, OR.

Harney County History Project, AV-Oral History #66, Ray Shaver & Russell Emery, August 16, 1991, Burns, OR p 5.

W. L. Jackson vs. R. V. Jackson, in the circuit court of the state of Oregon, for the county of Harney, case no. 666, filed October 20, 1902. Harney Circuit Court, 24th Judicial Dist., Harney County Courthouse, Burns, OR.

"Stolen Auto Recovered," *Oregonian,* September 5, 1923.

"Signs Found of Attack on Jitney Driver," *Central Oregon Press,* August 28, 1923.

"Kimzey Comes Here to Face Accusers," *Oregonian,* April 2, 1933.

"Kimzey Left In Portland When Sheriff Returns," *Bulletin,"* April 3, 1933.

"Fail to Identify Kimzey as Seller," *Bulletin*, April 3, 1933.

"Without Conscience, The Disturbing World The Psychopaths Among Us," by Robert D. Hare, Ph.D., 1993, The Guilford Press, New York, NY, p 65-68.

Harney County History Project, AV-Oral History #381, Shelby Petersen, August 4, 1991, Burns, OR, p 89.

Harney County History Project, AV-Oral History #380, Jess Gibson & Leora Houston Eggers, June 19, 1991, Burns, OR p 27.

Twelfth Census of the United States, Oregon, Clackamas County, Highland Precinct.

"Gave Him the Word," *Oregon Courier,* September 6, 1895.

"Slick Forger Arrested," *Oregon City Enterprise,* May 22, 1896.

"Circuit Court," *Oregon Courier,* June 12, 1896. Shows Jackson plead guilty to charge of forgery.

"Mysteriously Disappeared," *Roseburg Plaindealer,* March 17, 1904.

"Superintendent of Our Schools," *Lake County Examiner,* August 13, 1908.

"Kimzey is Back in Bend After 9 Year Search," *Bulletin,* March 17, 1933.

"Claude L. McCauley," *Bulletin,* October 23, 1973. Obituary.

"No Trace Found of 3 Bend Trappers," *Silver Lake Leader,* April 24, 1924. Article was picked up from the *The Central Oregon Press* at Bend.

"Trappers' Case Puzzles," *Oregonian,* April 17, 1924.

"Foul Play Fear Grows," *Oregonian,* April 16, 1924

"Elk Lake Remembrances," *Little Known Tales from Oregon History*, no. 117, by Carol Blackwell, p 56-59. Originally published in *Cascades East* magazine, winter 2003-2004.

"News from the Camps," *Deschutes Pine Echoes,* May 1924, editor Paul Hosmer, Brooks-Scanlon Lumber Co., Bend, OR, p12

"Trail of Murderer Ends at Fur Store," *Oregonian,* April 25, 1924.

U. S. Department of the Interior, Bureau of Land Management, General Land Office Records, Timber and Stone patent of Michael S. Mayfield, T 23 S, R 9 E, sections 26 and 35, ORLAA 051897, patented September 28, 1904. Available online at: http://www.glorecords.blm.gov/re sults/default.aspx? searchCriteria=type=patent|st=OR|cty=|ln=Mayfield|fn=Michae l|sp=true|sw=true|sadv=false. Michael's brothers Finis and Billy Mayfield patented claims in this same township in 1904.

Untitled, *Bulletin*, February 1, 1911, Short news items says Mayfields are wintering their cattle at "Brown Spring." Also known as Tim Brown Spring, in Klamath County, about 12 miles Northwest of Beatty.

U. S. Department of the Interior, Bureau of Land Management, General Land Office Records, Homestead patent of Ray B. Jackson, T 26 S, R 24 E, sections 8, 9, and 17, ORLAA 1066515, patented October 13, 1933. National Archives and Records Administration, Washington, D. C.

Ninth Census of the United States, Oregon, Clackamas County, Cutting Precinct.

"Martin Jackson," *Lebanon Express,* January 24, 1917. Obituary

Land Patent records of the Mayfield family in Clackamas County. U. S. Department of the Interior, Bureau of Land Management, General Land Office Records. Available online at: http://www. glorecords.blm.gov/results/default.aspx?searchCriteria=type=pa tent|st=OR|cty=005|ln=Mayfield|sp=true|sw=true|sadv=false. Father and uncles of Mike and Billy Mayfield took homesteads in 18741875
.

U. S. Department of the Interior, Bureau of Land Management, General Land Office Records, Homestead patent of Roy B. Jackson, T 23 S, R 9 E, Sections 25 and 26, ORLAA 1032174, patented November 18, 1929, National Archives and Records Administration, Washington, D. C. Ray Jackson used an alias in order to illegally obtain this homestead .

"Trapper is Injured at Lava Lake Camp," *Bulletin,* October 30, 1919.

"Bend Happenings From Day to Day, Thursday," *Bulletin,* May 27, 1920.

"20 Winters Spent in the Mountains," *Bulletin,* June 16, 1921.

"Bend Happenings From Day to Day, Tuesday," *Bulletin,* March 9, 1922.

"He Enjoys the Thrills of a Trapper's Life," by Fred Lockley, *American Magazine,* October, 1922, p 62-63.

"Shotgun Slips, Wounds Hunter," *Bulletin,* October 26, 1922.

An Illustrated History of Early Northern Klamath County, by Edward Gray, 1989, Maverick, Bend, OR, p 70, 76-83, 87, 170173, 254.

Historical Writeup of the Deschutes National Forest, 1950, by Gail C. Baker, unpublished manuscript, p 27-29.

"Pioneer Rancher Takes Own Life," *Harney County American,* February 4, 1938.

"Friends Pay Honor to Slain Trappers," *Oregonian,* April 27, 1924

"Charles Kimzey Held, Federal Man States," *Bulletin*, March 10, 1933. Agent George Costello of the U. S. Department of Justice is quoted as describing Kimzey as "one of the most dangerous criminals in the nation."

Bulletin, January 30, 1919, a brief news item stated "Grover Caldwell has moved his family from Paulina Creek to Bend where the children can attend school."

Deschutes, Crook and Jefferson Counties Directory, 1921, by Ralph Lane Polk, R.L.Polk & Co.Detroit, MI, p 45.

I have Lived in the Monster, by Robert K. Ressler and Tom Shachtman, 1977, St. Martin's Press, New York, p 109.

"Otis Self-administering Test of Mental Ability," by Arthur S. Otis, Ph.D., Charles Kimzey, inmate #12585, administered August 6, 1952. Inmate record of Charles Kimzey #12582, Department of Corrections, OISC, Wilsonville, OR. Kimzey scored 40, with an IQ score of 81. The test showed that he was reading at the 6th grade level.

"In Re: Charles Kimzey, Number 12585," a report to the Oregon State Parole Board for their meeting of April 18, 1940. Inmate record of Charles Kimzey #12582, Department of Corrections, OISC, Wilsonville, OR.

"Kimzey, Charles #12585, Hearing Transcript, April 18, 1940," Oregon State Parole Board, Inmate record of Charles Kimzey #12582, Department of Corrections, OISC, Wilsonville, OR.

Correspondent tracking form, Kimzey, Charles, no. 12585, 1943, Inmate record of Charles Kimzey #12582, Department of Corrections, OISC, Wilsonville, OR.

"Questionnaire of no. 12585, Kimzey, Charles," April 26, 1933. Inmate record of Charles Kimzey #12582, Department of Corrections, OISC, Wilsonville, OR.

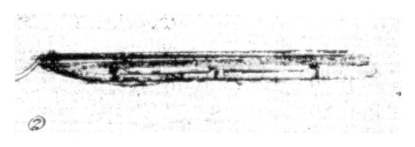

This small wooden tote sled, about the size of a child's sled, was found on the bank of Big Lava Lake, pointing to a hole in the ice and the spot where the bodies of the three victims were disposed. The victims owned two sleds, and the other was presumably used by the killers to make their getaway with a load of furs they had stolen from the cabin at Little Lava Lake.

Chapter Nine

Lava Lakes

When all that is known about Ray Van Buren Jackson and Charles Hyde Kimzey is put together in one base of knowledge, the possibility that Jackson was Kimzey's accomplice in the Lava Lakes triple murder cannot be ignored. Their family ties and mutual friends made it possible, and so did the fact that both lived in Lake and Harney counties at the same times. Remember Jackson's broad criminal versatility, including armed robbery, his love of money and material gain, and the fact that Jackson was always away from his Wagontire ranch from October through April. Then, there was the matching description of the partner as a glib and fast talking charmer who was hedonistic, neat and clean cut. If the Lava Lakes murders are approached with the supposition that Kimzey was one of the killers, then Ray Jackson is certainly worthy of consideration as his accomplice.

The 1924 investigation into the disappearance of three men at the Lava Lakes, about 25 miles southwest of Bend, was actually hatched in the worried mind of a mother. Sarah Wilson, mother of Roy Wilson, knew that something was wrong. She also knew how reliable her son was, and remembered that Roy said he would return home to Bend in February. She knew that Roy's real reason for being at the lake was to protect Ed Nickols from Charley Kimzey, the criminal, who was still at large. "Mrs. Wilson, who was severely shocked by the tragic death of her only son, has stated from the first that the three men had been murdered and would not listen to the consolation of her daughters and friends, who tried to persuade her the missing men were out on their trap line," was the version of the story told by the *Oregonian*. Sarah Wilson must have known that Ed Nickols was concerned about what might happen if Kimzey resurfaced, and that was the primary reason that he had asked Wilson and Morris to spend the winter with him.

"Reports are current that Kimzey had sworn to have revenge on the men at the lake for giving information to the authorities which nearly resulted in his capture in Boise," reported the *Oregonian* in the wake of the murders. "Kimzey still has a 14 year sentence waiting to be served in the Idaho penitentiary."

That article referred to the events of the previous summer, when Ed Nickols reported that Kimzey had robbed his cabin at Little Lava Lake, and probably also told the sheriff what he knew about Kimzey's past, that he was from Idaho, and where he might be found.

All of the folkloristic writing about the triple murder at Lava Lakes has romanticized the story by describing the victims as "trappers." But careful examination shows that trapping was only a recreational pastime for the three men. Morris and Wilson were both loggers by trade, and had worked together for about five years with Brooks-Scanlon Lumber Company. Indeed, the census of 1920 and the death certificates for both men gave their occupations as "logger." Nickols himself does not seem to have been much of a trapper either.

It was difficult to make a living solely from trapping in 1924, especially for novices. That was why Nickols also had the job caring for Logan's foxes, and why Kimzey and Nickols made moonshine to supplement their income. A somewhat comical photo, taken at the Little Lava cabin, tells the story that the trapping aspect of their stay was more for recreation than anything else, and may have been taken by Hervey D. Innis, Roy Wilson's brother-in-law, when he delivered the two young men to Little Lava Lake in October of 1923.

The cabin where Ed Nickols, Roy Wilson, and Dewey Morris stayed during that winter no longer exists, and the exact location of it is not known. But, the approximate location of it can be extrapolated from old newspaper articles, maps, and photographs. One of the articles published in the wake of the crimes described the location as one half mile from the main boat launching area at Big Lava Lake. The shadows cast behind the trapper's cabin and trees in old photographs show that the cabin faced south, more or less. And, since it was located at the edge of Little Lava Lake, that would mean that the cabin was probably somewhere on the northern shore.

For reasons of convenience, it would have made the most sense to place the cabin on the west side of the lake, for easy access to fishing opportunities at Big Lava Lake, and entry via the main trail into the area. That final consideration was probably the most important one, because of the difficulty of getting supplies and feed for the foxes to the cabin site in the winter. If the cabin had been on the south side of the outlet of Little Lava Lake, the channel would have cut off access to the main trail.

Combining all of those ideas narrows the probable location of the trappers' cabin down to the northwest corner of Little Lava Lake and, on the north side of the outlet of that lake where it forms the source of the Deschutes River. That spot is the current site of Little Lava Lake Campground, and the development of that area helps to explain why no trace of the cabin remains. On a fine summer day, the spot where the bodies were found can be reached by an easy half mile walk from the campground at Little Lava in just under 20 minutes.

The cabin itself was probably one of those built by Logan's former partner, trapper Robert A. Lewellen, around 1918. A photo of Bob Lewellen, published in *American Magazine* in 1922, shows him standing in front of the identical cabin where the triple murder took place.

Victims (from left) Dewey Morris, Roy Wilson, and Ed Nickols clowning around at the cabin. Note the the differences between this sled, probably stolen by the killers, and the bloodstained one on page 172 that was left at the body disposal site.

The last time that Sarah Wilson saw her son alive was over the Christmas holiday, when he and Ed Nickols traveled out from the lake to Bend for a visit. At that time, Roy told his mother that he would be home in February. No detail remains of how Dewey Morris spent the holidays, but it seems likely that he would have visited one or more of his brothers, who still lived in Deschutes County.

> *I spent three winters in this immediate area and at times was almost overcome by the knowledge that three men had been brutally murdered by a fiendish monster.*
>
> *Wayne Negus*

The investigation began as a missing persons case, and because Willcoxon was the last one to have definite knowledge of the whereabouts of the three men, the coroner's jury concluded that the date of death was "about the 15th day of January, 1924."

By April 13 the weather had started to warm a little and the roads had cleared enough that Owen Morris, Dewey's brother, and Hervey Innis gave in to the supposition that something must be wrong. The two men drove out to the nearest access point on Snow Creek Road, seven miles to the south of Little Lava, and snowshoed the rest of the way. In 1924 the popular loop drive of the Cascade Lakes Highway did not exist. The snow was still four feet deep in places when they arrived. They found the cabin deserted, with extra clothing and abundant provisions still there. Although they arrived in the middle of April, the calendar still showed the January page.

"Innis and Morris at the cabin Sunday, found every indication that the men had not been there for about two months. Their last meal judging from the dishes left on the table, was breakfast, and molded cooking utensils showed that food had been left simmering on the stove," reported the *Central Oregon Press*. "Rifles, traps, and heavy clothing were found in the cabin. No signs of preparation for a trip were evident." According to the *Oregonian*, "The place was not in orderly condition in which the trappers had always kept it.... Refuse had been thrown on the floor, magazines and papers scattered about, and the skin racks and dryers were in a neglected condition." Despite the mess, Innis said that he saw no indication of violence inside the cabin.

The valuable foxes were all missing from their pens, located at a spot only described as "nearby." Also missing were all of the furs that the men had harvested from their trap lines over the early part of the winter. Owen Morris and Innis knew that food had been delivered for the foxes on about January 13, but only two days' rations of it had been consumed, and the last ration was still in the feed pans, indicating that the theft occurred shortly after the foxes were last fed.

Innis and Morris noted that the trappers' boots and snow-shoes found about the cabin were clean, and from that they gathered that the men had cleaned their footwear in the evening, then disappeared the next morning, before those items were used. Their things seemed to have been prepared and left in readiness for the next day's excursion over the trap line.

They noticed a large blood stain in the snow at a point 30 feet west of the trappers' cabin. In another area, described only vaguely as "in front of the cabin," were five shotgun shells and three pistol shells. What appeared to be skull fragments were found about 10 feet east of the cabin. None of the evidence was really crystal clear, however, because a light blanket of snow covered up the blood stains, shells, and footprints.

The only other trace of the missing men was one of their wooden tote sleds, about six feet long and similar to a child's sled, that could be pulled by hand. Hervey Innis and Owen Morris found it by following a distinct set of tracks from the cabin all the way to Big Lava Lake, about a half mile away. It sat on the shore at the edge of the ice, and was stained with blood.

Meanwhile, Deschutes County Sheriff Bert Roberts launched his own investigation on the 15th of April, and Deputy Sheriff Clarence A. Adams of Redmond was assigned to the case. Adams was the best man for the job because he had previously been the district game warden and was very familiar with the area around the lakes, knew where cabins were located, and even knew the general layout of the trap lines of the missing men. His first assignment was to follow the trap lines and to try to determine if the foxes had truly been stolen, or if they had escaped from their pens.

The sheriff also contacted Herbert Lansing Plumb, Supervisor of the Deschutes National Forest, for assistance, and the Forest Service began contacting all of the ranger stations and fish hatcheries, and everyone else in the general vicinity of the Cascade Lakes. It was probably through Plum's phone canvassing that the last man to see the three men, Allen Willcoxon, was located. When Roberts interviewed Allen Willcoxon, he told the sheriff that there was nothing out of order at the cabin at that time of his visit, and that the trappers had collected about three thousand dollars in furs over the early winter.

On the 15th, Donald and Ben Morris, Dewey's other brothers, and the fox owner, Ed Logan, set out for the lakes from Bend because they were even more concerned now, since Innis and brother Owen had not returned. Sheriff Roberts decided to head off in the direction of Crane Prairie, and searched that lake with a motor boat. The sheriff theorized that the missing men had accepted Willcoxon's invitation to meet those other trappers.

The Brooks-Scanlon Lumber Company newsletter in Bend, *Deschutes Pine Echoes,* seems to have contained the first published account about the missing men in a short article, probably written by Editor Paul Hosmer, on April 15. "Dewey Morris, who used to run the jammer at Camp 2 for a number of years, has mysteriously disappeared from his trapping camp at Lava Lake, and a crew of searchers have been in the woods for several days trying to discover some trace of the trappers. That search party found things in their cabin in such a state that the conclusion is they had left the lake in a hurry, but nothing was missing except their furs. Seven pairs of webs, three or four pairs of skis, all their guns except one revolver, and their entire camping outfits were still in the cabin and it is thought that they may have all perished. At this writing nothing definite has been established. Owen Morris, who is running the Camp 2 jammer, has left to help in the search for his brother."

Deputy Adams returned briefly to Bend on the 16th to pick up supplies and to make a short report to the sheriff. He brought with him a sample of blood from the trappers' sled that the sheriff sent off for an 'analysis' that consisted of someone viewing it under a microscope, probably a local physician. The carcasses of Ed Logan's five foxes seem to have been located during that second search effort, minus the pelts, in the brush near their pens. On April 18, Sheriff Roberts received the results from the blood test that was negative for human blood. Despite that finding, Roberts suspected that the bodies of the three missing men would be found in Big Lava Lake, and decided to try sending a second sample off to the University of Oregon Medical School. By that time, Adams and his party had completed their search of the first of the two trap lines, without result, other than the conclusion that the traps had not been tended for quite some time.

The sheriff and his men got their first decent clue in the case on April 19 when they learned that four of the missing fox pelts had been purchased by the Schumacher Fur Company, at the intersection of Third and Main, in Portland. The *Oregonian* had begun covering the story of the three missing men and the stolen foxes on April 16, and Carl Schumacher, being in the fur business, was naturally interested in the story. Then, Schumacher's store was visited by Edward H. Clark, a deputy game warden who noticed four fox pelts that seemed out of place and asked Schumacher where they had come from. Clark had apparently also heard of the theft of the valuable pelts near Bend, and the missing trappers. "I told him that I got them from a trapper from Bend," Schumacher told the *Oregonian*. "We began comparing notes and in my purchase book I found the entry on January 22 that showed that the furs were sold by a man purporting to be Ed Nichols (sic)."

When Schumacher contacted the police department at Portland, news of the sale of the stolen furs reached the ears of a traffic cop by the name of Walter C. Bender, who recalled that he had chatted with a couple of trappers back in January. "W. C. Bender, police officer, said he talked on a street corner with two men who carried furs and asked directions to fur dealers' establishments."

Bender had been on duty and stated that the two men first stopped at a fountain at Third and Morrison, took a drink, and then walked out to his semaphore. Bender remembered that the men were neatly dressed, but looked like men who had "lived out in the open." He also remembered that he had chatted with the men about hunting and trapping, understood that they were just in from the mountains west of Bend, and that neither of them appeared nervous or in a hurry.

The witnesses were able to provide partial descriptions, and were shown a photograph of Ed Nickols. Both Bender and Schumacher stated that Nickols was definitely not one of men that they had met. The Portland end of the case was turned over to the Multnomah County Sheriff's Department, under Thomas M. Hurlburt who, incidentally, does not seem to have been related to the Hurlburts of Harney County. "The trail is an old one and it is cold," said Multnomah Deputy Christopherson to the *Oregonian*. "The fact that the murders were committed about January 15 and that the furs were sold here a week later would indicate that the man who sold the furs and who exhibited Nichols' (sic) trapper's license is the man responsible for the triple killing."

On the same day that Schumacher contacted the police, and despite the observation that the ice was beginning to melt, Ed Logan decided to venture out onto the frozen surface of Big Lava Lake, following the trace of the sled's runners. About 100 yards from shore, Logan found a hole, that had not been broken, but had been deliberately chopped in the ice with some instrument, like a hatchet. There was blood around the hole, and Logan noted the diameter of it was about right to shove a body through. He called out to Deputy Adams, Owen Morris, and Innis, who were watching from shore, and Adams came out onto the ice to have a look. At the edge of the hole, stuck in the blood, Adams found a single hair that appeared to be human. It was light brown in color and rather fine. It now became pretty plain that one or all of the missing men had been killed and then shoved through that hole in the ice, and the difficulty of recovering the bodies was discussed. Because of his intimate knowledge of the seasons around the Cascade Lakes, Logan told Adams that he believed the ice would start to break up and go out of the lake in about four days, so the men decided to wait it out.

The next day, April 20, Sheriff Roberts received a tip from an unnamed person that the fifth fox pelt, previously unaccounted for, had turned up in Klamath Falls. deputies Adams and Stokoe went to investigate on April 21, leaving Logan and Innis at Big

Lava Lake. On April 21 the search of the second trap line was begun, probably by Ben and Donald Morris. On Tuesday the 22nd, the party returned from their trap line search with no news. They found remains of twelve marten, four wild foxes, and a skunk in the traps, that had obviously not been tended for quite some time. And, Adams and Stokoe came back to Bend with the word that the trail to Klamath Falls had been a false one.

The three bodies were "sighted" some distance from the shore of Big Lava Lake, at the present-day location of the main boat ramp, at 5:30 p. m. on April 23 by Deputy Adams and Hervey Innis, who had just spent another day searching one of the trap lines. They walked over from Little Lava to catch some fish and to check the lake surface again when they saw three dark objects floating close together off shore. Adams and Innis got into a small boat and set about the awful task of trying to identify the bodies. Ed Nickols and Roy Wilson were found floating face downward, in the way that human bodies typically float in water, but Dewey Morris was found floating on his back. After making a quick identification, they put ropes around the bodies to keep them fromdrifting away and towed them to within 16 feet of shore. Deputy Adams went off to Bend to report what had been found, and Logan and Innis stayed behind to make sure the bodies were not tampered with.

Sheriff Bert Roberts told the newspapers what he had learned in the first days of the investigation. That some unsubstantiated rumors were circulating that the three missing men had been seen around the lakes or in Bend since January, and that he was checking into that mysterious horseman who had appeared at La Pine. Roberts had also received a report of a 'Kimzey sighting,' with the information that Kimzey had spoken to "a trapper who knew him well," around January 12 near Prineville. Kimzey told that man that he was going to Cultus Lake. The lake referred to lies at the end of the same road that was used to access the Lava Lakes, known today as Road 40, that crosses Snow Creek about seven miles south of the victims' cabin.

Both the *Oregonian* and the *Bulletin* reported the discovery of the bodies and both articles were based on information provided by Deputy Adams, who arrived at Bend around 10:30 p.m. Adam's handled the bodies first, and given his duty to report findings with accuracy, his observations should be taken literally. However, it is not known exactly how the information in the articles was obtained. Adams was paraphrased, although not quoted. And, there were some discrepancies between the two versions, so they seem to have not been based on an official, written report.

In the *Oregonian* version of Adams' story, "two of the bodies were coatless, two of the men had their hats on, and Nichols' (sic) glasses still were in place. The third hat was found in the ice a short distance from where the bodies were sighted."

The *Bulletin* version of Adams' account was that "a cap and a hat floated nearby" and, "Nichols (sic), the oldest of the three, still had his glasses on." Those details about who was wearing what are useful information for anyone trying to piece together the chain of events on the day of the murders. It is interesting to note that Coroner Niswonger, when he examined the bodies the following day, said that Nickols' "reading spectacles were on his body when it was taken from the lake."

Gravestone of victim Dewey C. Morris at Greenwood Cemetery, just south of Pilot Butte in Bend, Oregon. Morris was a Brooks-Scanlon logger and the youngest of the three victims.

The *Oregonian* article stated a mistaken opinion of Adams,' that "each of the victims had been shot in the back of the head." And, that observation in itself tells a story about the limited extent to which Adams examined the bodies. Adams also reported that he believed the men had been shot from ambush by a high-powered rifle, suggesting that he had seen at least two severe gunshot wounds. He and Innis would have seen the horrible state of Dewey Morris' face, because he was found floating face up, and was probably unrecognizable. At any rate, Adams did not examine Morris closely enough to understand the nature of his injuries. The bodies of Nickols and Wilson were probably turned over briefly in an effort to identify them. Nickols would have been barely recognizable because of the shotgun blast to his face, and if Adams only saw part of the injury, it might have been mistaken for a shot from behind that left considerable damage as it exited. Innis would have recognized Wilson's face when his body was turned over, and would have seen the bullet hole behind his ear. Those were very bad things to see, to say the least, and both Adams and Innis must have been very shaken by the experience.

On April 24, Sheriff Roberts named Charles Kimzey as a suspect in the murders. Perhaps feeling the strain of the investigation of the horrific crime, Roberts told the *Oregonian* that he believed the killers had lived in the cabin at Little Lava for a time after they had committed the murders. Roberts already knew from questioning Willcoxon that the victims were seen alive on the 15th, and had the report that Schumacher gave to the police, that the killers reached Portland by the 21st of January. That time line gave the killers only six days to make the rather arduous trip out of the mountains and half way across the state, and eliminated the possibility that they had lingered around the crime scene. Looking back on the investigation now, it seems remarkable that the sheriff did not conclude that the cabin, which was also the scene of a robbery, was in disarray because it had been searched by the killers.

On the 24th, the day that the bodies were pulled from the water, Multnomah County Deputy Sheriff Roy Kendall met Officer Bender at Portland and showed him a photo of Kimzey. Bender said that he recognized Kimzey as one of the men who had approached him back in January. Deschutes County Coroner C. P.

Niswonger went to the recovery scene to conduct an initial examination, but county doctor Ray W. Hendershott seems to have remained in Bend. That evening, Niswonger returned to Bend with the bodies and told reporters that a shotgun, revolver, and hammer were the murder weapons, and that the victims' clothing was in good condition, other than showing the effects of having been in the water for over three months.

Photographs were taken at the scene by Paul Hosmer, Editor of *Pine Echoes,* as Niswonger examined the bodies. A few of those photos survived and eventually made their way into the collection of the Des Chutes Historical Museum in Bend, probably via Phil Brogan of the *Bulletin,* and through the hands of another journalist, Mary Fraser. That collection includes a group photo of a bunch of men gathered around the recovery site, looking on as Dewey Morris was wrapped in a body bag; another photo of the three bodies floating near shore; a picture of Niswonger examining Roy Wilson's shoulder wound; and a close-up of Wilson's face and shoulder.

When we compare the injuries of the three Lava Lakes victims, the injuries of Dewey Morris far exceeded those of Ed Nickols or Roy Wilson in both number and severity. Someone put considerable effort into killing Morris, whereas the other two met death at the pull of a trigger. "His head practically had been beaten to a pulp with a hammer," wrote a reporter for the *Oregonian.*

It is clear that multiple blows were dealt to Morris, far beyond what was necessary to kill him, in what is commonly referred to as "overkill." Why did that happen? What made Morris different? Was it because his size and youth made him seem threatening to the killer? Could there have been some motive or malice behind it? Or, was Morris' killer a malicious psychopath with poor impulse control who simply 'lost it' when the attack began? Morris died during that attack, and blunt force trauma to the head was given as his official cause of death.

Dewey was the 24 year-old son of John A. and Hattie Morris, and the youngest of four boys. He had told his mother that he would see her again at Easter. According to family folklore, when he did not arrive home, his mother became concerned and sent his oldest brother, Owen, to go to the lake with family friend,

Hervey D. Innis, to search for Dewey and the others. Owen Morris and Innis did, in fact, arrive at the trappers' cabin on April 13. But, 1924 was a leap year, so Easter came late, falling on April 20th, so that family tale cannot be true. Also, Morris' mother lived in Portland at the time, so it seems much more likely that Innis and Owen Morris actually embarked on their search at the urging of Mrs. Wilson, who had stated that she believed Roy had met with harm when he failed to return home in February, as promised.

Dewey Morris was born in Iowa on February 12, 1899. His sister, Janeva B., was the wife of Charles Carroll, a well-known real estate developer of Bend. Two brothers, Ben of Odell Lake, and Owen, were also loggers for Brooks-Scanlon. Brother Donald R. Morris had a ranch near Bend. Dewey had a thirteen year-old sister, Vera, who was living with their mother in Portland at the time of the murders.

Hattie M. Wood married John A. Morris in 1888 and the couple lived in South Dakota until about 1895. John's sister, Anna A. "Effie" Morris, who was born in New York in 1851, married Thomas R. Negus, who lived in the Dakotas from at least 1880 through 1929. The marriage of Anna Morris to Thomas Negus explains the relationship of writer and trapper, Wayne Negus, to Dewey Morris, who referred to Dewey as a "cousin," and Dewey's mother, Hattie, as "aunt."

In 1900, the Morris family was living on a farm near Little Sioux, in Woodbury County, Iowa. Hattie had lost two children by that time, and the remaining five lived at home, including baby Dewey, who was 4 months old when the census was taken. They lived next door to John Henry and Elizabeth A. Wood, Hattie's parents,.

The family arrived in central Oregon about 1903, and lived in the Lytle development north of Bend. Dewey's father, John A. Morris, invested in a freight team and went to work hauling freight from the rail head at Shaniko to Bend. Hattie's parents seem to have arrived in Bend about the same time, and lived near the Morrises in the Lytle neighborhood. The youngest child, Vera, was born in Bend on August 3, 1906. The Morris children all attended public school in Bend, and John Morris passed away around 1915.

The 1920 census found Dewey Morris living in southern Deschutes County, where he boarded at the house of Max Berger, and gave his occupation as "foreman in a logging camp." The rest of the census page was populated with many other laborers and teamsters who were residents of Brooks-Scanlon's Camp Two.

The grief-stricken, surviving family members of victims of violent crime have the unfortunate habit of lapsing into sentimentality in the wake of their tragedy. Overwhelmed as they are with feelings of remorse and love for those that they have lost, their statements do nothing to forward the purposes of a serious and careful investigation. For example, during the inquest in the Lava Lakes case, Hervey D. Innis testified that, as far as he knew, none of the trappers had any enemies.

One little known detail about the short life of young Dewey Morris is that he was tried for rape less than nine months before the Lava Lakes murders. In November of 1922, Dewey Morris had allegedly attacked a young widow from Sisters by the name of Mary Pednault. The trial took place on April 11, 1923. "Sordid testimony marked the entire case," reported the *Bulletin*. The prosecution presented their material to the jury in under 15 minutes, and five character witnesses appeared for Dewey Morris, who was not required to take the stand. The attack, according to the prosecution, had taken place in Morris' automobile, and although very few details of the alleged assault survive, but if it happened today, it might be characterized as 'date rape.' The jury deliberated for only seven minutes, and found Morris not guilty of the crime.

The trial was the subject of crude jokes and foul humor all over the county, and must have been a source of great pain and consternation for Mary Pednault's family. Even Morris' employer, the Brooks-Scanlon company, dealt with the subject in a biased and unsympathetic manner. "The camps were greatly interested in the Dewey Morris case in circuit court last week," wrote Paul Hosmer in *Pine Echoes*, "as Dewey is an old hand around all the camps and well known. Dewey was arrested and charged with a statutory crime, but when the case finally reached a jury it only took them seven minutes to bring in a verdict of not guilty." Perhaps Hosmer would have dealt with the matter in a more serious and unbiased way if he had known that, one year later, he would be writing about the brutal murder of the young logger. It is not known exactly why Morris chose to spend the winter at that isolated cabin, but he may have welcomed the opportunity to get away from some of the gossip and unwanted attention that came after the trial.

Mary Pednault was about five years older than Morris, and was the youngest child of the prominent Peter J. Leithauser family of Sisters. Her real name was Gertrude, but she preferred to be called by her middle name, "Mary."

It appears from the photographs taken at the recovery scene that Coroner Niswonger removed the body of Dewey Morris from the lake first. An *Oregonian* article also offered the detail that "Morris, who was a man of powerful physique, and who had suffered only an arm wound from the shotgun, was believed to have fled east after his companions fell. Fragments of his head were found 10 feet east of the cabin."

The death certificates were comprised of three basic sections. At the top was the most basic information, such as the name and address of the deceased, certificate number, and place of death. The left side of the form, "personal and statistical particulars," contained sex, race, marital status, age, date of birth, and occupation of the deceased, as well as the names and birthplaces of the parents of the deceased. At the bottom was a space for the name of the person who supplied the information, usually a family member, and the signature of the person who filed the certificate with the county and the date filed.

The right side of the form, headed "coroner's certificate of death" held the date of death, cause of death and contributory causes, and the method used to determine the cause of death, by inquest, autopsy, or inquiry. On the right was also the signature of the examining physician, the place and date of burial, and the name of the undertaker.

Morris' certificate was very badly botched, and why neither the county coroner or the county doctor considered it objectionable is not known. There was no birth date given, other than the year, 1900, although his brother, Owen was present. The left side, personal information about Dewey Morris, was typewritten, but contained three typographical errors, with his sex given as "Mail," and birthplace given as "South Dakato."

County doctor Hendershott failed to mention the arm wound at all when he filled out the right side of the form, although the handwriting was plainly his. Worst of all, Hendershott recorded the cause of death as "gunshot wound by unknown person. Homicide," when Morris had clearly died of blunt force trauma to the head. The certificate stated that gunshot as the cause of death was determined by an inquest, when the true inquest finding was that Morris "was killed by being hit on the head with some blunt instrument."

Additionally, when Coroner Niswonger brought the bodies to Bend on the evening of the 24th, he told reporters that Morris "had been shot with a shotgun, the charge entering his left forearm above the elbow" and "his head practically had been beaten to a pulp with a hammer." The first observation was a bit confusing, because the forearm of the human body is not located above the elbow, but below it. So all we can really say for certain is that the blast struck somewhere near the middle of Morris' arm.

As County Physician, Hendershott was required to examine the bodies himself, and he testified at the inquest that Morris had been killed by a blow from a blunt instrument. It might be safe to assume that both the county doctor and coroner were so emotionally disturbed by what they saw that they found it difficult to perform even their most basic duties. Bend was just a sleepy little town in 1924, barely over 20 years old, and the gruesome triple murder was probably the worst thing that either of those officials had ever dealt with.

Edward D. Nickols was born in Ohio on June 12, 1870, and was the oldest of the eight children of Thomas and Rachel A. Nickols, who were also Ohio natives. The family farm was located near Marion, in Morgan County.

Nickols was married in 1895 to a Canadian woman named Elizabeth or "Liza" Ann Young, and in 1896 their first daughter, Anna Belle, was born at Lake City, Michigan. After leaving Michigan around 1899, the family lived in Harlem, Montana, in Chouteau County, for a few years, and their second daughter, Jannetta, was born there in 1904. Ed worked as a blacksmith in Harlem with a man named Ellis, and lodged above the saloon of Gerald Ringwald.

Gravestone of Edward D. Nickols, who invited two younger men to spend the winter with him at an isolated cabin at Little Lava Lake in 1924. Nickols was worried that his former partner, Charles Kimzey, might return and cause trouble.

The 1910 census found Nickols and family in Whatcom County, Washington, in the town of Deming, where Ed worked as a donkey engineer for a logging company. That same year, Roy Wilson's sister, Leoella, who liked to be called by her middle name of "Margaret" also lived in Deming with her husband Dan McLennan, and it seems that Nickols became friendly with the Wilson family during that period. At the time of the Lava Lakes murders, Nickols' sister, Estella A. Marquette, and brother, Cliff, still lived near Bellingham, Washington.

Ed Nickols came to north Lake County, Oregon in 1913 from Washington, and filed on a homestead on April 16. In October of that year, he established residence on his claim. That "residence" consisted of a 12' x 16' box house, outhouse, a well that was 24 feet deep, and fence posts on the corners of his 320 acres. His younger brother, Guilford J. Nickols, can be found in the Silver Lake census for 1910. Ed Nickols proved up on his homestead claim in township 26 south, range 19 east, section 32 on November 14, 1916, and his younger brother, Guilford J. Nickols, proved up on a claim, that adjoined Ed's to the south, in 1914. Both claims were located about five miles east of Christmas Lake. "Ed Nichols (sic) and Roy Wilson were known to many in Silver Lake," reported the *Silver Lake Leader* in the wake of the murders, "both having resided here ten or twelve years ago."

Nickols' marriage seems to have ended about the same time that he arrived in Lake County in 1913. Perhaps Liza decided that the windblown and gritty life of the "Great Sandy Desert" was not right for her. In any case, she divorced Nickols and married an older man by the name of Sylvester Burns from Bellingham, and Ed Nickols never remarried. In 1920, Nickols lived alone in Bend, Oregon at the Bartlett Hotel on Hastings Street, between Franklin and Hill. He seems to have quit working for the big mills by that time, and gave his occupation as "general laborer" when the census was taken. His brother, Guilford, also lived in Bend, next door to Roy Wilson's mother, Sarah, and worked as a laborer for one of the lumber mills.

At the time of his death Nickols was 53, and his daughter, Jannetta, was living in Bellingham, in Whatcom County, Washington, and Anna Belle was married to Jerome E. Ward, a teamster for Brooks-Scanlon at Camp Four. Guilford later went back to live in Whatcom County, and was buried there at Bellingham when he died in 1970.

The close ties between the three victims are made obvious by their backgrounds. The author found several suggestions that the Wilson and Nickols families may have been more than just good friends, and may have been remotely related by blood, but was unable to definitely prove that connection. For example, both Roy Wilson and Ed Nickols had a sister with the first name "Leoella." That name was very rare, and a variant of the slightly more common name of "Leonella," with an "n." Uncommon names such as that are often handed down through the generations of a family. Also, during the time around 1900 when Nickols lived in Harlem, Montana, he lodged with a man named Frank Wilson, although no definite connection was discovered between that man and Roy Wilson's family. Ed Nickols had married a Canadian, and so had Wilson's sister, Leoella, who married Dan McLennan.

From photos taken at the second crime scene, the 'dump site' at Big Lava Lake, it appears that Nickols' body was the second pulled from the water. When Niswonger returned to Bend that evening, he told a reporter for the *Oregonian,* "Practically the whole of Edward Nichols' (sic) jaw had been carried away by a shotgun charge, part of which entered his neck. A .38-caliber revolver bullet had wounded him in the throat." That article also contained the information that "Nichols (sic) owned two pairs of spectacles, one of which he wore in the house, and the other outside. His reading spectacles were on his body when it was taken from the lake. Nichols' (sic) watch, found in his pocket, had stopped at 9:10 o'clock."

It is worth noting that the slug found in Nickols' neck must have later been determined to be a slug of heavy game shot, because after the autopsy and during the inquest, no mention was made of a pistol bullet, and there was no such wound on Nickols' death certificate either. At the inquest, Dr. Hendershott told the jury that Nickols had been killed by "a shotgun wound of the right lower jaw and breast."

Nickol's daughter, Anna Ward, provided the personal information for his death certificate. The cause of death, in Hendershott's handwriting, was given as "gunshot wound by unknown person. Homicide." The only real irregularity in Nickols' certificate was that Coroner Niswonger forgot to date his signature when he signed it.

At the age of 29, on May 26, 1917, Harry LeRoy Wilson enlisted in the United States Marine Corps and stated that he was a resident of Silver Lake, Oregon, but was born near Rifle Creek, Colorado. He was working as a logger for the Brooks-Scanlon Lumber Company when he enlisted, and stated that his mother was solely dependent on him for support. The registration card gave few other details about Wilson, other than his physical description, 5' 9 1/2", 165 pounds, light hair and blue eyes, and his birth date of January 12, 1888. He was called "Roy" by his friends and family.

Wilson served in the Eighth Regiment of the 108th Company of the Marine Corps, and despite his rather small size, he was described as "a very rugged individual" by writer Wayne Negus in his book, *Wilderness Tales and Trails*. As we wade through the details of the Lava Lakes murders and try to reconstruct events, we must bear in mind the problem of Roy Wilson. That problem being, just how does one go about murdering a marine? The life of a marine is not an easy one to take, even for an armed assailant. His death certificate gave his official cause of death as a bullet wound to the head (behind the right ear, to be exact). He had only one other wound, from a shotgun, fired at point blank and from the rear, that took off the point of his right shoulder.

The Eighth Regiment of the Marine Corps was originally activated in October of 1917 at Quantico, Virginia, about six months after the U.S. entered into World War I. On October 13, Roy Wilson's company, the 108th, joined the regiment at Virginia, after two months of basic training at Mare Island, California. His commanding officer was Major Ellis B. Miller.

The 108th was not deployed to Europe, but was sent to Fort Crockett near Galveston, Texas on November 9 to stand ready in case the U.S. needed to protect oil fields at Tampico, Mexico. Relations between the U.S. and Mexico were rather strained at the time, and the allied forces were dependent on the flow of oil from Tampico. Wilson and the rest of the 108th arrived at Galveston in the Gulf of Mexico on November 16 on the U. S. S. Hancock. The company remained stationed at Galveston until the end of the war to remind Mexico that the US was ready to intervene if oil interests were threatened, and the 108th functioned as a typical garrison force until it was decommissioned on April 25, 1919.

According to *A Brief History Of The 8th Marines*, by James S. Santelli, Wilson's unit did not see combat during World War I. But, the case could easily be made that all of the men of the 108th, who filled most of one and a half years with drilling for a possible intervention in Mexico, were very thoroughly trained. When confronted by an attacker, Roy Wilson's reaction to the threat would have been automatic, programmed into his muscle memory and his subconscious mind. He would have simply reacted, quickly and without thinking.

Before moving to Roy's birthplace in Colorado, the Wilsons had lived in Nebraska, and moved to Colorado around 1887. Roy's parents were Lavina S. Jones, who liked to be called by her

The gravestone of Harry LeRoy "Roy" Wilson matches those of his two friends, who were murdered on the same date, except for the Marine Corps insignia at the top. The life of a marine is not an easy one to take, and Wilson's murder posed a problem for the killers, and the author as well.

middle name of "Sarah," and Charles Wilson. He had two sisters, Leoella Margaret, who married Dan McLennan, and Rose B., who married Hervey D. Innis. The family lived in Washington state from about 1895 to about 1909, and the 1900 census found the Wilsons in Bellingham, Whatcom County, with Charles Wilson working as a mine prospector there.

In 1910, Wilson's family was living at the homestead of his brother-in-law, Hervey Innis, outside of the homestead era town of Viewpoint, located in north Lake County, seven miles east of Christmas Valley at a spot known as "Vaughn Well." The well got its name from Albert and Jennie Vaughn, who were an aunt and uncle of Roy Wilson. Ed Nickols' brother, Guilford, lived nearby. Coincidentally, another resident of the Viewpoint area at the time of the 1910 census was Mrs. Samson, who lived on the claim of her deceased son, Julius Wallende, who was identified in *The*

Sandy Knoll Murder, as another probable victim of Ray Jackson's, having been murdered in 1907.

Charles Wilson, Roy's father, filed on a homestead before 1914 in township 28 south, range 15 east, sections 13 and 14. The claim was just southwest of Table Rock, a familiar landmark northeast of the town of Silver Lake, and only about 10 miles from where Creed Conn had operated his mercantile store. Charles Wilson died in 1915, and was buried at the Silver Lake Cemetery.

In 1920, Roy's mother, Sarah, was living in Bend on Division Street with her mother, Mary A. Jones, next door to Guilford Nickols. That last census before the murders found Roy working at Brooks-Scanlon's Camp Two in southern Deschutes County with another of the Lava Lakes victims, Dewey C. Morris and his brother, Owen A. Morris, as a logging camp laborer.

A brief bio at the time of the funeral for the three victims offered the details that Wilson was a member of the Moose Lodge. "Innis, whose wife is a sister of Wilson, and Owen Morris, a brother of the trappers, visited the lake April 13," reported the *Oregonian.* "They had feared that the men had met with trouble, for Wilson and Nichols (sic) had spent the Christmas holidays in Bend, and at that time had announced their intention of coming out in February."

Roy Wilson's military training and close friendship with Ed Nickols probably strongly influenced Nickols to ask him to spend the winter with him at the isolated cabin at Little Lava Lake. Roy Wilson was 36 years old when he was killed.

The body of Roy Wilson was apparently removed from the lake last. Niswonger, after his initial examination, told the *Oregonian,* "a shotgun charge had carried away the point of Roy Wilson's right shoulder, and a revolver bullet had entered his head back of the right ear. Evidently both shots had been fired from behind."

At the inquest, Dr. Hendershott told the jury that Roy Wilson "had a shotgun wound in the right shoulder and back of the shoulder and what appeared to be a bullet wound in the back of the head in the region of the right ear." Then clarified that statement with "a bullet killed Wilson." On Wilson's death certificate, Hendershott gave the cause of death as "gunshot wound by unknown party. Homicide." No mention was made of the shoulder wound on the certificate.

The entire top and left hand sections of Wilson's certificate were very carefully filled out with what was obviously the hand-writing of his brother-in-law, Hervey D. Innis, who was named as providing the personal information. That seems a bit unusual, because the same sections of the certificates of the other two victims were typewritten. Innis obviously paid careful attention to all matters connected with the investigation, and was actively involved throughout.

The inquest took most of Friday the 25th, and while it was going on, the bodies were prepared for burial, which took place at the end of the day at Greenwood Cemetery in Bend. Also, toward the end of the day, the coroner's jury released its findings to the public. Despite their having fixed the approximate date of death at January 15, that date did not appear on any of the death certificates of the victims. The date of the inquest, April 25, 1924, was recorded as the official date of their deaths.

Additional findings during the inquest and autopsy were that the shotgun wounds were inflicted with heavy game shot, and it was believed that the trappers' own weapons had been used to kill them. The information about the ownership of the weapons used in the murders was later contradicted at the crime scene.

The *Oregonian* noted that the hole in the ice had been rather small, and just big enough to shove a man through. It was not until April 24, the day after the bodies were found, that the Deschutes County officials heard back from the University of Oregon Medical School about the test of the blood taken from the trappers' sled. No one was surprised at the result. Pathologist R. L. Benson reported "stain on wood gives test for human blood."

In the matter of the deaths of Ed Nichols (sic), Roy Wilson, and Dewey Morris, deceased.

We, the jury impaneled and sworn to inquire into the cause of the death of the above named deceased persons, find that they all came to their death about the 15th day of January, 1924, in the following manner:

Ed Nichols (sic) was killed by a shotgun wound.

Roy Wilson was killed by a bullet wound through the head. He was also shot with a shot-gun.

Dewey Morris was killed by being hit on the head with some blunt instrument. He was also shot with a shotgun.

All these men were killed by a person or persons unknown to this jury.

Foreman A. B. Taylor
Leroy Fox
Ora D. Ollingham
Lavorn Taylor
William N. Box

This fisherman was kind enough to position his canoe in the outlet of Little Lava Lake at the source of the Deschutes River. Photo was taken from the probable location of Logan's cabin. The killers chose not to place the bodies here, even though the current would have carried them down the Deschutes River and away from the crime scene.

Bodies of Dewey Morris, floating face up at left; Roy Wilson, second from right; and Ed Nickols, far right, just before they were removed from Big Lava Lake. Ropes were placed on the bodies the day before by Deputy Adams and Hervey Innis when they towed them to shore .

SOURCES:

U. S. Department of the Interior, Bureau of Land Management, General Land Office Records, Homestead patent of Ray B. Jackson, T 26 S, R 24 E, sections 8, 9, and 17, ORLAA 1066515, patented October 13, 1933. National Archives and Records Administration, Washington, D. C.

"Trail of Murderer Ends at Fur Store," *Oregonian,* April 25, 1924.

"Captive Taken in Death Case Not Identified," *Bulletin,* January 22, 1925.

"Slain Trappers Shot to Pieces," *Oregonian,* April 25, 1924.

Photographs 12302, 6162, 6425 and 6310. Collection of the Des Chutes Historical Museum, Bend, OR.

Fourteenth Census of the United States, Oregon, Deschutes County, Bend.

Field research conducted by author, summer 2012.

"Trapper is Injured at Lava Lake Camp," *Bulletin,* October 30, 1919.

"He Enjoys the Thrills of a Trapper's Life," by Fred Lockley, *American Magazine,* October, 1922, p 6263.

Wilderness Tales and Trails, by Wayne Negus, 1990, Maverick Publications, Bend, OR, p 157-162.

"In Re: Charles Kimzey, Number 12585," a report to the Oregon State Parole Board for their meeting of April 18, 1940. Inmate record of Charles Kimzey #12582, Department of Corrections, OISC, Wilsonville, OR.

Historical Writeup of the Deschutes National Forest, 1950, by Gail C. Baker, unpublished manuscript, p 27-29.

"3 Slain Trappers Buried at Bend," *Oregonian,* April 26, 1924.

"Bodies of Trappers Found in Lava Lake," *Silver Lake Leader,* May 1, 1924.

"No Trace Found of 3 Bend Trappers," *Silver Lake Leader,* April 24, 1924.

"Foul Play Fear Grows," *Oregonian,* April 16, 1924.

Untitled article, *Deschutes Pine Echoes,* vol 5, No. 12, April 1924, p 12.

"Murder Theory Upset," *Oregonian,* April 19, 1924.

"Fox Hides Sold Here," *Oregonian,* April 20, 1924.

"New Clew is Found in Trapper Mystery," *Oregonian,* April 21, 1924.

"Fox Pelt Sale Probed," *Oregonian,* April 22, 1924.

"Clew Proves Fruitless," *Oregonian,* April 23, 1924.

"Trappers Shot, Bodies in Lake," *Oregonian,* April 24, 1924.

"Three Lured From Cabin to Meet Fate, is Theory; Lava Lake Gives up Dead," *Bulletin,* April 24, 1924.

"News From the Camps," Phil Brogan, editor, *Deschutes Pine Echoes,* vol 5, No. 13, May 1924, p 12.

"Kimzey Not Alone in Triple Slaying," *Oregonian,* March 12, 1933.

"The Little Lava Lake Murders," by Don Burgderfer, *Little Known Tales From Oregon History*, Vol. III, No. 61, *Cascades East Magazine*, Bend, OR, p 27-33.

Twelfth Census of the United States, Iowa, Woodbury County, Little Sioux Township.

Oregon State Board of Health, Certificate of Death #43, Dewey Morris, filed April 25, 1924, Deschutes County, Oregon State Archives, Salem, OR.

Fourteenth Census of the United States, Oregon, Multnomah County, Portland.

"Local Bits," *Bulletin,* August 10, 1906.

"News From the Camps," Phil Brogan, editor, *Deschutes Pine Echoes,* vol 4, No. 12, April 1923, p 10.

"Pick Jury for Morris Case; Garage Wins in Damage Suit; Car Was Too Old to Insure," *Bulletin,* April 11, 1923.

"Dewey Morris Case Will Go to Jury Today," *Bulletin,* April 12, 1923.

"Morris Freed by Trial Jury," *Bulletin,* April 13, 1923.

"Central Oregon Neighborhood News, Sisters," *Bend Bulletin,* August 2, 1917.

Fourteenth Census of the United States, Oregon, Deschutes County, Sisters.

Tenth Census of the United States, Ohio, Morgan County, Marion Township.

Oregon State Board of Health, Certificate of Death #42, Edward Nickols, filed April 25, 1924, Deschutes County, Oregon State Archives, Salem, OR.

Homestead patent application file of Edward D. Nickols, serial #ORL 0006587, Township 26 south, Range 19 east, section 32, Bureau of Land Management, records of the General Land Office, National Archives and Records Administration, Washington, D.C. Patented April 14, 1917.

Homestead patent of Guilford Nickols, serial #ORL 0002743, Bureau of Land Management, records of the General Land Office, National Archives and Records Administration, Washington, D.C., Township 26 south, Range 19 east, section 32, . Patented June 11, 1914. Available online at: http://www.glo records.blm.gov /details/patent/default.aspx?accession= 413128&docClass=SER&sid=pssyiqsx.4vf

Snohomish County Auditor, Marriage Records, 18672008, Liza Young Nickols to Sylvester Burns, August 26, 1916, document #nwsnomc8512. Washington State Digital Archives: http://www.digitalarchives.wa.gov/Record/View/49D538A61FC BF94A9BF8CAB89DD77D0B

Find A Grave page for Guilford J. Nickols, Bayview Cemetery, Bellingham, Whatcom County, WA. Available online at: http://www.findagrave.com/cgibin/fg.cgi?page=gr&GSln=

Nickols&GSbyrel=all&GSdyrel=all&GSst=50&GScnty=2989&GS
cntry=4&GSob=n&GRid=7820142&df=all&

Twelfth Census of the United States, Montana, Chouteau County, Harlem Township.

Draft Registration Card of Harry LeRoy Wilson, May 26, 1917, P. J. Hardisty, Registrar, Bend, OR. National Archives and Records Administration, Washington, D. C.

Oregon State Board of Health, Certificate of Death #44, Harry LeRoy Wilson, filed April 25, 1924, Deschutes County, Oregon State Archives, Salem, OR.

A Brief History Of The 8th Marines, by James S. Santelli, 1976, History and Museums Division, Headquarters, U.S. Marine Corps, US Government Printing Office, Washington D.C., p 13.

Twelfth Census of the United States, Washington, Whatcom County, Bellingham.

Thirteenth Census of the United States, Oregon, Lake County, Silver Lake (and Viewpoint area).

Find A Grave page for Charles Wilson, Silver Lake Cemetery, Lake County, OR. Available online at http://www.findagrave. com/ cgibin/fg.cgi? page=gr&GSln=Wilson& GSfn=Charles&GS-byrel=all& GSdyrel=all&GSst=39&GScnty=2223&GScntry=4& GSob=n&GRid=13078223&df=all&

Homestead patent of Charles Wilson, serial #ORL0004304, Bureau of Land Management, records of the General Land Office, National Archives and Records Administration, Washington, D.C., township 28 south, range 15 east, sections 13 and 14. Patented September 9, 1914. Available online at: http://www.glo records.blm.gov/details/patent /default.aspx?accession=429669 &docClass=SER&sid=wnh5eqqw.r4i

Fourteenth Census of the United States, Oregon, Deschutes County, South Side #6, (Brooks Scanlon Camp #2).

"Friends Pay Honor to Slain Trappers," *Oregonian,* April 27, 1924.

Deschutes County Coroner removing the body of Marine Corps veteran Roy Wilson from Big Lava Lake. The killers shoved the bodies through a hole in the ice, just off shore from the main boat launch area.

A group of family members and other searchers look on as Deschutes County Coroner Niswonger examines one of the three victims.

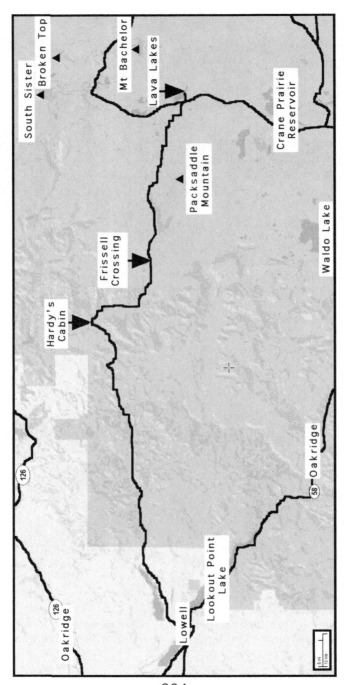

Chapter Ten

Sheriff Bert Roberts received an important piece of correspondence on either the 23rd or 24th of April that seems to have been put aside for a couple of days. The 23rd was the day that the bodies were first spotted, and from that moment on, the small department of the Deschutes County Sheriff was a flurry of activity and media attention. It wasn't until after the victims were buried, late on the 25th, that Roberts had a chance to follow up on the letter, written by Arthur P. Runey, whose family owned a resort at Foley Hot Springs. The information in the letter moved the probable date of the murders forward in time, by about two days, to the 18th of January.

Runey wrote that some men, supposed to be Kimzey and his partner, had broken into a cabin around the middle of January at a place called Frissell Crossing, about 12 miles west of the Lava Lakes on the South Fork of the McKenzie River, Also, that the men seemed to have spent the night there, stolen most of the food in the place, and headed west. Officer Roy Kendall of the Multnomah County Sheriff's Department followed up on the lead, and discovered that a similar break-in had happened on the night of the 20th at Hardy's cabin, also on the South Fork. Foley Springs, Hardy's cabin on Hardy Creek, and Frissell Crossing are all in the northeast corner of Lane County, and can still be found on modern maps. Kendall told the *Oregonian* that he believed the new timeline would have given the killers adequate time to reach Portland by the 22nd of January.

If Runey and Kendall were right, then the killers followed an old established route west that was "along the line of most direct exit from Little Lava Lake." The route out of the mountains, the historic McKenzie River Trail, was used by early trappers and settlers, and probably by indians long before that. It starts at a point between the two Lava Lakes and bears toward the northwest, over a low pass on Williamson Mountain, and out of the Cascades. The killers would have reached the source of the South Fork of the McKenzie River after the first five miles. And, that route would have taken them within two miles of Packsaddle

Mountain in the Cascades, the same place where they told Carl Schumacher that they had trapped the foxes.

It was about a twelve mile hike to Frissell Crossing, and a pretty remarkable hike, considering the time of year. It indicates that at least one of the men knew the route well, and the distance and difficulty of that journey shows that the killers probably left Lava Lakes on the morning of January 19, the day after the murders.

If we base our timeline on the information about the break-ins, then on the 20th the killers traveled about nine more miles to Hardy's cabin, located where Hardy Creek empties into the South Fork, and spent the night there. On the 21st they would have had to cover a lot of territory, about 35 miles, along the Fall Creek Road to the town of Lowell. That would not have been impossible if they managed to catch a ride on a wagon or automobile. At Lowell, they got on a train along the Natron Cutoff rail line on the morning of the 22nd, and made it to Portland and the Schumacher Fur Company before noon.

Some of the sequence of events during the murders is known from the facts of the case and the physical evidence found at the scene. Most of the rest of what happened can be extrapolated or surmised from photographs, through deductive reasoning, and from simple research. Although a few holes remain, a likely scenario can be pieced together, based upon the supposition that the killers were Ray Van Buren Jackson and Charles Hyde Kimzey.

For example, it is probably safe to assume that the killings happened in the evening, and not the morning, as Sheriff Roberts had supposed. Here is how we might arrive at that conclusion: The killers would have probably needed some time at the outset to meet up, to talk, to premeditate, and otherwise organize their plan. Then, if the killers had begun their hike in from the main road to Lava Lakes in the morning, a hike that probably took at least three hours, they would have arrived at the cabin around midmorning, and would have lost the element of surprise. Starting for the lakes in the morning decreased the chance of catching the three victims at the cabin. Additionally, it probably would have been impossible for the killers to have carried out the murders and disposed of the bodies by 9:10 that same morning, that being the time that Ed Nickols' watch stopped.

If the killers had instead started their hike later, and waited around the cabin site until the three men retired for the evening, they could have caught all three unawares. Roberts seemed to be working off of the 'food evidence' at the crime scene, the remains of a stew and some breakfast dishes, but exactly who ate what was never very clear. Nickols was probably the man who made the stew that was found. After all, it was his home and his kitchen, and he had been surviving as a bachelor with no one to cook for him for quite some time.

Kimzey's partner was indispensable in carrying out the murders. After all, how could Kimzey, the disorganized and not-so-bright hoodlum, gain the upper hand against a burly young logger, an ex-marine, and a sworn enemy, all inside of a very well-fortified log cabin containing numerous firearms and other weapons? The very necessity of an accomplice to pull off even a simple robbery under those circumstances points to some advance planning and premeditation. It also stands to reason that, if Kimzey had acted alone, at least one of the three trappers would have survived, whereas Kimzey himself may not have.

Events fall into order when we suppose that the killers met and made preparations in the morning, hiked into the lakes in the day time, and waited for evening. Working forward, it seems logical that the killers would have spent the night after the murders at the cabin, after all of the time and labor of hauling the bodies to the other lake, and after searching the cabin for Nickol's trapping money and other valuables. And, they would have wanted to wait until the next morning to skin the foxes, so they could do it in daylight, and had some breakfast before getting an early start.

The $1,800 foxes were the big payoff in the crime, and provided at least a partial motive. They had to be, if we consider all of the effort that went into killing the foxes, skinning them, and traveling all the way to Portland in the winter to sell them. It is clear that the killers wanted that money, regardless of any other motivations they may have had. But, regardless of the value of the pelts when they were 'on the hoof,' by the time they reached Mr. Schumacher, there were only four of them, two of the silver variety, and two cross foxes, and they were not in the best of condition.

"There were four of them," Schumacher told the *Oregonian*. "I could tell that they were wild and not farm foxes; that, though a trapper had skinned the animals, the skins were poorly stretched, detracting much from their value." Here again the clumsy and disorganized criminal style of Charles Kimzey shines through. Because of the time that Kimzey had spent around the Cascade Lakes, he would certainly have known something about the proper care of fresh hides, and at least one of the killers had a degree of expertise in skinning animals and handling pelts. Schumacher said that 'the talker' knew the market price of the pelts. Yet, the problem of caring for the hides while making a getaway to Portland seems not to have dawned on the killers until later. Schumacher's comment about the foxes being "wild" can only mean that Ed Logan had obtained his breeding stock from his own trap line.

The detail about the foxes having not finished eating their last ration of food before the murders is only of limited value. If they were fed a large amount of food only once per day, then there would probably have been at least some food in their pans at all times. For example, if Nickols had fed them late in the day, just before the killers arrived at the cabin and before supper time, there could have still been some food left in the pans early the next morning.

Equipment such as snowshoes and heavy boots were found in readiness for the next outing, and that could suggest that the trappers had returned to the cabin for the day.

Just after he made his first, cursory examination of the crime scene at Little Lava, Sheriff Roberts told the *Oregonian* that he believed that the trappers' own firearms had been used to kill them. However, that statement was never substantiated with other information, such as evidence that guns found at the scene had been fired, or ballistics matching. It also conflicted with another statement, made by Deputy Adams, that he believed the trappers had been ambushed outside of their cabin. And, one must recognize that getting inside of the cabin and separating the three men from their weapons would have been very difficult and risky.

A shotgun loaded with heavy game shot was and is to this day a popular choice for its stopping power, and the very use of that particular weapon on Nickols, Morris, and Wilson suggests premeditation. Kimzey knew that Nickols kept guns at the cabin, and would have wanted enough fire power for a confrontation. It stands to reason that the killers brought shotguns to the lake with them, perhaps of the double-barrel variety, and loaded with heavy game shot.

The Lava Lakes were a pretty isolated spot in 1924, but were not completely cut off from the outside world. The Forest Service had put in phone lines to their ranger stations by that time. When Cephas Gott, Logan's old trapping partner, accidentally shot himself in the shoulder in 1922, he was able to walk to a nearby cabin and phone for help. In 1920, construction had been completed on a wagon road connecting Bend to Sparks Lake and Elk Lake. Eventually, other roads in the area were connected to create what was known as "Century Drive," so named because it was about 100 miles long. Various improvements over the years have shortened that loop road to about 87 miles, and it is now known as "Cascade Lakes Scenic Highway."

The killers made the seven mile walk on the Lava Lake trail from the Snow Creek Road on January 18, and would have discussed their plan to rob and kill Nickols along the way. Supplies and food for the foxes had been dropped off five days earlier, on January 13, and the tracks from the food drop may still have been visible in the snow.

The fox food and other supplies must have been left at the usual drop off point, on a prearranged date, along Snow Creek Road, and then someone with a tote sled and snowshoes had walked out from the lake to drag the stuff back in. This stands to reason, because the newspapers, which provided good details about all of the comings and goings from the lakes around the time of the murders, like the original arrival of Wilson and Morris at the lake; the departure and arrival of the trio for the holidays; and Willcoxon's visit, made no mention of any other person having seen the trappers in January.

Surely, if a delivery had been made 'to the doorstep' of the cabin by a resident of Bend on the 13th, that person would have been interviewed and would have told what he had seen around the cabin. Nickols probably made arrangements for the food delivery around the first of January, before he returned from the holidays, and it is very possible that Logan himself delivered it.

The trappers had at least two tote sleds that they used for hauling gear, supplies, and water, and they can be seen in two different photographs. One sled was pictured in that snapshot of the three men in front of their cabin, probably taken by Hervey Innis when he brought Wilson and Morris out to the lake in the fall. The second sled was the one that was found encrusted with blood at the edge of Big Lava Lake. A photograph of it was printed in the *Oregonian* on April 26. Maybe Nickols asked Wilson and Morris to go down to the road and fetch the supplies on January 13, or maybe all three men did the errand together. Either way, there would still have been evidence of more than one set of footprints and sled tracks along that trail, and by the time the killers arrived, they probably knew that Nickols had company. If not, then they certainly would have realized it when they crept up on the cabin, in the peace and quiet of the Cascade Lakes, and heard the voices of the men inside.

Ed Nickols seems to have been shot first. Unlike Morris and Wilson, who both suffered injuries to two parts of their bodies, Nickols was leveled with a single fatal shotgun blast. Kimzey, because of having lived at the cabin himself, would have known that Nickols had a ritual of going down to the pen to feed the foxes, and probably recognized that as an opportune time to catch Nickols out in the open and unarmed.

Some shotgun shells were found around the cabin yard by the investigators, who apparently sifted through the snow to find them. But, using the information about those shells to reconstruct events is problematic. For starters, the methods used in locating the shotgun shells and the condition of the crime scene were far from ideal. Hervey Innis and Owen Morris arrived at the cabin on April 13, and from that day onward, the crime scene was continuously occupied by various friends, relatives, and officials. As late as April 23, Sheriff Adams still believed that the three men had been shot by someone at a distance using a high-powered rifle. He and his deputies would have been more interested in searching through the surrounding shrubbery for rifle shells than they would have been in any shells located in the cabin yard. Meanwhile, shotgun shells around the cabin were trampled underfoot, or ignored altogether, for ten whole days.

It wasn't until the coroner had a look at the bodies that the sheriff learned that at least one of the murder weapons was a shotgun. That state of affairs probably explains why the newspapers had such poor information about the number of shells and where they were found. In an article written on the 24th, the *Oregonian* offered that the trappers *"were fired upon by the murderer or murderers from a point in front of the cabin where five shot gun shells and three revolver shells were found."* A statement that could not possibly have been more vague.

A conflicting, yet equally vague remark about the shells came from Ed Logan during the inquest. *"He told of finding empty shotgun shells 12 feet from the cabin in two spots where blood had stained the snow and where it is believed that Morris and Wilson met their deaths."* Logan must have been recalling shells that he found around the cabin sometime after he arrived on April 15. Those statements by the sheriff and Logan clarify nothing. Were there shells found in two places, or just one? Were they in front of the cabin, or were they 12 feet away? Exactly how many shells were there?

Then, there is the problem of how the shotgun shells came to rest in the spots where they were found, wherever that was. Unlike spent shells from an automatic revolver that are ejected from the weapon and land at the spot where they were fired, shotgun shells remain in the weapon until the shooter or someone else ejects them intentionally. They could have been carried across the cabin yard inside of the weapon and ejected at a different location, and at a later point in time. Maybe even on the following day. Bearing those things in mind limits the value of any information about their location.

From the injuries of the murdered men we know that at least two shots were fired from a shotgun, a fact that sets the minimum number of shells at two--or four-- depending upon whether the weapon was of the double barrel variety, and whether or not both barrels were discharged separately. There is also the problem of matching the shells to any particular weapon, and that was never done. The question of whether the shells found were all fired by the killers on January 18, or at an earlier date by someone else, remains unanswered.

If the crime scene had been treated with more care and had not been so badly trampled; if the location of evidence, such as the gun shells, had been carefully catalogued; or if the shells had been matched to any particular weapons; if the sheriff would have arrived on the scene a bit sooner than he had, then information about the shells might have been very valuable to anyone trying to recreate the actions of the victims and the killers. But, having been handled the way that it was, the shotgun shell information is of almost no value.

When the bodies were removed from Big Lava Lake in April, the *Oregonian* reported that "two of the bodies were coatless," so by exclusion we might safely assume that the third man was wearing a coat and had been outdoors just prior to his death. Photographs were taken at the recovery scene, probably by Paul Hosmer, as the bodies were removed from the lake and examined, and show that Morris was wearing a shirt, suspenders, and jeans, and Wilson was wearing a shirt, lightweight sweater, and jeans. By process of exclusion, we can assume that it was Nickols who had his coat on.

The way that Nickols was dressed suggests that he did not bolt out of the cabin in a hurry, but took the time to put his coat on. He did not swap his reading glasses for everyday glasses, so he was not out on a long, planned excursion, just a short jaunt. But, wearing those reading glasses outdoors would have been rather uncomfortable and made him shortsighted. The failure to change his glasses suggests that something may have distracted him from an indoor activity, like cooking that stew. The foxes might have been stirred by the approach of the strangers. Although it is not known just how close the fox pen was to the cabin, foxes do make a variety of sounds like barks, howls, and yips, similar to other canines. Nickols may have thought that the animals were merely hungry, or maybe he just wanted to go see what all the ruckus was about.

Months later, just after Deputy Adams had flipped each of the victims over in the lake in order to identify them, he told the *Oregonian* that Nickols "wore his reading spectacles," and that "Nichols' (sic) glasses still were in place." Likewise, the coroner told the paper that Nickols' "reading spectacles were on his body when it was taken from the lake." Those descriptions lead us to believe that either the glasses were on a chain about his neck, or they were pressed in place by the shotgun blast.

The angle of that shot, fired from Nickol's right side and at close range, suggests that the killer was standing behind something, a structure or a tree, and pulled the trigger as Nickols passed by. Blood evidence and a piece of a tooth, both believed to have come from Nickols, were found in the snow 30 feet west of the cabin. Although the newspaper accounts only gave a vague description of the location of the fox pen, it could have been located west of the cabin, and the killers could have positioned themselves in that area, watched as Nickols went to feed the animals, then struck as he was returned to the cabin. Remember that Deputy Adams stated that he believed the killers had waited in ambush, and he may even have found some tracks, impressions in the snow, or other evidence of that activity in the surrounding woods. From the moment that first shot on Nickols was fired, things began to happen very quickly. Much more quickly than can possibly be described here.

Wilson and Morris would have jumped at the sound of the shotgun blast, being so loud and so close to the cabin. Morris may have been a bit too startled by it to react very effectively, but Wilson, with all of his Marine Corps and weapons training, would have recognized it at once as arms fire. He would have snatched up a weapon, a weapon that he knew to be loaded. He also would have went outside quickly with the thought of protecting Nickols and without putting his coat on. In an instant, he would have felt concern for Ed Nickols, thought him shot, and thought of his agreement to protect Nickols over the winter from the criminal, Charles Kimzey. Probably one or both of the younger men called out to Nickols as they moved outside.

Because there was no evidence of violence, bloodshed, or gunfire found inside of the cabin, we have to assume that Morris followed Wilson out, and that they probably exchanged a few words about Charles Kimzey, the bad man who they had been expecting all winter. It would stand to reason that Wilson and Morris were together during the next phase of what was, essentially, a surprise attack.

What happened next is indicated by some of the pistol shells found at the scene. Deputy Adams told reporters that three revolver shells were found at a point about 10 feet in front of the cabin. As the investigation unfolded, and after the bodies had been brought in to Bend, the *Oregonian* reported that, based upon the location of those spent pistol shells, the sheriff was working off of a theory that the trappers were fired upon from a point in front of the cabin. Sheriff Roberts may not have taken Wilson's military training into account, and the author believes that it was Wilson himself, and not one of the killers, who fired a pistol into the woods from that point in front of the cabin, shooting at whoever had shot Nickols.

Wilson and Morris crept around the cabin toward the west, toward the direction of the shotgun blast. They caught sight of someone moving through the woods, and Wilson positioned himself near the southwest corner of the cabin and fired three shots at the shadowy figure he caught sight of near where Nickols lay. And, the man who Wilson was firing upon was probably Kimzey himself. Wilson's supposed choice of the Luger pistol as his weapon can be explained by the shell casings that were found; by the simple coincidence that the pistol had been kept handy and loaded because he halfway expected Kimzey to show up; and by the fact that Wilson was later killed with a pistol.

When Hervey Innis delivered Morris and Wilson to the lake in October, he must have made a mental note of all or most of the guns that the cabin contained, because he gave a list of seven weapons to the coroner's jury. But, when the search for the missing men began, it was discovered that two of the guns were missing, a ".22 Colts revolver," and a "Luger automatic." Although Roy Wilson never went to Germany during his service in the Marine Corps, it stands to reason that the Luger was probably his. During World War I, the somewhat exotic Luger pistol became a popular souvenir for soldiers, and thousands were taken home to Britain and America.

Roy Wilson's first wound was the shotgun blast to his right shoulder. That was obvious because, the other injury, the pistol wound to the right side of his head, was definitely fatal. The shotgun blast was fired from behind him, at point blank, and took off the point of his shoulder. It was an odd wound, and not the result of a clear shot. It was more like half of a shotgun wound. It was a glancing sort of injury, and the shooter was not able to get a clear shot, so Wilson was probably in motion when the trigger was pulled.

According to the FBI *Crime Classification Manual*, in a multiple murder, the most damage is usually done to the victim who seems the most threatening to the killer. To a man who knew Wilson's background, Wilson would have posed the greatest threat. And, a man like Kimzey, who was well acquainted with Ed Nickols, would have heard about his friend, the marine, who he was particularly close to. But, to a man who did not know any of the victims personally, Dewey Morris would have superficially presented the greatest threat because of his size and youth. From that detail, we might extrapolate that it was probably the second killer, the more aggressive partner, and not Kimzey, who made the attack on Morris.

Through all of those long, dark, and cold winter nights that the three men spent in the remote cabin, the topic of Charley Kimzey had come up often. Nickols would talk at length about how much he loathed the man, how he regretted that he had ever trusted him, and how the cowardly lowlife had stolen his money and left town. Nickols viewed Kimzey as a no-good hoodlum, and during those rants, Wilson would try to assure him that he and Morris would run Kimzey off of the place if he dared to show his face. The significance of those talks over a period of three months was that they focused Wilson's mind on Kimzey as a threat, but just Kimzey and Kimzey alone, a fugitive and loner, wanted in two states. A man trying to hide his identity. None of the three residents of Little Lava Lake seemed to consider the possibility that Kimzey might show up there with a partner. If they had, they might not have spent the winter there at all.

An armed marine is not an easy person to kill. Killing a marine requires a special skill set or a special set of circumstances. The man who goes after a marine can only get the upper hand in a couple of distinct ways, one of which is to use the element of surprise, and another is to not be seen. The sun had already set and the light was getting poor as Wilson fired from that point at the southwest corner of the cabin. The cabin itself would have blocked most of his field of view to the right. And, Morris and Wilson both failed to realize a couple of important things. First, that Kimzey had someone with him; and second, that the instant the criminals heard Wilson or Morris call out to their fallen friend from inside of the cabin, Ray Jackson had split off from Kimzey and circled around behind the cabin toward the east. As Wilson began firing his pistol into the woods, Jackson recognized the opportunity to creep up on the shooter, and did so. Wilson and Morris had no idea that Jackson existed, or that he was right on top of them.

In one startled instant, Morris looked up, and was almost simultaneously struck by the shoulder of his friend, Roy Wilson, and the shotgun blast that shredded his left arm. Wilson tackled him with one of the takedown moves that he had learned in the Marine Corps. Jackson followed the motion of Wilson, and with the end of the gun barrel almost touching Wilson's shoulder, pulled the trigger. The blast struck Wilson and Morris at the same time, and Wilson rolled off, his right arm now useless at his side, and bolted off into the woods to the west. Many hours of drills had taught him the importance of remaining on his feet, and he would have automatically jumped back up.

Wilson had dropped the pistol the moment he was shot, because his hand had gone limp. Despite that brief tussle, the shot was a rather lucky one for everyone concerned. Wilson and Morris had both survived what would have certainly been a fatal shot for either one of them, and it was a lucky shot for Jackson, because it swiftly disabled both men.

The shotgun wound that Morris suffered, like Wilson's, was a peculiar one. Coroner Niswonger said that Morris had been shot in the region of his left elbow with a shotgun, yet there was no mention of game shot damage to any other part of his body. There were only two ways that a wound like that could occur, a wound that was essentially half of a wound. The arm could have been held out from the side of his body at a right angle when the shot was fired. Or, the rest of his body was shielded from the blast by something, or someone.

Kimzey saw Wilson run off into the woods clutching his right arm, and Jackson shouted out an order to pursue him. Because Kimzey was more of a thief, a coward, and a bully than he was a bloodthirsty killer, and because Wilson was loosing blood fast,

Kimzey caught up with him shortly and ordered him back to the cabin. In the back of his mind, Kimzey was thinking that he still needed to find out where Nickols had hidden his money over the winter, and that Wilson might now be frightened enough to tell him. So, Kimzey did what he usually did in a robbery, he ordered Wilson to march at gunpoint.

Photographs of Wilson's body, taken on the day that it was removed from the lake, show that someone, probably Wilson himself, had pulled the right hem of his sweater up and over his injured right shoulder and arm to serve as a sort of temporary sling. That tells us that some time must have passed between when Wilson was first hit in the shoulder and when he was killed, execution style, with a shot to the head. With such a large portion of his shoulder joint gone, his right arm would have been practically useless.

A takedown move like this one, from the U.S. Marine Corps training manual for close combat, could have been used by Roy Wilson to remove his buddy, Dewey Morris, from the line of fire. Note the position of the right shoulder of the marine (in camo clothing) relative to what would have been Morris' left elbow.

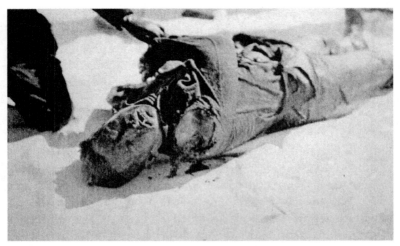

Coroner Niswonger examines the body of Marine Corps veteran Roy Wilson and the unusual shoulder wound. Someone, probably Wilson himself, had pulled his sweater up and around his right elbow and injured shoulder as a makeshift sling to support the arm. That evidence shows that some time passed between the shotgun blast to Wilson's shoulder and the pistol shot to this head that ended his life.

From Kimzey's broad criminality and the paper trail that it generated, we know that he was not the sort of killer to fly into a rage and produce overkill. He did not seem to have impulse control problems. There were documented instances when he had the opportunity to kill, but turned away. So, when we consider the Lava Lakes murders, it seems likely that it was the partner, Ray Jackson, who bludgeoned Dewey Morris. A spot of blood found 20 feet east of the cabin contained skull fragments, and was identified as the place where Morris was killed.

During the few minutes that Kimzey pursued Wilson, Jackson picked up Wilson's Luger pistol and crammed it into his belt. Morris writhed in pain, but still had enough sense about him to try to get away, and that was what he did. He found his feet, and like Wilson, clutched his injured arm and took off, but in an opposite direction, toward the east. Jackson dropped the shotgun now and nimbly overtook Morris, delighted, in his own twisted way, by the opportunity to brutalize a frightened and vulnerable young man.

Jackson grasped a heavy, blunt instrument. It may have been a hatchet with a hammer head that he carried on his belt, or it may have been a hatchet that was stuck in a chopping block nearby. Or, there is the possibility that a hammer was used as a weapon. The sheriff and his men later found a hammer beneath the surface of the dirt floor of the cabin, and suspected it of being the weapon that had killed Morris. But, why would the killers have made that one, isolated effort to hide evidence of the crime, to hide that one item, when they otherwise so deliberately displayed everything else? An axe or a hatchet was also referred to early in the investigation. On April 19, when Ed Logan ventured out onto the frozen surface of Big Lava Lake, he reported that a hole had been "chopped" in the ice. It is quite possible that the same instrument used to kill Morris was used to create that hole, and that it was left in the lake.

Jackson swung the heavy weapon at the staggering young logger, and struck a savage blow to the right side of his head. Once Morris was on the ground, Jackson crouched over him and went into a killing frenzy, striking his face repeatedly. Morris probably expired moments after that initial, savage blow, but a detail like that did not matter to Ray Jackson, who was essentially a sadist.

Kimzey returned Wilson to the cabin yard with a shotgun pointed at his back, and found Jackson standing breathlessly over the badly mutilated Morris. Wilson was totally horrified by what he saw, and probably realized that Nickols was fatally wounded as well. He may have caught a glimpse of Nickols lying west of the cabin, in the half light with his face blown off. Kimzey himself could not help feeling a bit sheepish, as he began to realize just how malicious his partner was. Kimzey had been in prison, and he had known some bad men in his day, but, up until that time, he had never killed anyone. Jackson demanded to know why Kimzey had not killed Wilson, and why he had brought him back. The only explanation that he could offer was that he wanted Wilson to tell them where Nickols had hidden his money.

After asking Wilson a few pointed questions, Jackson pulled Wilson's own Luger pistol from his belt and shot him behind the ear with it. Because Jackson and Kimzey searched the cabin and left it in a state of total disarray, it could be reasoned that Wilson refused to tell them what they wanted to know. That, if they were going to steal Nickols' trapping money, he was not going to help them do it.

The killers searched the cabin that evening, then disposed of the bodies the next morning, in a way that was very telling. There must have been a pathology at work, because the actions after the murders were not logical, and the decisions that they made were not sound, or even wise. A 'normal' motivated killer, such as one who kills out of revenge or purely for material gain, would have made more of an effort to hide the evidence and the bodies. Someone who wanted to hide the crime would have shoved the sled through that hole in the ice, as well as the bodies. Or, would have put the bodies inside of that remote cabin and lit it on fire.

At least one of the killers seems to have been a psychopath because, instead of trying to hide the crimes, the decision was made to move the bodies half of a mile to Big Lava Lake. One of the sleds that they were hauled on was deliberately left on the shore pointing to the hole in the ice. And, the bodies were left in an area where they would surely be found in the spring. Just after the bodies were located, the *Bulletin* reported:

> "*The discovery was made near the large hole in the ice found by searchers several days ago, which was in a line with tracks made by the sled on which the bodies of the victims are supposed to have been hauled from the trappers' cabin at Little Lava lake to the edge of the ice.*"

The location of the bodies could not have been made any more obvious, and the spot where those bodies were placed was and is the main boat launching area at Big Lava Lake, an almost legendary fishing spot. Every fishing season, the boat launch area swarms with people and their vehicles trying to get into and out of the water. It is the focal point of the entire Lava Lakes recreational area.

The psychopath wanted the bodies to be found, and knew that the nature of their injuries would make the fact of murder obvious. He knew that whoever found the bodies, some good and decent person, would be horrified by the discovery, and he wanted that as well. There was something about the ice and the water that appealed to that killer. It was a part of a pattern and his signature behavior. Hauling the bodies to Big Lava Lake was a lot of work, and so was chopping that hole in the ice. But, that behavior was not based upon any kind of reasoning or practicality. It deviated from what was necessary to carry out the crimes. It was driven by the internal motivations and the pathology of that dominant partner.

If we work backward from the time that Ed Nickols' watch stopped, 9:10, presuming that it stopped when his body went into the water, we can piece together a rough timeline of the events of January 19. According to NOAA, the National Oceanic and Atmospheric Administration, sunrise occurred at 7:46 a.m., and the sun set at 4:56 p.m. on that date. With two sleds, the killers could have probably completed the whole task of hauling the bodies to Big Lava Lake, located one half mile away, and chopped that hole in the ice, in under two hours.

If the killers spent the night of the 18th at the cabin, they could have gotten up on the 19th around 7:00 a.m. and skinned the foxes; hauled the bodies of Wilson and Morris on both sleds to Big Lava by 7:45; chopped a hole in the ice by 8:15; got back to the cabin by 8:30; loaded one sled with Nickols' body and the other with the furs by just before 9:00; hauled both sleds to Big Lava and deposited Nickols' body by 9:10; then left the area heading west with the one sled and furs. On a slow walk through snow they probably could have covered the 12 miles to Frissell Crossing in about six to eight hours. They decided to leave one of the sleds, the inferior one with low clearance, at Big Lava Lake, and kept the higher, better sled for their journey.

Considering the violent way that Morris and Nickols were killed, it stands to reason that, if they had been wearing hats at the time, their hats would have been knocked off of their heads. Even Wilson, with his terrible shoulder wound, seemed unlikely to have still had his hat on his head when all was said and done.

Yet, all three hats somehow made it all the way over to the dump site at Big Lava Lake. They were deliberately collected and carried there, possibly on the heads of the victims. When the bodies were found, the *Oregonian* added the detail that two of the victims *"had their hats on... the third hat was found in the ice a short distance from where the bodies were sighted."* Here we see another trace of Jackson's signature behavior, because the same thing had been done to Creed Conn's body with his hat in 1904. Jackson had stored the body for a time, but before he deposited it on the Sandy Knoll outside of Silver Lake, with the face mutilated like Morris and Nickols, he had crammed Creed Conn's hat down tightly on the back of his head.

After they reached Portland and sold the fox furs, with cash in hand, Kimzey dropped from sight and went to California, and Jackson may have joined him for a time.

On April 25, 1924, the bodies of Harry LeRoy Wilson, Dewey C. Morris, and Edward D. Nickols were laid to rest at Greenwood Cemetery in Bend. Instead of burying the three men separately and in their family plots, the surviving relatives chose to bury them side-by-side, like a final monument to the singular and awful tragedy that took their lives. The graves have matching headstones, and seem to have been squeezed into a space designed for two coffins. Reverend F. H. Beard, chaplain of the local American Legion post, spoke at the service on the behalf of Roy Wilson and his family, and called the Lava Lakes murders "an inhuman catastrophe that causes us to cry for justice and vengeance."

Many years later, a set of three adjoining buttes about six miles east of Crane Prairie were named "The Three Trappers" in memory of the Lava Lakes victims, by the Oregon Geographic Names Board. The continuing investigation was complicated by the death of the deputy in charge of the case, Clarence Adams, who was killed in an automobile accident in 1927. The Lava Lakes murders were never solved.

It wasn't until March 10, 1933 that Charles Kimzey was finally arrested on that bad check charge, in Montana. At that time, he knew that he was wanted in Nevada for the 1925 murder of William R. Howard, and was still wanted in Idaho due to his escape from prison there in 1915. But, in yet another vivid display of his alleged 'criminal genius', Kimzey opened his big mouth, and in so doing, heaped even more suspicion upon his own head. When he was taken to jail in Kalispell, instead of acting like he didn't know anything about the Lava Lakes murders, and even before anyone brought up the subject, Kimzey told the arresting officers, "They think I killed those trappers, but I didn't. I was in Colorado working on the Moffat Tunnel at the time."

The tunnel that Kimzey referred to was the project of David Moffat that passed through the Rocky Mountains. It was started in 1902 to connect Denver to Salt Lake via the Denver, Northwestern and Pacific Railroad. Moffat died in 1911, and the tunnel was finally completed in 1927. The railroad itself was eventually taken over by the Union Pacific.

"Whether Kimzey will be tried on the triple murder charge will not be determined until his alibi, that he was working on the Moffat tunnel, Colorado, at the time the murder of the trappers was committed, is checked," reported the *Bulletin* on March 13, 1933, along with the information that Kimzey would be returned to Deschutes County. "Immediate steps to check the alibi are to be taken. If Kimzey's name, or some of the many aliases he has used, can be found on the Moffat tunnel payroll or if canceled checks can be produced, the solution to the Lava Lake murder may be just as remote as it was on that April day in 1924."

On March 16, when Kimzey was returned to Bend, he thought he had been brought in purely for questioning about the Lava Lakes murders. And, there were, indeed, three outstanding warrants against him for first degree murder, one for each of the three victims. Kimzey knew that the case against him was weak, and thought that he might have outwitted the prosecutor by cleverly employing the alibi that he was working in Colorado as "Tom Collins" at the time of the murders. Even the newspapers were saying that the evidence against him was "purely circumstantial."

Hervey Innis also wanted to question Kimzey about what had happened at the Lava Lakes. He had been more than a brother-in-law to Roy Wilson. He was also a true friend, and his continuing actions showed just how loyal of a friend he was. Innis had originally taken Morris and Wilson out to the lake in the fall of 1923, and he had been involved in the search effort from the first day. He was with Deputy Adams when the bodies were sighted, and was in the boat when they were identified and brought to shore. He guarded the bodies and waited, was present when the coroner came, signed Wilson's death certificate, and was there for the inquest and funeral. Hervey Innis had also known Kimzey way back in 1923, before the attack on the driver, Harrison, and he wanted some answers. But, all that Kimzey would say to Innis during his visit at the county jail was that he had been unjustly accused in the Lava Lakes murders.

Kimzey did not know that there was also a warrant against him for the Harrison crimes, because he had left Oregon in haste after dumping the driver into that cistern in 1923, and probably did not even know that Harrison had survived. Kimzey was not around when Harrison told his harrowing story to the local papers. District Attorney Boylan knew that the charges in the Harrison case would 'stick,' so he wisely decided to pursue that case, the case that was practically a sure thing. Kimzey found out that he was in hot water on March 18 when he was questioned about the triple murder and the Harrison case as well. On March 20, he was charged with three counts of first degree murder in the Lava Lakes case, and "assault and robbery while armed with a dangerous weapon" in the Harrison matter. After that, he was held in the Deschutes County Jail pending further investigation.

District Attorney Bert Boylan questioned a number of local people in 1933. He was trying to find someone who could remember that Kimzey, alias Lee Collins, had been in the Bend area in January of 1924. And, that was really a two part challenge. Kimzey had indeed worked at the Moffat Tunnel near Denver as "Tom Collins," and payroll records showed that he had been employed from December 16 through January 6, 1924. A report created for the Oregon State Parole Board in 1940 contained specific details about Kimzey's movements around the time of the Lava Lakes murders, and stated that he had left the Moffat Tunnel work camp on January 7, and that he was seen "about January 12th, 1924... near Prineville, Oregon, by a trapper who knew him well." Even if the account of that Prineville witness was faulty, Kimzey certainly had adequate time to reach central Oregon by January 18. The second part of the challenge involved proving that Kimzey had been at the Lava Lakes on the day of the murders, and that was where the investigators' case fell apart.

Kimzey was taken to Portland on April 1, 1933, and on April 3 he was put in a lineup in front of Carl Schumacher and his partner, Gotthilf J. Bofinger, and the traffic cop, Walter C. Bender. It was hoped that his connection to the murders could be proven, but all three men failed to pick Kimzey out of that lineup nine years later. "Bender said one of the men resembled Kimzey, but he could not be sure," reported the *Oregonian* on April 3, 1933. Bender's statement came as a great disappointment to the district attorney because, back in 1924, Bender had been shown a photograph and recognized Kimzey as one of the men who had approached him with that big bag of furs.

It was plain from Carl Schumacher's account that Kimzey had remained very much in the background during their meeting, and had allowed the other man, his partner with the glib and superficial charm, presumed here to be Ray Jackson, to do all of the talking. All of the attention of the fur dealers and the traffic officer was focused on the more dominant partner, the talker, and for that very reason, Kimzey remained only a vague shadow in the memories of the three witnesses.

Schumacher was not able to identify Kimzey for the simple reason that he never got a good look at him. Officer Bender said that, on that morning, he was approached by two men with a sack of furs. But, Schumacher only talked to one of the men, who then left the store to go and get some furs to show him. It must be that Kimzey waited outside with the bag of furs, not wanting his face to be associated with Nickols' trapping license and Logans' stolen foxes. It was Ray Jackson, 'the talker' and thinker, who went inside to shoot the breeze and make the sale.

"This fellow," said Schumacher, "whom I remember as a neat, clean shaven, and respectably dressed man, came into the store on the morning of January 22 and asked if we bought raw furs." It is worth noting again that those observations of Schumacher about the dominant partner's personal appearance matched Ray Jackson's style as a hedonistic psychopath. "I told him that we did, and he said he had some fox and would be back later. He came back with the furs in a gunny sack. I remember, when he was ready to leave, that he walked to the front of the store, made the remark that he had some martens and that he would be back with them. He never came back."

While he was being held in the Multnomah County Jail, Kimzey was paid a visit by an *Oregonian* reporter. "I was working on the Moffit tunnel in Colorado during January 1924, and was not in Bend or anywhere in that country," Kimzey said. "Bend authorities are checking my story and I think they'll find I'm stating the fact. They have already found that my name was on the employment roll at the tunnel at that time. Now they are attempting to get the canceled checks with which I was paid so they can check my signature. When they get them, they will find I was at Moffit (sic) tunnel and not in Oregon."

Proving that Kimzey had left Colorado and that he was seen near Prineville was not the same thing as proving that he was present during the murders at Little Lava Lake. Without more evidence or a confession, investigators were not able to try Kimzey for the triple murder. The investigators needed the sworn testimony of an eye witness. They needed a signed confession from Kimzey or some physical proof that he had been present at the scene of the Lava Lakes murders, but, they had nothing of the sort.

Back in Bend on April 12, Kimzey was indicted for the crimes against Harrison. The trial started on April 20, and he was convicted on April 22. The next day he was sentenced to life in the Oregon State Penitentiary by Judge T. E. J. Duffy, the same judge who, ten years earlier, had tried Dewey Morris for the rape of Mary Pednault.

Apparently, Judge Duffy could imagine no motive for the Lava Lakes murders beyond Kimzey's hatred of Ed Nickols, and seems to have drawn no connection whatsoever between the murders and Morris' alleged attack on Mary Pednault. Duffy sentenced Charles Kimzey to life in prison for his assault on Harrison, a sentence that was later described by the Oregon parole board as disproportionately harsh and not in keeping with the crime for which he was charged. When Duffy passed sentence on Kimzey, he seemed to be punishing him for more than just the attack that Harrison survived. He seemed to be punishing him for the Lava Lakes murders.

In a statement written just after Kimzey was committed to the penitentiary in May of 1933, Judge Duffy wrote that he believed Kimzey was "absolutely without any moral responsibility," and had intelligence, "above the ordinary. Cunning." The judge then, very strangely, described the attack in which Harrison was not killed, but knocked out and thrown into a cistern, as *"the most heinous crime ever committed in the most cold blooded manner."*

While Kimzey was serving out his sentence in Oregon, he made several requests for parole. For all of the time that he was in prison he denied his guilt. Even in the Harrison matter, of which he was certainly guilty, and with the victim, Harrison, appearing as a witness, Kimzey insisted that he was innocent. The following exchange was recorded in the transcript of Kimzey's hearing before the Oregon State Parole Board on April 18, 1940. Items marked "A" are Kimzey's answers.

Regarding the assault on Harrison:

> A. *It is in the court records that it was nearly 10 years before I was tried after the crime was committed. This man admitted he couldn't identify me. He admitted he couldn't identify me in the court. On the stand, he identified me. My attorney asked him whether he admitted he couldn't identify me. My attorney asked him and he says it was none of his business. That is the kind of evidence I was convicted on.*

> Q. *MR. MASON Are we to understand from you this morning that you had nothing to do with assaulting this man Harrison?*

> A. *No sir.*

> Q *You never did drive out on that desert country and stand him on his head in the sistern (sic)?*

> A. *No.*

Regarding the Lava Lakes murders:

A. I am not a criminal. I never was a criminal. I worked hard all my life. There is to (sic) recommendations I could give you, people that is got pretty good influence, Harry Hopkins, superintendent of the First National Bank, Wisdom, Montana.

Q. What is the other one?

A. Ellen Wilcoxin (sic), Bend, Oregon.

Q. Since 1924, in May, the 27th of May, Deschutes County, you were wanted for murder. What about that?

A. That was dropped. They brought me back from Montana on that charge and it was dropped.

Q. Was there anything to that murder charge?

A. No.

Q. You were alleged to have killed three trappers in their cabin without giving them a chance for their lives. There was a reward of $1500 in that and you were brought from Montana and you had that court charge and they dropped it for lack of evidence?

A. Yes. I know this murder was done but I don't know who did it. I was in Chicago* (sic) but they got my name on pay checks. That is how it was dropped.

Q. That is all, Mr. Kimzey.

The word "Chicago" appears in the transcript, followed by a question mark with a backslash through it. It is not known what was meant by that notation, unless Kimzey actually stated "Colorado" and the court recorder misheard the word as "Chicago."

Another report from the Oregon parole board, located in Kimzey's prison file, contained more information about Kimzey's 'career' during the years after he left Oregon in 1924. Kimzey was never charged in the murder of William R. Howard, the man that he killed outside of Las Vegas, possibly due to insufficient evidence and the lack of a confession. But, what would the outcome have been if any of the official investigators or the Burns detective agency had pursued a different course, and focused their efforts during that period on Jackson, the talker, instead of Kimzey, the disorganized partner?

The men who attempted to solve the Lava Lakes triple murder seem to have approached it as an isolated and singular incident. They were not thinking along the lines of similar crimes. They focused on Kimzey's financial grudge against Ed Nickols as the primary motive, without much consideration of the influence of Kimzey's pathological and more dominant partner. That man's modus operandi would change with the circumstances of each crime, but his pathology, his signature aspect, would run through his crimes like a thread. It evolved from one to the next, but was still recognizable. Contrary to popular belief, serial killers do not commit a series of identical crimes. They adapt to prevailing circumstances with each murder they commit. According to the *Crime Classification Manual* of the FBI, "an investigator who rejects an offense as the work of a serial offender solely on the basis of disparities in M. O. has made a mistake."

The author believes that is was Ray Van Buren Jackson who shot Creed Conn on the bank of Silver Creek in 1904, when it was frozen over in the early spring, and that he later mutilated the man's head and face. The attack on Conn's head also left a strange hole that was not a bullet entry wound, but seemed to have been punched through the skull in the right temple by a heavy, blunt weapon, such as a hammer or hatchet with a hammer head. The author also believes that, four years later, Jackson murdered Julius Wallende, another resident of north Lake County, by bludgeoning, and later took the body of the young man to Silver Creek, to a spot very near where he had murdered Conn four years before, and anchored it in the stream.

The same thread runs through the trapper murders as a signature aspect in the way that the bodies were disposed of, and particularly in the attack on Dewey Morris. Jackson was a sadistic psychopath with a predilection for young men. Remember what Earl F. Moore wrote, "The bigger the teenager, the more Jackson seemed to enjoy the cruelty," and Dewey Morris was only 24 years old and the youngest of the three victims.

Once Jackson began his bludgeoning, he lost all control and lapsed into overkill mode, inflicting wounds far beyond what was needed to simply render the victim dead. Overkill was evident in attacks that Jackson made on some of his other victims. like Wallende, and Ira Bradley. The killing in the cold winter months, transporting the body to an icy body of water, were themes that followed the thread from Conn, to Wallende, to Lava Lakes.

A wound found in Dewey Morris' skull, believed to have been the fatal one, is a detail of great interest. It was not caused by a bullet, but had been punched through the bone. County doctor Hendershott described it as *"a hole crushed by a blunt instrument in the right side of the skull back of the ear. The hole was about the size of a a half dollar."*

When the body of Creed Conn was recovered in 1904, his face and head had been mutilated. The *Crook County Journal* said that his face was "maimed" and "mangled." The *Oregonian* said that his features were "obliterated" to such an extent that his gold watch had to be used to identify the body. The *Crook County Journal* noted "a bullet hole in the right temple," and that article seemed to be based on a conversation with a witness at the Sandy Knoll where Conn's body was found. But, the two physicians who examined Conn's body for the inquest documented only two wounds from bullets, both in the chest. Was it a mere coincidence that Dewey Morris was found to have suffered a similar, peculiar wound, and on the same side of the head?

Charles Hyde Kimzey at age 67, five years before he was pa-roled from the Oregon State Penitentiary and went to live out the remainder of his days in Idaho.

SOURCES:

"3 Slain Trappers Buried at Bend," *Oregonian,* April 26, 1924.

Oregon Geographic Names, 7th edition, 2003, by Lewis A. McArthur and Lewis L. McArthur, Oregon Historical Society Press, Portland, OR, p 952.

Find A Grave page of Peter Runey, available online at: http://www.findagrave.com/cgibin/fg.cgi?page=gr&GSln=Runey&GSfn=Peter&GSbyrel=all&GSdyrel=all&GSst=39&GScntry=4&GSob=n&GRid=48775348&df=all&

Fourteenth Census of the United States, Oregon, Lane County, McKenzie Precinct, .

"Fox Hides Sold Here," *Oregonian,* April 20, 1924.

"Trail of Murderer Ends at Fur Store," *Oregonian,* April 25, 1924.

"Slain Trappers Shot to Pieces," *Oregonian,* April 25, 1924.

"In Re: Charles Kimzey, Number 12585," a report to the Oregon State Parole Board for their meeting of April 18, 1940, and hearing transcript. Inmate record of Charles Kimzey #12582, Department of Corrections, OISC, Wilsonville, OR.

"No Trace Found of 3 Bend Trappers," *Silver Lake Leader,* April 24, 1924.

"Trail of Murderer Ends at Fur Store," *Oregonian,* April 26, 1924.

"Fox Hides Sold Here," *Oregonian,* April 20, 1924.

"Bodies of Trappers Found in Lava Lake," *Silver Lake Leader,* May 1, 1924.

"Three Lured From Cabin to Meet Fate, is Theory; Lava Lake Gives up Dead," *Bulletin,* April 24, 1924.

Luger P08, a history of the Luger pistol, with design details, available online at: http://guns.wikia.com/wiki/ Luger_P08
NOAA ESRL, Sunrise/Sunset Calculator, Web site of the National Oceanic and Atmospheric Administration, http://www.esrl.noaa.gov/gmd/grad/solcalc/sunrise. html

"News from the Camps," *Deschutes Pine Echoes*, May 1924, editor Paul Hosmer, Brooks-Scanlon Lumber Co., Bend, OR, p12

"No Trace Found of 3 Bend Trappers," *Silver Lake Leader*, April 24, 1924.

"New Clew is Found in Trapper Mystery," *Oregonian*, April 21, 1924.

Wilderness Tales and Trails, by Wayne Negus, Maverick, Bend, OR, 1990, p 63-67, 157-162.

Crime Classification Manual, by Burgess, Burgess, Douglas, and Ressler, 2006, John Wiley & Sons, San Francisco, CA, p 19-40.

Close Combat, MCRP 302B, J. E. Rhodes, Lieutenant General, U.S. Marine Corps, Commanding General, Marine Corps Combat Development Command, 12 February 1999, Department of the Navy, Headquarters, United States Marine Crops, Washington, D.C.

Photographs 12302, 6162, 6425 and 6310. Collection of the Des Chutes Historical Museum, Bend, OR.

"The Little Lava Lake Murders," by Don Burgderfer, *Little Known Tales From Oregon History*, Vol. III, No. 61, *Cascades East Magazine*, Bend, OR, p 27-33.

"Stolen Auto Recovered," *Oregonian*, September 5, 1923.

"Signs Found of Attack on Jitney Driver," *Central Oregon Press*, August 28, 1923.

Convict Record of Charles Hyde Kimzey #2316, Idaho State Penitentiary. Idaho State Archives, Division of the Idaho State Historical Society, Boise, ID. Kimzey was convicted on a charge of grand larceny for theft of grain in Blaine County on June 3, 1915.

Field research by author at Lava Lakes, summer 2012.

"First in Heart," *Oregonian*, July 14, 1904. Article criticizes the investigation of the Conn murder, and mentions that Conn's hat had been pulled down tightly over the back of his head.

"J. C. Conn's Body Found," *Crook County Journal,* April 28, 1904.

"J. C. Conn Murdered," *Roseburg Plaindealer,* May 12, 1904. Article states that Conn's facial features had been "obliterated."

Editorial, *Crook County Journal,* June 23, 1904.

The Sandy Knoll Murder, Legacy of the Sheepshooters, by Melany Tupper, 2010, Central Oregon Books, LLC, Christmas Valley, OR. p 125-135, 237-244.

"Friends Pay Honor to Slain Trappers," *Oregonian,* April 27, 1924.

"Shotgun Slips, Wounds Hunter," *Bend Bulletin,* October 26, 1922.

Brief history of Century Drive, GORP web site: http://www. gorp.com/weekendguide/traveltascenicdrivesbendlapineoregons idwcmdev _052631.html

"Elk Lake Remembrances," by Carol Blackwell, *Little Known Tales from Oregon History, No. 117,* Cascades East Magazine, Winter 2003-04, p 56-61.

"Charles Kimzey Held, Federal Man States," *Bend Bulletin,* March 10, 1933.

"Kimzey Not Alone in Triple Slaying," *Oregonian,* March 12, 1933.

"Kimzey Waives Extradition, to Face Trial," *Bend Bulletin,* March 13, 1933.

"Moffat Tunnel," Wikipedia, http://en.wikipedia.org/wiki /Moffat_Tunnel

"Kimzey is Back in Bend After 9 Year Search," *Bend Bulletin,* March 17, 1933.

"To Tell Kimzey of Second Case," *Bend Bulletin,* March 18, 1933.

Oregon State Board of Health, Certificate of Death #42, Edward Nickols, filed April 25, 1924, Deschutes County, Oregon State Archives, Salem, OR.

Oregon State Board of Health, Certificate of Death #43, Dewey Morris, filed April 25, 1924, Deschutes County, Oregon State Archives, Salem, OR.

Oregon State Board of Health, Certificate of Death #44, Harry LeRoy Wilson, filed April 25, 1924, Deschutes County, Oregon State Archives, Salem, OR.

"Kimzey to Get Surprise," *Oregonian*, March 19, 1933.

"Kimzey Appears at Bar," *Oregonian*, March 21, 1933.

"Kimzey Comes Here to Face Accusers," *Oregonian*, April 2, 1933.

"Kimzey Left in Portland When Sheriff Returns," *Bend Bulletin*, April 3, 1933.

"Fail to Identify Kimzey as Seller," *Bend Bulletin*, April 3, 1933.

"Kimzey Indicted by Jury," *Oregonian*, April 13, 1933.

"Kimzey Enters Plea of Not Guilty Here," *Bend Bulletin*, April 13, 1933.

"Kimzey Case Opens Today," *Bend Bulletin*, April 20, 1933.

"Harrison Tells of Journey Into Desert," *Bend Bulletin*, April 21, 1933.

The State of Oregon vs Charles Kimzey, judgment #4225, Circuit Court of the State of Oregon for Deschutes County, April 25, 1933. Inmate record of Charles Kimzey #12582, Department of Corrections, OISC, Wilsonville, OR.

"Jury Convicts Kimzey," *Oregonian*, April 23, 1933.

"Kimzey Given Life Term in State Prison," *Bend Bulletin*, April 25, 1933.

"Kimzey Given Life Term," *Oregonian*, April 26, 1933.

"Dewey Morris Case Will Go to Jury Today," *Bend Bulletin*, April 12, 1923.

"Howard Hired Holmes Pair, Newest Story," *Salt Lake Telegram*, January 6, 1926.

"Howard Feared Attack During Trip, Declared," *Salt Lake Tribune,* January 7, 1926.

"Sheriff Rebels in Howard Case; Blames Citizens," *Salt Lake Tribune,* January 8, 1926.

"Howard Case Given Over to Burns Agency," *Salt Lake Tribune,* January 9, 1926.

"Howard Last Seen in Mohave Desert, Belief," *Salt Lake Tribune,* January 12, 1926.

"Sheriff Finds No Trace of Howard," *Salt Lake Tribune,* January 20, 1926.

"Nationwide Search For Alleged Slayer of Howard Planned," *Salt Lake Tribune,* December 9, 1927.

"Nevada Attorney Probes Case," *Salt Lake Tribune,* December 10, 1927.

"Tourist Held Murdered," *Oregonian,* December 12, 1927.

Western Echoes, by Earl F. Moore, 1981, Paul Tremaine Publishing, Klamath Falls, OR, p 72-73.

Draft Registration Card of Harry LeRoy Wilson, May 26, 1917, P. J. Hardisty, Registrar, Bend, OR. National Archives and Records Administration, Washington, D. C.

A Brief History Of The 8th Marines, by James S. Santelli, 1976, History and Museums Division, Headquarters, U.S. Marine Corps, US Government Printing Office, Washington D.C., p 13.

"Adams Dies in Auto Accident at Tumalo," *Bend Bulletin,* May 17, 1927

INDEX:

Barnum, Orva Ann, 58, 62
Barnum, William E., "Earl," 58, 62
Barry, John P., "Jack," 56
Barry, S. W., 47
Bartlett Hotel, 190
Batavia, Illinois, 116-118
Bath, L. H., 92
Beard, Reverend F. H., 222
Bellingham, Washington, 189-190, 193
Bend, Oregon, vii, 9, 18, 34, 70-73, 105, 133, 135, 138-140, 147, 153, 155, 159-162, 165, 173, 176, 178-181, 184-185, 188, 190-191, 194-195, 209, 214, 222, 224, 226, 228
Bender, Walter C., 179, 180, 183, 225
Benson, Henry L., 91
Benson, R. L., 195
Berger, Max, 186
Big Lava Lake, vii, 154, 172, 174, 177, 179-181, 191, 198, 203, 210, 212, 219-220, 222, 699
Big Stick Creek, 10, 32, 120-122
Billings, Ethel Ewing, 17
Billings, Nelson, "Jay", 17
Black Butte, 11
Blackwell, Carol, 136
Blaine County, Idaho, 132
Bloss, John, 11, 57
Blue Mountains, 159
Bofinger, Gotthilf J., 225
Boise, Idaho, 131, 135, 145, 148, 173
Bonanza, Oregon, 36
Bourne, Jonathan, 73
Box, William N., 196
Boylan, Bert, 137-138, 153, 224
Bradley, Harold, 35-36, 61, 81
Bradley, Ira, 81, 230
Brattain, P. J., 33
Bridge of Sighs, 78, 83, 86, 93, 98
Brogan, Phil, 184
Broken Top, 204
Brooke, William H., 114

Chewaucan River, 74
Chewaucan State Bank, 73
Chilton, Dr. W. L., 91, 93, 96
Chouteau County, Montana, 188
Christmas Lake, 19, 190
Christmas Valley, Oregon, 20, 193
Christopherson, Deputy, 180
Citizen's Bank and Trust Co., 142
Clackamas County, Oregon, 163
Clark, Edward H., 179
Clevenger, George W., 107-109, 111-113
Collins, Fred, 13
Comet Lodging House, 87, 97
Conn freight team, 7-9, 14, 121
Conn, George, 10, 21, 33, 55
Conn, Henry Sr., 7
Conn, John Creed, viii, 3-8, 10-17, 19-22, 33, 36, 38, 55, 57, 61, 79, 81, 121, 153, 155, 158, 194, 222, 229-230
Conn, Lafayette, "Lafe," 6, 13-15, 20-22 54-56
Conn, Virgil, 10, 15, 21, 33, 36, 70
Costello, George, 153
Crane Prairie, 161-163, 178, 222
Crane Prairie Dam, 162
Crane Prairie Reservoir, 152, 162, 204
Crook County, Oregon, 135
Crooked River, 163
Crowley, James, 82
Cultus Lake, 152, 160, 162
Currier, M. C., 33
Curron, F. W., 47
Cuttingville, Oregon, 164
Daly, Bernard, 49, 53-54, 56-57, 63
Davis County, Oregon, 115
Davis Lake, 152
Davis ranch, 80
Davis, Alexander A., 51, 69
Deer Flat, Idaho, 145
Degermark, Carin, 133, 136
Deming, Washington, 189

Harney Lake, 32, 106, 120, 124

Harper, George, 39

Harries, Benjamin R., 143

Harrison, Dr. Tillson L., 108

Harrison, William, 133-135, 138-141, 146-147, 154, 158-159, 224, 226-227

Hendershott, Ray W. 184, 188, 191, 194-195, 230

Henry, Mr., 38

Highland School District, 164

Highland, Oregon, 164

Hirsch, Otto, 108

Holmes, James F. and William, 144

Homedale Work Farm, 29, 133

Hoover, J. Edgar, 146

Hopkins, Harry, 228

Horton, Jack, 36

Hosmer, Paul, 136-137, 178, 184, 186, 212

Hotel Paisley, 70

Howard, William R., 142-145, 222, 229

Howe, Carrol B., 7

Hudson, C. S., 70

Hunsaker, Jesse, 83

Huntington, W. H., Sheriff, 31

Hurd, W. O., 144, 147

Hurlburt family, 121

Hurlburt, Anna, E. "Annie" Bardwell, 32, 120-121

Hurlburt, Augustus ranch, 124

Hurlburt, Thomas M., 180

Hutchins, R. Vance, 97

Hutton, Leona, 61

Hutton, Link, 35-36, 61

Hyde, Henry H., 131

Idaho State Penitentiary, 29, 140, 143, 159, 173

Illinois Department of Corrections, 107

Imlay, J. W., 143

Ingersoll, W. H., 143-144

Innes ranch, 13

Innis, Hervey D., 174-178, 180-181, 183, 185-186, 193-195, 198, 210, 214, 223-224,

alias Tom Rose, 146
alias W. R. Howe, 143
alias William Becker, 143
Kimzey, Earl, 132
Kimzey, James (Kimsey), 131, 133
Kimzey, John B., 132
Kimzey, Mary Basil Peasley, 131
Kimzey, Mary E., 132
Klamath County, Oregon, viii, 38, 75, 80-81, 98, 163, 165
Klamath Falls I.O.O.F. Cemetery, 98
Klamath Falls, Oregon, 17, 22, 55, 75, 78-81, 83, 86, 88, 91-92, 95-96, 180-181
Klamath Flats, 75
Klamath Marsh, 51, 69, 163
Klein, Peter, 118
Kuklinsky, Richard, 62
Kuykendall, Delman V. 55-56
La Pine, Oregon, 139-140, 152, 157, 160, 162-163, 181
Laborence, Charles, 110
Lake City, Michigan, 188
Lake County, Oregon, viii, 7, 11, 15-16, 18, 22, 32, 34-36, 45-47, 50, 54, 56, 60, 69, 73, 75, 79, 86, 120, 122, 124, 132, 154, 158, 173,189, 193, 230, 6999
Lake Euwana, 86
Lake Lowell, 145, 147
Lakeview school, 49
Lakeview, Oregon, 21, 33, 35-36, 45, 51, 56-57, 74-75, 79-80, 111, 132
Lamb, E. O., 37
Lane County, Oregon, 16, 22, 205
Lane, Martha, 10, 12, 21-22
Langell, William, 82
Las Vegas, Nevada, 143, 145, 229
Last Chance ranch, 134, 139
Lava Lakes, 133-137, 141, 146-148, 152-153, 155-157, 159-164, 173-174, 178, 184, 186, 189, 192, 194, 204-206, 209, 218, 222-224, 226, 228-230
Lava River Cave, 137
Lawrence, J. M., 73

Martin, Ethel, 9
Martin, J. S., 18
Mason, Gerald W., 159, 227
Mayfield family, 163-164
Mayfield ranch, 152
Mayfield, Green W., 164
Mayfield, Jackson, 164
Mayfield, Michael S., "Mike," 163-164
Mayfield, Tennessee, 164
Mayfield, William G., "Billy," 164
McCauley, Claude L., 136-137, 146, 153, 161
McKenzie Pass, 35
McKenzie River Trail, 205
McKinley sawmill, 136
McKinley, William R., 136
McLennan, Dan, 189, 191
McLennan, Leoella Margaret Wilson, 189, 191, 193
Mehama, Oregon, 147
Melbourne, Faye, 88-89, 91, 95-96, 98
Messner, policeman, 96
Miller, Bill Y., 47
Miller, Judge, 105
Miller, Major Ellis B., 192
Millican, Oregon, 134
Moffat Tunnel, 141, 160, 223-224, 226
Moffat, David, 223
Moore, Earl F., 18, 20, 230
Moore's Creek, 145
Morgan County, Ohio, 188
Morgan, V. O., 33
Morris, Addie L., Ranger, 22
Morris, Anna A., "Effie", 185
Morris, Ben, 178, 181, 185
Morris, Dewey C., 139, 154, 156, 162-163, 173-176, 178, 181-188, 194, 196, 198, 209-219, 221-223, 226, 230
Morris, Donald R., 178, 181, 185
Morris, Hattie M. Wood, 184-185
Morris, John A., 184-185
Morris, Owen A., 176-178, 180, 184-185, 187, 194, 210

Morris, Vera, 185
Moss, Stephen P., 47
Mt. Bachelor, 204
Mt. Shasta, 75, 80
Mud Lake, 32, 124
Multnomah County Jail, 226
Multnomah County Sheriff's Department, 180, 205
Murray, Rosette, 91
Mush Spring, 11
Nampa, Idaho, 145
Narrows, The, 10, 32, 120, 124
National Oceanic and Atmospheric Administration, NOAA, 221
Natron Cutoff, 206
Negus, Thomas R., 185
Negus, Wayne, 137-138, 176, 185, 192
Nelson, Jesse, 47, 53
New York Harbor, 117
New York, New York, 89, 145
Newell, Sam, 134
Nicholas, T. F., 87
Nichols, Addie, 88
Nichols, Arthur S., 144
Nickols, Anna Belle, 188
Nickols, Cliff, 189
Nickols, Edward D., 135, 137-142, 154, 157-160, 163, 173-175, 179-183, 188-191, 194, 196, 198, 206, 208-209, 212-215, 217, 219-222, 225-226, 229
Nickols, Guilford J., 189-190, 193
Nickols, Jannetta, 188, 190
Nickols, Leoella, 190
Nickols, Rachel A., 188
Nickols, Thomas, 188
Niswonger, C. P., 156, 182-184, 187-188, 191, 194, 203, 211, 216, 218
North, K., 92
Northwest Townsite Co., 73
Oak Avenue Canal, 92
Oakridge, Oregon, 204
Obenchain, Silas, 86

Odell Lake, 185
Odell, Oregon, 16-17
Old Military Road, 16, 22
Ollingham, Ora D., 196
Ontario, Oregon, 115
Oregon Geographic Names Board, 222
Oregon State Insane Asylum, Oregon State Hospital, 116-117
Oregon State Land Board, 54
Oregon State Parole Board, 147, 153, 155, 160, 224, 226-227, 229
Oregon State Penitentiary, 8, 10, 31, 106, 114, 116, 119, 131, 133, 135, 147, 153, 159, 226-227, 231
Oregon State Police, 146
Oregon State Teachers' Association, 49
Oregon Trail, 7
Oregon Valley Land Co., 54, 57-58
Otis, Eugene, 118
Overland Hotel, 143
Owsley, Ernest E., 105, 107, 109
Owsley, William B., 80
O'Brien, M. W., 47, 53
O'Neill, C. M., 88
Pacific Coast Underwriters, 135
Pacific Livestock Co., 106
Packsaddle Mountain, 204-206
Paisley I.O.O.F. Cemetery, 50, 59
Paisley Mercantile Co., 47
Paisley National Bank, 73
Paisley school, 35, 75
Paisley, Oregon, 7, 10, 18, 33-34, 36-38, 50, 52-53, 55, 69-72, 74, 79, 163
Pasco, Washington, 136
Passtime pool hall, 154
pathology, sociopathy, psychopathy, vii-ix, 1-3, 5, 8, 16-17, 37-38, 48, 52, 56, 98, 121-122, 132-133, 142, 153, 158, 184, 220-221
Paulina Prairie, 139
Payne, Frank W., 10, 36, 39, 47, 49, 53-54, 56-58, 61-63, 72, 80, 121
Payne, Frank and Florence, 59
Payne, Myrtle Simpson Barnum, 63

victimology, 122
Viewpoint, Oregon, 193
Vollmer family, 112, 122
Vollmer farm, 124
Vollmer, August C., 104, 110-111, 113-115, 119-120, 123
Vollmer, Della, 122
Wagontire Mountain, 35, 61, 73, 120, 157-158, 163, 173
Waldo Lake, 204
Walker, Samuel L., 86-89
Wallace, William, 60
Wallende, Julius, 15-20, 79, 81, 163, 193, 230
Ward, Anna Belle Nickols, 190-191
Ward, Dorothy, 91
Ward, Jerome E., 190
Warm Springs, Oregon, 104, 106-107, 112, 119-120
Warner, Archie A., 154-155
Waterloo, Oregon, 11
Webster, George R., 102-106, 108-113, 115-116, 119-121, 123-124
West, Oswald, 70, 73
Whatcom County, Washington, 189-190, 193
White, Mr., 96
Whitechapel, London, England, 5
Whitlock, Earl, 83, 92
Wickiup Reservoir, 152
Wild Billy Lake, 163
Wilkins, M. G., 92
Willamette University, 10
Willcoxon, Allen W., 135-137, 159, 161-163, 178, 183, 209, 228
Willcoxon, Arba Roe, 135-136
Willcoxon, George, 135
Willcoxon, George Reeves, 136
Willcoxon, Harriet, 135
Willcoxon, Lucy B., 135
Willcoxon, Reeves A., 136
William J. Burns International Detective Agency, 142-145, 229
Williams, Andrew S. "Clubber", 89
Williams, J. H., 146
Williams, Jessie Bardwell, 32
Williamson Mountain, 205

The author, on the trail at Little Lava Lake with her faithful research assistant, Tonka, who provided chipmunk data.

Titles by Melany Tupper:

Trip, Nomadic in America
2001

High Desert Roses,
Significant Stories from Central Oregon
volume one
2003

The Sandy Knoll Murder,
Legacy of the Sheepshooters
2010

High Desert Roses
Lake County for the Curious
volume two
2011

The Trapper Murders
A True Central Oregon Mystery
2013

Printed in Great Britain
by Amazon

42992316R00155